Bringing Down the House
The Crisis in Britain's Regional Theatres

Bringing Down the House
The Crisis in Britain's Regional Theatres

Olivia Turnbull

intellect Bristol, UK / Chicago, USA

First Published in the UK in 2008 by
Intellect Books, The Mill, Parnall Road, Fishponds, Bristol, BS16 3JG, UK

First published in the USA in 2008 by
Intellect Books, The University of Chicago Press, 1427 E. 60th Street, Chicago,
IL 60637, USA

Copyright © 2008 Intellect Ltd

All rights reserved. No part of this publication may be reproduced,
stored in a retrieval system, or transmitted, in any form or by any means,
electronic, mechanical, photocopying, recording, or otherwise, without
written permission.

A catalogue record for this book is available from the British Library.

Cover Design: Gabriel Solomons
Copy Editor: Poppy Keeling
Typesetting: Mac Style, Beverley, E. Yorkshire

ISBN 978-1-84150-208-3

Printed and bound by Gutenberg Press, Malta.

Contents

Acknowledgments   7
Introduction   9

Part One: The Build-up   15

Chapter 1   The Unsteady Foundations and the Post-war Cultural Unsettlement   17

Chapter 2   Plural Funding, Multiple Problems   47

Part Two: The Crisis   67

Chapter 3   Thatcher Gets Down to Business   69

Chapter 4   Major Dramas   87

Part Three: Casualties and Survivors   111

Chapter 5   Salisbury Playhouse   113

Chapter 6   Thorndike Theatre, Leatherhead   129

Chapter 7   Redgrave Theatre, Farnham   145

Chapter 8   Yvonne Arnaud Theatre, Guildford   157

Chapter 9   Merseyside Everyman Theatre and Liverpool Playhouse   167

Chapter 10 Harrogate Theatre   187

Part Four: The Legacy   197

Chapter 11 Tony's Council: artful or armless?   199

References   221
Index   229

Acknowledgements

On the long road to publication, the many friends, colleagues and professionals who have kindly provided information, suggestions and inspiration are far too numerous to mention here. It goes without saying that my gratitude to them is immense. I would, however, particularly like to mention those very busy practitioners, the pressures of whose workload, documented here, need no further comment, but who nevertheless kindly gave up their time to talk to me about their experiences. I would also like to extend my appreciation to my advisers at Tufts University, who helped oversee the doctorate that provided the foundation for this work, and to my editors at Intellect, Melanie Harrison and Sam King, for their sympathy and humour during the long haul. Above all, my many, many thanks go to my mum for her unwavering encouragement, patience and help with this work, something that went far above and beyond anything words can describe. And equally to my dad, for very sweetly providing the much needed support for the support. Without them, there is a distinct possibility that this book would still just be a pile of notes collecting dust in the corner.

Introduction

Working in British Theatre today feels like working in a certain hotel in Scarborough. We are all wondering which one of us will go over the cliff next.[1]

In December 2007, a cloud descended over the nation's theatre community as the Arts Council announced a change in policy that would see its grants to thirty-seven theatre companies cut or withdrawn. Amongst them, four of the nation's regional producing houses were earmarked to lose their entire funding, and predictions for their futures were gloomy. A threat to regional theatres was widely perceived as a threat to theatre across the nation, for they had long been recognized as the bedrock of the art form in Britain and the training ground for many of the country's most celebrated practitioners. Despite a widespread recognition that the Arts Council was long overdue for a rethink, and that many companies benefited substantially from the changes, the announcement caused an outcry the likes of which had not been heard for a decade and a public meeting with the theatre community at the Old Vic resulted in a vote of no confidence. Six months earlier, outgoing Prime Minister Tony Blair had stood on a platform in the Tate Modern and announced that Britain was experiencing a 'golden age' for the arts, the implication being that the state of the arts was a far cry from the dark days under the previous government. If true, this might go some way in explaining the extent of the anger from theatre practitioners that greeted the Arts Council's proposed cuts. The previous regime under the Conservatives had produced an era dominated by low levels of funding, bureaucracy and political infighting. For regional theatres, it had meant a prolonged period of crisis where robbing Peter to pay Paul to stay afloat had been very much the order of the day. For many, evidence that such problems had not, in fact, been laid to rest was apparently too much to bear.

During the Conservative Party's eighteen-year period in government between 1979 and 1997, the number of regional producing theatres operating in Britain fell by a quarter. When the Tories finally left office in 1997, the remaining forty-five playhouses, referred to as producing theatres because they staged their own shows rather than receiving toured-in productions, were carrying a combined deficit of £6 million, a sum that exceeded their collective annual subsidy.

At this time, over three-quarters of these theatres claimed to have such serious deficits as to threaten imminent closure within the next two years if the situation were not to improve. Almost all claimed that mounting difficulties over the previous decade had forced them to reduce their operations radically, in ways that ranged from scaling down their programming to safe, small-cast productions, taking in growing numbers of touring dates and cutting fringe and outreach activities, to going dark for extended periods of time.

This crisis had been recognized as ongoing in regional theatres since the beginning of the 1980s, a phenomenon that directly followed Margaret Thatcher's election as prime minister at the end of 1979. The factors that led to this situation, however, had been accumulating for decades. While the Conservatives' enterprise culture and their scant regard for the arts during the 1980s and 1990s sounded the death knell for many producing houses, the roots of the problems can be traced much further back.

Conservative government policy directly and indirectly reduced state funding of the arts and forced subsidized provincial playhouses to operate in the real world, where they were subject to the blast of market forces. But tracing the history of Britain's regional theatres back to the advent of state funding of the arts reveals a catalogue of problems that have returned time after time to ensure that the fabric base of regional theatre has been consistently fragile.

Matthew Arnold's call in 1879 to 'organise the theatre' heralded the beginning of decades of struggle to establish a state-funded national theatre and a network across Britain of subsidized repertory theatres, where an ensemble company stayed for a season and performed a series of different plays (Arnold 1879). At that time, proponents of state funding of the arts presented subsidy as a means to oust the perceived insidious effects of the Victorian and Edwardian theatrical establishments. The commercial emphasis of the star system and the 'long run' that dominated the period were loudly criticized as adversely affecting the quality of the nation's theatre, undermining production standards and compromising opportunities to develop new dramatic talent. The repertory idea, most cohesively presented in William Archer's argument for a National Theatre, provided a model for theatre that was entirely different from the dominant commercial practices of the time. Not least, the repertory idea was heavily linked to the growing awareness of theatre's potential importance as an educational as well as artistic medium and, therefore, its significance in the cultural life of the country.

Arnold's call was effectively answered with the acceptance of state funding of the arts at the end of the Second World War, something most clearly demonstrated with the establishment of the Arts Council of Great Britain, the national arts funding body, in 1945. In many ways, the arrival of state funding provided the budding regional repertory movement with the resources to develop and expand on a scale Arnold could only have dreamed of. Not least, it provided a safety net to cushion the theatres against historical events such as the technological revolution that might otherwise have destroyed their support base. By 1970, only a quarter of a century after the Arts Council had been established, more than sixty subsidized building-based regional producing theatres were operating across the country.

The advent of state funding offered regional theatres huge opportunities. But it could equally be argued that the act of giving subsidy distorted the shape of Britain's provincial theatres in the decades after the war, and in a way that was both restrictive and destructive. In particular, the growth of subsidy meant government bureaucracy became an increasingly important determinant in these theatres' operations and state funding an increasingly vital condition of their survival. Unfortunately, the fluctuating nature of government cultural and economic policy, coupled with the erratic basis on which the national funding body historically allocated funds, ensured that these were insecure grounds for any theatre to rely on.

The nature of the Arts Council's creation after the war was quasi-accidental, and the practice of giving subsidy in Britain was created obliquely by a series of circumstances that owed more to fate than to any thoroughgoing survey of the nation's artistic practices and needs. Consequently, for many years, the criteria for allocating funds and the methods of distributing them were largely ad hoc. In the case of regional theatres, the circumstances behind the foundation of arts subsidy and the Arts Council's subsequent policy of day-to-day response meant that, before 2001, no national policy for theatre was established to offer its regional clients any consistent, coherent guidelines for funding (ACE 2001).

Decades of changing and ambiguous ideas about the nature of subsidized theatres and state funding of the arts combined to put increasingly burdensome and often conflicting demands on provincial producing houses across the country and set the stage for the move towards the idea of buying services in a contract culture rather than funding art for its intrinsic value. The stamp placed on the Arts Council by its first chairman, John Maynard Keynes, with his emphasis on the civilizing nature of art, defined the post-war years. The organization's prioritization of cultural excellence, seen largely in terms of text-based drama for a minority elite as defined by the metropolis, has continued to be an important credo in state funding of regional theatres. Since the 1960s, however, this emphasis has coexisted uneasily alongside an accent on the social utility of art. This emphasis was initiated by Jennie Lee, the Labour politician and first minister for the arts, under whose leadership regional theatres also had to assume a wider social purpose. The 1965 Labour Party's *A Policy for the Arts* set the main agendas as participation, access and community provision, on which increased subvention, particularly from non-statutory bodies such as the local authorities, was subsequently based. Rather than accepting the innate value of high art, local authorities and metropolitan county councils increasingly demanded a clearer social emphasis as a way of measuring regional theatres' contributions to the welfare of the local community. If Keynes' civilizing mission and Lee's socializing mission have on occasion proved incompatible, they have also been constantly at odds with the demands of the popular audience. Pressure from public funding bodies to answer the demands established by Keynes and Lee has often made it difficult for regional theatres to adjust their programmes to take in the dominant tastes and requirements of the theatres' target audiences.

While the idea that regional theatres should 'earn their keep' was most forcefully realized during the Conservative administration of 1979 to 1997, unresolved ideas about the playhouses' primary function and the nature of subsidy itself combined to ensure that few theatres were in a position to generate adequate revenue during this period. And while a new agenda under New Labour has seen increased state support, few of these ideas have been resolved. Since the advent of state funding, regional theatres have increasingly been required to be different things to different masters. But the fact that the theatres' main funding bodies have rarely been in agreement, and that their agendas have further been subject to the fluctuations of politics, the economy and internal dissension, has resulted in a situation whereby producing houses have had to expand consistently and adjust their programmes over the years, but have rarely been allowed to scale back their activities, even in times of extreme financial hardship.

As I will discuss in the first two chapters, the quasi-accidental circumstances of the Arts Council's foundation and consequent unresolved issues surrounding the funding body's role and responsibilities translated into a lack of firm central control or coordination for regional theatres in the decades after the war. Until the 1990s, the Arts Council was the primary funding body for the majority of Britain's provincial producing houses. However, there were perennial problems in the organization's operations. The Arts Council's ideological 'arm's length' status, whereby it was intended to function as an autonomous intermediate body between the government and artistic organizations to prevent politics from influencing artistic decisions, was always questionable. Similarly, constant concerns over the issue of central or regional control and the prioritization of funding for national and metropolitan companies meant that regional theatres were often as much victims of internal dissent within the Arts Council as beneficiaries of its protection and munificence. In affluent circumstances, the lack of resolution in such issues might not have proved so problematic. But state funding of the arts since 1945 has constantly failed to keep pace with the increasing demands of the arts community. And the ambiguity of the Arts Council's position meant that in the face of metropolitan bias, for instance, presenting a bureaucratically orthodox programme was not necessarily enough.

Inherent problems of this system were compounded for regional theatres by the move into plural funding with the introduction, in the 1950s, of new sources of funding from other public bodies, namely the regional arts associations and local authorities. The agendas of the new funding bodies were often diametrically opposed to those of the Arts Council and equally subject to the fluctuations of politics and the economy. As such, while the move towards plural funding and the increasing arguments put forward for devolution at this time were intended to benefit the regional theatres, they actually complicated rather than eased the situation.

The unresolved issues in funding policies discussed in the first two chapters, and the long-term effects they have had on the operations of provincial producing houses in Britain, meant that regional theatres were already in a vulnerable position when Margaret Thatcher and the Conservative Party came to power in 1979. With the new government, the commercial bias whereby 'everything is costed; nothing is valued' meant an entirely new approach for theatres in the provinces. The New Right ideology, with its emphasis on a free-market economy and scant regard for the arts as a non-vote-catching issue, resulted in policies that placed many regional theatres in an increasingly difficult position. Consistently low funding whereby the government's annual grant-in-aid often failed to keep pace with inflation was exacerbated by the Conservatives' insistence that theatres should operate like any commercial business and be equally subject to market forces. Such an idea undermined the very basis of subsidy and was antithetical to regional theatres' traditional relationship with the Arts Council and other public funding bodies. These bodies, in turn, were often left powerless to defend the theatres when their own existence was threatened by other governmental changes. The abolition of the arts-friendly metropolitan councils in 1986, for instance, not only involved a substantial financial loss for the arts community in Britain but, in the threat it posed to plural funding, jeopardized the whole system by which arts funding was organized. Similarly, the Arts Council's position, already compromised by years of meagre funding, was weakened by a series of attacks on its structure. Right-wing appointments to key positions in the establishment undermined its arm's length principle and cost it the confidence of the arts community, and several government-commissioned reports were highly critical of its operations and suggested a severely reduced role.

During the Conservative administration, a crisis built up in the regions. By the time Thatcher's successor, John Major, left Downing Street in 1997, approximately three-quarters of Britain's provincial producing houses had had to severely pare down activities and had proclaimed imminent closure in the face of enormous accumulated and operational deficits.

On 15 January 1995, the people of Salisbury awoke to find their theatre had gone dark. A staple of cultural life in the conservative cathedral city since the Second World War, following substantial financial losses the Playhouse was forced to close for seven months to avoid bringing down the curtain forever. The Redgrave Theatre in Farnham, also in dire financial straits, went dark the same day. The following year, the Harrogate Theatre closed temporarily, and hot on its heels was Leatherhead's Thorndike Theatre, which went into liquidation in 1997. In 1998, the Merseyside Everyman Theatre went into receivership. The individual experiences of these and three other affected producing houses provided in this book vividly illustrate the straits to which provincial theatres were reduced as they battled to survive. Their stories reveal definite trends in the nature of regional theatre's operations and problems under the Conservative government, demonstrating that regional theatres were subject to many of the same forces during the 1980s and 1990s.

New Labour's election victory in 1997 did not immediately bring any relief to the theatres' troubles despite the party's recognition that the arts were an influential tool in compassionate conservatism, their aim of creating a caring and economically successful society. It was not until the 2000 report by consultants Peter Boyden Associates into the state of regional theatre, followed by the creation of the country's first ever national policy for theatre, that substantial extra funding, to the tune of £25 million, was promised to provincial theatres. For the first time in twenty years, regional playhouses saw some blue in the sky. But this only applied to England, and inevitably the extra money came with strings attached: more bureaucracy, more governmental pressures and more dependence on the vagaries of central policy. The position of regional theatres may have been less precarious in the first decade of the twenty-first century, but as an economic recession looms, many issues remain unresolved.

Since the foundation of the first regional theatre in Britain, the Gaiety Theatre in Manchester in 1907, the burgeoning repertory movement has played an increasingly vital and dominant role in shaping the nation's theatre. The substantial development and growth of provincial producing houses across the country, particularly after the Second World War, led to a position whereby the network of subsidized regional theatres became central to the craft base of the national theatre system. In addition to their function as centres of excellence providing quality theatre to the majority of the population living outside the metropolis, regional theatres have traditionally been a forum for new and experimental dramatic ideas, a touchstone for local community access, education and entertainment, and a training ground and employment industry for a large part of the country's theatre profession. For such reasons, a crisis in regional theatres does not just threaten the erosion of one of 'the nation's greatest cultural assets' (ACE 1995: 4), but threatens to undermine the entire fabric of British theatre.

Note

1. Philip Hedley, artistic director, Theatre Royal, Stratford East, quoted in 'Making a drama out of a crisis', *The Independent*, 23 February 1995. Referring to the Holbeck Hall hotel in Scarborough, which collapsed into the sea in 1993.

PART ONE: THE BUILD-UP

1

THE UNSTEADY FOUNDATIONS AND THE POST-WAR CULTURAL UNSETTLEMENT

The whole ludicrous set-up happened by accident but could not have been better designed if the object was to ensure that cultural unity is avoided at all costs. It is a tribute to the strength of British culture that its separate manifestations manage to survive as well as they do.

(Jenkins 1979: 21)[1]

Britain's current system of regional theatres can be traced back to the repertory movement at the end of the nineteenth century and the efforts of pioneers including Harley Granville Barker, J.T. Grein, George Bernard Shaw, William Archer and Matthew Arnold. By the beginning of the twentieth century, their new repertory idea played a central role in the developing anxiety about the future of British theatre. Concern for its increasingly wretched state had been mounting for some time, concern that focused most heavily on the debilitating influence of the long run and star system that dominated the national scene. The overwhelming emphasis on profit was considered particularly harmful. Popular dramas, among which musical comedies were particularly prevalent, were pervasive in the West End. Many ran for years at a time and were often mass-produced and sent out from London via second-rate, subsidiary companies to tour the regions in ill-equipped venues. The oft-voiced accusation that the provinces were receiving 'smudged carbon copies of last year's West End success' (Jackson and Rowell 1984: 3) refers to one specific anxiety that was related to this system: the insidious effects of London's dominance on the nation's theatrical scene. But the paucity of quality drama translated into other concerns that remained problematic even with the development of subsidized regional theatres after the Second World War: the lack of continuity in theatre companies, particularly owing to a shortage of ensemble work, the prohibitive risks of staging innovative and experimental drama, and the insecurity of the acting profession and dearth of good training forums for actors.

The repertory idea emphasized a permanent ensemble maintaining a broad programme of work rotating throughout the season, and provided one possible way to tackle the problems of the period. Under the dominant system of the long run, tired actors lacked vitality and inevitably undermined quality. Equally, the star system's emphasis on the lead actor negated any possibility of uniform excellence amongst the cast and routinely led to a complete disregard for the script. The repertory idea was also considered pivotal to other concerns harboured by Archer and his friends: in particular, the need for a state-funded national theatre with a programme organized on a repertory basis, improved production standards and the nurturing of new dramatic talent across the country.

Behind such ideas was a growing belief in the educational as well as the entertainment potential of theatre and, beyond that, its ideal role in the cultural life and heritage of the country. Just as the repertory system was inextricably bound up with ideas for renewing the vitality of the theatre across Britain and for re-establishing its links with the community, it was equally tied to the belief that playhouses should also be cultural amenities – a public right supported by public funds, just as museums, libraries and art galleries had long been.[2]

While the repertory movement made some important progress in the first half of the twentieth century, major advances were checked by numerous events. The outbreak of the First World War in 1914 threatened to destroy the movement, with wartime conditions cutting staff and support. The war saw the closure of two of the major pioneer theatres in Bristol and Glasgow, while a third, the Manchester Gaiety Theatre, was only able to continue, even with private patronage, by reverting to its previous role as a 'touring date'. Conditions hardly improved in the two decades following the war and any further progress was impeded by the economic depression of the 1930s and the appearance of the cheaper and more spectacular rival for the theatre's audience, the cinema.[3]

In the years before state funding of the arts, the vicissitudes of history were compounded by the existence of strict legislation and an initial lack of popular and financial support for the repertory movement. The idea offered little by way of commercial appeal, and using public funds for entertainment purposes was strictly prohibited. Under these conditions, the building and maintenance of true repertory theatres at this time was very much a 'rich man's privilege' (Jackson and Rowell 1984: 54). The burden of fostering repertory theatres was left to the enthusiasm and initiative of a few privately wealthy individuals. Most important amongst these were the ventures at the Manchester Gaiety and Birmingham Repertory Theatre. The first was led by the eccentric Rosicrucian English tea-heiress and amateur enthusiast, Miss A. E. F. Horniman. Following her difficult and somewhat turbulent experience with the nationalists at the Abbey Theatre in Ireland, in her second outing she decided to put her wealth behind a more solidly British venture and founded the Manchester Gaiety in 1907. Miss Horniman's forays were quickly followed by those of Barry Jackson, son of the founder of the Maypole Dairies, who built the Birmingham Rep in 1912 and installed his own company, the Pilgrim Players, there.

Fuelled by her belief in the educational and uplifting potential of theatre, Miss Horniman poured substantial funds into the Gaiety. Between 1907 and 1921, during the theatre's lifetime under her fourteen-year patronage, more than a hundred new plays by British dramatists were first produced at Manchester. Sadly, the Gaiety never had the impact she desired. As Miss Horniman's protégé, Basil Dean, a company member until 1913 who left to start the Liverpool Repertory Theatre on a similar basis, wrote, 'the general public regarded the Gaiety productions as lying outside the normal run of play-going, a foreign body in the corpus of theatrical entertainment' (Elsom 1971: 22). By 1921, Miss Horniman felt she could no longer afford to finance such a costly venture and withdrew her backing. Few efforts were made to find an alternate source of funding and the theatre was forced to close later the same year.

The Birmingham Rep had a longer and more distinguished career, but at no less cost to its proprietor. Jackson single-handedly financed the theatre for over twenty years, with estimated losses in excess of £100,000. It is said the scale of his investment prompted George Bernard Shaw to comment that he could run a steam yacht for the same amount of money. Jackson replied, 'Ah, but a theatre is much more fun' (Elsom 1971: 21).

Adding to the challenges of realizing the repertory idea across Britain were a number of ongoing problems incumbent on theatre in the regions, prominent amongst them being the issue of parochialism. The belief that there was an intrinsic lack of cultural sophistication in the provinces was a vital and often destructive factor in the development of the country's subsidized regional theatres throughout the twentieth century. This was by no means a new belief, but rather one that extended back through the modern era, something powerfully demonstrated in the works of the Restoration dramatists, amongst others. In the first half of the twentieth century, before the creation of the Arts Council, attempts to create a network of repertory theatres were undermined by the widespread belief that culture was the preserve of the capital. Certainly, the lack of interest in sustaining the Manchester Gaiety after Miss Horniman's departure was due in part to the idea that the provinces were 'dead areas':

> People were convinced, even those who worked at the Gaiety, that cultural leadership should come from elsewhere, from London, that the provinces were 'dead areas,' and that only the West End could bestow the accolade of success. A company which tried to generate its own light, and did not use the reflected glory of London, was fighting a hard battle for recognition. The Birmingham Rep only received recognition in Birmingham after Barry Jackson had taken over two theatres in London and could claim several West End hits.
>
> (Elsom 1971: 22)

Aggravating this problem was the fact that many of the playhouses operating in the first half of the century were so poorly constructed and inadequately equipped that they could not have coped with the frequent changes of bill demanded by the repertory system. Nor was there a ready-made audience for the type of theatre proposed by the repertory idea. The regional population in particular had become very conservative in their theatre-going habits. People expected plays to run for a week and asking them to change their routine to find out which play was to be given on which evening and plan ahead accordingly was a tall order. At the outbreak of the Second World War in 1939, only two theatres, Birmingham and Liverpool, could be said to be operating a true repertory system in the provinces. The twenty-odd other resident companies that called themselves repertory theatres usually offered twice-nightly programmes of 'popular' plays at 'popular' prices.[4] Although the double bill such theatres offered on an average evening would typically differ, the 'product offered was cheap in every sense' (Jackson and Rowell 1984: 73) and effectively undermined everything the repertory idea had originally represented.

Initially, it looked like the war would repeat the devastation caused by its predecessor. In the first weeks of what came to be called the 'phoney' war of 1939 to 1940, all entertainment facilities across Britain were shut down. In some cases the closure proved to be temporary, but those theatres that did renew activities did so under significantly altered circumstances. The Sheffield Repertory, for instance, moved to Southport for the duration of the war, while the Liverpool and Birmingham Repertories closed for several months. When, with municipal encouragement, each eventually reopened, they were to function as, respectively, a satellite theatre for a provincial branch of a prestigious London company and as a partial receiving house for tours from the capital. With hindsight, these changes foreshadowed many of the ideas that were to shape the regional theatre movement after the war.

The circumstances of World War Two, ranging from the blackout, the bombings and wartime austerity, to the enforced control of labour, collectively brought about important changes in patterns of theatre-going in Britain. For a time it appeared as if these changes presented a potentially fatal threat to the theatrical life of the country and regional theatre in particular. In retrospect, they actually laid the foundations for the establishment, after the war, of a network of regional theatres that came closest to realizing the repertory idea as relates to quality, longer rehearsal periods and new and experimental drama than attempts at any other time. The harshness and restrictions of wartime conspired to produce conditions ripe for fostering new audiences for theatre in the regions. Perhaps more importantly, the war created conditions under which the authorities recognized the importance of the arts above and beyond mere entertainment, to the extent that it led to financial subvention for the arts on a previously unimagined scale. But while the establishment of a network of regional theatres 'of manifestly superior quality in ever-multiplying quantity' (Jackson and Rowell 1984: 76) owed its development to the beginnings of subsidy, the very condition of requiring state funds for their survival has equally meant that regional theatres have constantly existed on an insecure basis. While the potential problems such a system could pose were most forcefully and destructively realized under the Conservative administrations of Margaret Thatcher and John Major in the 1980s and 1990s, the roots of the difficulties can be traced back to the beginnings of subsidy itself.

* * *

By the time theatre subsidy became a fact in Britain at the end of the Second World War, the idea of state funding had been resisted by theatre businessmen for over a century. From the end of the nineteenth century, idealists had argued that the use of public funds would provide a degree of security to the acting profession, ensure that theatre functioned as an agency for the moral improvement of society and create a stimulating centre of prestigious work that would be the envy of the world. This was particularly true in terms of the building and maintenance of a national theatre. Hostility, voiced most loudly by the prosperous actor-managers who made their fortune in the commercial theatre, focused on the belief that government bureaucrats who did not understand the mysterious nature of professional theatre would inevitably take over. In the words of the actor Henry Peat in 1879, a subsidized theatre would 'be staffed by actors well past their prime playing to a well-heeled audience too polite or too inept to notice the senile incapacity of the whole organisation' (Pick 1986: 8). In the years since the introduction of state funding for the arts, both sides of the argument have been realized and the discord never fully resolved.

The lack of resolution can partly be attributed to the almost accidental nature through which state funding of the arts in Britain was established. Hugh Jenkins, arts minister between 1974 and 1976, puts it succinctly: 'a series of decisions were taken – for little reason other than in response to immediate wartime pressures – which effectively set the parameters of the subsidy system operating in the contemporary theatre. They may be said, therefore, to be at the root of many of the tensions and muddles in modern theatre management' (Pick 1986: 8).

The Arts Council of Great Britain, the public body at the centre of state funding ideals, grew directly out of the Council for the Encouragement of Music and the Arts (CEMA).[5] CEMA was an ad hoc wartime institution set up in 1940 'in the best tradition of political expediency and the old boy network' (Hewison 1995: 30). Foreshadowing the Arts Council's constant problems in obtaining sufficient levels of support, not to mention its doubtful arm's length status, funding for CEMA came initially from an independent educational charity called The Pilgrim Trust, an American-funded organization established to conserve British heritage. Under the guidance of its secretary, Dr Thomas Jones, a long-time advocate of adult education, it sent exhibitions and music and drama organizers to distressed areas around Britain. When the Treasury refused the Board of Education's request for increased funds to address the wartime threat to culture and education, The Pilgrim Trust was able to offer £25,000 to set up CEMA, on condition it was matched by £25,000 from the government.

Given the wartime circumstances, it is perhaps not surprising that the ideological issues and practical details of the state's responsibility for maintaining national culture were not at the forefront of the minds of the nine hastily appointed council members when they drew up CEMA's constitution.[6] The founding principles of the memorandum sent to the Treasury in March 1940 to formally establish CEMA failed to address numerous practical and theoretical issues. Closer examination reveals inherent contradictions among the principles, which, with a limited budget, could easily force prioritization of one claim over another. Most notably, the first clause, which asserted the goal of 'preservation in wartime of the highest standards in the arts of music, drama and painting' (Sinclair 1995: 30), echoed a patrician concern for the arts and put it somewhat at odds with the more democratic sentiments of the second clause. This voiced the need for 'the widespread provision of opportunities for hearing good music and the enjoyment of the arts generally'(Sinclair 1995: 30). While these two principles foreshadowed the future struggle over whether to prioritize standards or accessibility – something that has been a perennial concern in the Arts Council – both coincided in their privileging of the professional artist. This focus, in turn, was inconsistent with the emphasis of the third article, which advocated 'the encouragement of music-making and play-acting by the people themselves'. As the cultural historian Robert Hewison has commented, the terms of CEMA's founding policy 'established the fundamental confusion of purpose that was to bedevil public funding of the arts in Britain' (Hewison 1995: 34).

These contradictory ideals affected CEMA's practices from the start. The majority of the Council's early undertakings were based on the personal predilections of the powerful Dr Jones, who saw CEMA operating primarily in a social service capacity, effectively as an extension of The Pilgrim Trust's activities before the war. Its initial work thus focused on bringing drama and music to areas of the country deprived by the war. Sponsoring new or existing theatre companies was very much a secondary consideration. During CEMA's first two years, about half a dozen professional theatre companies were sent out under the Council's aegis to bring drama to theatre-less areas and wartime factories.[7] The first company to be sponsored was Martin Browne's religious dramatic society, The Pilgrim Players, who toured the besieged south coast with intentionally faith-inspiring productions of T. S. Eliot's *Murder in the Cathedral* and James Bridie's *Tobias and the Angel*. The idea behind sponsoring such companies was explicitly directed towards serving audiences. Even so, it should be noted that for practitioners, the precedent and advantages of association with CEMA were first realized here.

The prioritization of social welfare in CEMA's early operations also set the scene for debates over other issues central to the subsequent funding and artistic policies of Britain's regional theatres. In particular, it foreshadowed the question of what constitutes the highest standards of art and both who and what should be responsible for setting these standards. Already, in the first year of CEMA's operations, the antecedents of the ongoing struggle for cultural dominance between London and the regions can be seen. It was at this time that Dr Jones introduced the practice of using 'animateurs', unemployed artists who travelled around the country to areas deprived in wartime, to help organize and encourage amateur cultural activities such as local drama and music. If nothing else, the introduction of animateurs is noteworthy as the precursor of the later local representatives of the provincial playhouses, the regional arts associations, which, from the 1950s, sporadically acted as the primary funding bodies for many regional theatres. Since their foundation, the regional associations' tenuous and constantly changing affiliation with the Arts Council has often been cited by provincial playhouses as contributing to the difficulty of maintaining their operations.

One other event that happened at this time was also to have profound effects on the later developments of the country's regional theatres: CEMA's decision to sponsor the Old Vic.

Under the directorship of Tyrone Guthrie, the Old Vic theatre company was celebrated for its output of classical works. Prior to the war, it was held up by those hostile to state funding of the arts as a shining example of a theatre that did the work of a national theatre without the aid of subsidy. Nevertheless, until this time, the Old Vic had been a purely London venture. When, at the beginning of the war, the company's resident home in Waterloo Road was closed, Lewis Casson, CEMA's director of professional drama and a long-time actor with the Old Vic, offered the company an association with the Council. Initially CEMA's involvement stuck to its brief and simply entailed sponsoring Old Vic tours to culturally deprived areas (*Macbeth* to Welsh mining villages with Casson in the title role; *Twelfth Night* and *She Stoops to Conquer* to the industrial centres of the north west). A successful performance at the Victoria Theatre in Burnley, Lancashire, however, saw the building become a temporary wartime venue for the company. After taking up residence in November 1940, they were joined by the Sadler's Wells companies and opened an eight-week season of opera, ballet and drama. The programme note read:

> Burnley, with the combined season of opera, drama, and ballet, suddenly becomes the most important creative centre in the English theatre. The event is symptomatic of the times. For too long London and the great metropolitan cities have owned altogether too much of the cultural life of the country. One of the most important and encouraging symptoms of the turmoil which we are now enduring is the dispersal of the treasure of art and culture throughout a wider area of the land, and a wider range of the people.
> (Landstone 1953: 22)

Although the Old Vic company returned to London the following year, the time spent in residence in Burnley was a huge success, with performances of *Macbeth*, *King John*, *Twelfth Night* and *Trilby* well received by local audiences. And the company's temporary residence there set a number of precedents. Although anomalous to CEMA's constitution, this was the first major incidence of state support being used to sustain a professional theatre company and it was done in such a way as to emphasize 'good' drama as a right of the nation, not just the metropolis.

> In this war-time effort there was laid down, for the first time, the principle that the best the arts have to offer is not the sole perquisite of big centres; the many in smaller centres have an equal right to its enjoyment. It is a principle that has been argued over, praised and derided, and proved right and equally wrong in practice ever since.
> (Landstone 1953: 21)

In recognition of the fact that good drama should not be the exclusive property of the capital, when the Old Vic company returned its headquarters to London in 1942, Guthrie arranged for a second, subsidiary company to take up residence at the newly reopened Liverpool Playhouse. This event both promoted the regional cause and sowed the seeds for the struggle between the claims of London and the provinces that was so heavily to affect subsequent operations in regional theatres, as evinced by the decision, despite the success of the Old Vic's tenure at

Burnley, to return the main company to London as soon as it was safe to do so. There, as Charles Landstone, the drama panel's first director, noted, few attitudes had changed:

> In my wanderings around the usual haunts of Shaftesbury Avenue and Leicester Square I was annoyed to find supreme indifference to the work accomplished in Burnley. London, superbly self-satisfied and self-sufficient, was quite certain that nothing that mattered could have been achieved outside its own orbit.
> (Landstone 1953: 35)

From the outset, the company set up at Liverpool Playhouse was considered very much a subsidiary group.

The belief in metropolitan superiority was one that penetrated all areas associated with the provincial theatre. If this attitude existed before the war, the introduction of subsidy exacerbated the situation under the auspices of the national funding body. Although its initial investment in professional theatre was concerned with sending companies out to tour the provinces, CEMA was always a London-based operation and continued to be so in its later incarnation as the Arts Council. As such, it has consistently been seen as prioritizing the claims of specifically London-based, national companies, a bias underscored by the person who, more than anyone else, was to influence the principles and policies of the Arts Council and its clients after the war: John Maynard Keynes.

In March 1942, with commitment to amateur work and touring weakening, The Pilgrim Trust withdrew from its involvement in CEMA leaving the organization the exclusive responsibility of the government, financially and otherwise. At this point, it fell to the Board of Education to appoint a new chairman. The new minister for education, the Conservative politician R. A. Butler, invited his old Cambridge colleague and the unofficial economic adviser to the wartime Treasury, the economist Keynes, to take the post.[8]

A robust personality and a great patron of the arts, Keynes was nevertheless not an obvious choice for the role. He had limited sympathy with CEMA's work in the arts and believed that, under its patronage, welfare was being developed at the expense of standards. His artistic preferences were for quality above all. His administrative practices were very much those of an economist and financier. Both ran almost entirely contrary to the practices espoused by CEMA. He was not interested in amateur theatricals, or taking music and drama to parts of the country deprived by the war, as Jones had been. And in bringing such contrary ideas to the table, his leadership of CEMA and the blueprint he provided for its successor, the Arts Council, saw the realization of all the potential contradictions in the organization's constitution. As Andrew Sinclair, biographer of the Arts Council, comments:

> Two characters, Dr. Jones and Lord Keynes, would bequeath to the embryo Arts Council of Great Britain their emphases and contradictions, which were never to be resolved.
> (Sinclair 1995: 36)

Under Jones, CEMA had acted primarily in the interests of social welfare; under Keynes, the funding body became more an arbiter of artistic excellence as embodied primarily by London-based professional companies.

Keynes had long been a passionate lover of the arts and had a long history of personal cultural patronage. In addition to founding and supporting the Arts Theatre in Cambridge in 1936, he was married to the former Diaghilev dancer Lydia Lopokova, served on the board of the Covent Garden Royal Opera House, was a trustee of the National Gallery – in 1919 he had purchased a key collection of Degas paintings for the nation while attending the Versailles Treaty conference – and had been a personal collector of precious books and art all his life. He was also a strong personality with firm convictions about what constituted good art and how cultural policy should be shaped and administered. Keynes was single-minded and confident enough in his own judgement to believe that 'the things he enjoyed everybody should enjoy'.[9] In the chairmanship of CEMA, he saw the chance to forge a national policy of his own making.

Keynes espoused a mandarin view of the arts and, when he arrived at CEMA, he emphasized that the focus should be on quality above all else, something he believed could be achieved almost exclusively by professional companies operating primarily in the metropolis. Under his leadership, the Council's responsibilities shifted to include the high art forms of ballet and opera, while CEMA's welfare activities were significantly reduced, or dropped altogether. The key to Keynes' plan in pursuing his policy of excellence was the creation of national companies, organizations that could represent the very best the country had to offer of their respective art forms. CEMA already supported the Old Vic, the nearest thing Britain had to a national drama company; under Keynes, it also began to support the Sadler's Wells Opera and Ballet companies. A vital part of Keynes' plan was the concentration of these companies in the capital. Such close proximity would allow CEMA, and subsequently the Arts Council, to be heavily involved in the operations of the major companies – if not actually direct them – and would glorify the metropolis itself. Speaking on a radio broadcast in 1945, Keynes noted, 'It is…our business to make London a great artistic metropolis, a place to visit and to wonder at' (Hewison 1995: 44).

Believing that 'in its beginnings, the Arts Council needed the publicity of association with resplendent theatrical productions' (Sinclair 1995: 62), Keynes had CEMA actively link itself with established professional theatre companies, well respected for the quality of their work, amongst which there were a number of high profile, glamorous London-based companies. The first and most important association with an established company came in 1942 with CEMA's sponsorship of H. M. Tennent Productions Ltd., Hugh ('Binkie') Beaumont's production company. Although the initial association simply saw CEMA subsidizing a single tour, the alliance threw up a large number of problems. H. M. Tennent Ltd. was one of the largest commercial organizations operating in the West End, and there were obvious difficulties in the idea of CEMA being seen to use taxpayers' money to support a clearly profit-oriented operation. As much as anything, the Council was prevented from doing so under its own constitution, despite a clause included in the Standard Drama Agreement whereby 'financial arrangements of varying kind and degree may be made with each company to assist its work; and for each the Council is prepared to act as sponsor with Government Departments and public bodies' (White 1975: 47). A solution was found by Beaumont, one of the canniest theatre producers of the last century, and supported by Keynes in the face of a resistant drama panel. With hindsight, it was responsible for bringing about some of the most momentous changes in administrative practices and arts funding, and, by extension, the British theatre community in the years that followed.

As a commercial company, H. M. Tennent Ltd. was subject to the heavy financial burden placed on it by the 1916 Finance Act, which imposed a general tax on entertainment. After the toll was raised in 1941, this levy claimed one-third of a company's gross profits. Only two clauses in the act offered the possibility of exemption from the tax, namely 'if the entertainment is of a wholly educational character, or if the entertainment is provided for partly educational or partly scientific purposes by a society, institution, or committee not conducted or established for profit'.[10] Certain classical theatre companies had managed to gain exemption on the grounds that their work was of a sufficiently high standard to be considered 'wholly educational' – amongst them the Old Vic, Stratford-upon-Avon Shakespeare Memorial Theatre, Regent's Park Open Air Theatre, Wolfit's Advance Players and Keynes' Cambridge Arts Theatre. However, Beaumont was the first to see the possibilities involved in gaining exemption through the not-for-profit aspect of the clause. In 1942, he set up a second distributing company called Tennents Plays Ltd. with a board of directors almost identical to that of H. M. Tennent Ltd. and a charitable, not-for-profit constitution. Rather than producing shows itself and taking the profits, Tennents Plays Ltd. simply charged a fixed fee to other companies for managing their productions. This followed a practice established during the depression years of the 1930s, when such a fixed fee would be given to small, specially formed, limited private companies to run a production. The fee was intended to cover the normal running expenses, administrative costs and salaries of the management personnel, with all profits going to the production company. Thus the profit motive was removed. Tennents Plays Ltd. had a ready client in its sister-company and was able to charge large management fees without ever technically making a profit. So long as the plays they produced were 'of a standard which conformed roughly to...that of the better class plays of the B.B.C. Home Service' (Landstone 1953: 70), they were able to qualify for tax exemption and association with CEMA.

For its part, CEMA gave Tennents Plays Ltd. aid in the form of guarantee-against-loss, a practice initiated and preferred as the most cost efficient by Keynes. This form of funding meant accounts had to be drawn up and the loss accounted for before the deficit would be paid off by CEMA. Ironically, given its legacy, the 1942 tour of *Macbeth*, including its finale in the West End, was so successful that CEMA did not have to give Tennents a penny in funding. However, from this time on, guarantee-against-loss became one of the primary systems of support used by CEMA to fund its clients and continued to be favoured by its post-war successor, the Arts Council.

The problem with this policy, particularly insofar as it went on to affect regional theatres, was that it ultimately evolved into a form of deficit budgeting. Over time, the theatres began to include the promised loss as part of planning their budget, expecting the Arts Council or relevant regional arts associations to make good the loss in the form of the subsidy provided at the beginning of each fiscal year. As a result, according to John Pick, cultural economist and vocal critic of public funding of the arts, 'This habit became so ingrained in the 70s and 80s, taking an enormous state grant for theatre work came to be called '"breaking even"' (Pick 1986: 9). Understandably, as will be seen, this kind of practice ultimately put the regional theatres in a very vulnerable position when the annual arts budget was consistently reduced under the Tory government in the 1980s and 1990s, and when Britain's regional theatres were expected suddenly to reverse a practice evolved over decades of subsidy and start 'earning their keep'.

Keynes' insistence on CEMA's liaison with Tennents had another far-reaching consequence. While Keynes was adamant that CEMA's liaison with Tennents should go ahead, the drama panel, one of CEMA's three panels with executive powers, was opposed to the association. They argued that not only was there enormous room for abuse of such associations, but that the higher level of expenses possible in the areas of royalties, salaries and rentals in subsidized companies would cause inflation in the theatre and set a precedent for competition and commercial success rather than artistic integrity. As such, supporting such companies would undermine the integrity of the Council itself. Keynes' outrage at resistance by the 'troublesome' drama panel ensured that when CEMA was remoulded into the Arts Council in 1945 he saw to it that power was concentrated exclusively in the hands of an executive committee (council), with the staff carrying out the committee's policies and the panels operating in an advisory capacity only. The result has been a lack of consistency in policy – a national policy for theatre was not created until 2001 – and an Arts Council that was 'always to give the appearance of consulting the experts in the respective art forms, [while] the real power of decision lay with members of the Council and their executive officers' (Hewison 1995: 42).

With regard to the development of regional theatre, from the outset the establishment outlook of the executive committee constantly differed from that of the Arts Council's drama department and drama panel's more practical concern for the welfare of the form. While the difference in priorities often led to a fundamental breakdown in communication between the various divisions of the Arts Council, on other occasions it created a situation whereby the executive committee disregarded the views of the drama department or panel altogether. Such problems can be seen in the Arts Council's earliest operations, with the London bias of the council contributing to the failure of the drama department's first attempts to sustain a subsidized repertory theatre in Salisbury, a situation documented more fully later in this chapter. Similarly, the notorious Neville Affair, which threatened the success of the Nottingham Playhouse in 1968 when the board of directors tried to wrest power from the artistic director, was not helped by the fact that the Arts Council chairman and drama panel were separately offering contradictory advice and support to opposing parties involved. Such situations are by no means isolated. By 1985, the problems encouraged by the divided system had escalated so far within the drama panel that overwhelming feelings of impotence concerning the executive committee's persistent disregard of its views, combined with frustration at its inability to help improve the parlous state of the contemporary theatre, caused more than half the panel to walk out on the national funding body in protest.

While such incidents primarily illustrate Keynes' ambitions for central control and the privileged claims of professional and capital enterprises, he was somewhat restricted by CEMA's existing constitution and practices at the time of his arrival. In his 1945 radio broadcast for the BBC, he was forced publicly to reject the idea of metropolitan bias:

> Nothing can be more damaging than the excessive prestige of metropolitan standards and fashions. Let every part of Merry England be merry in its own way.
> (Keynes 1945: 32)

On arriving at CEMA, the rival claims of the provinces had provided a number of obstacles to the changes he wanted to make. In trying to get around these, however, it may be argued that Keynes unwittingly gave support to future arguments for devolution.

The legacy of Jones' animateurs, and their association with 'inconsequential' amateur work, was something Keynes was determined CEMA should be rid of. In looking for ways of doing this, it was noted that the current arrangements of provincial centres of civil defence might equally offer appropriate subsidiary bases for controlling regional arts. In addition to raising the alarm for air raids, in 1942 the ten early warning regions for Britain became the platform for local drama, concerts and arts exhibitions. A regional office was set up in each of these areas, and most of the animateurs and travelling musicians were absorbed into the small organizations to make up the staff – an officer and two assistants per office, each one specializing in either drama, music or the visual arts. These offices were the harbinger of the regional arts associations, and, as Sinclair comments, 'although these bodies were initially given little autonomy, they were "the germ of a great idea" of future devolution, which was far from the current thinking of Lord Keynes' (Sinclair 1995: 37).

In one other significant action, Keynes facilitated the development of the provincial theatres. When he referred to 'Merry England' in the radio broadcast, he was probably referring to the Bristol Theatre Royal, whose lease had been assumed by CEMA in 1942. The 175-year-old Georgian building was Britain's oldest working theatre and had been described by David Garrick on its opening as 'the most beautiful playhouse in Europe' (Landstone 1953: 44). It had nonetheless been in danger of being converted into a warehouse after the previous commercial management had ended its association with the theatre in 1941. Determined to prevent such a tragedy, Keynes saw the theatre's potential in his plan to create 'centres of excellence'. Stepping in on behalf of CEMA, he offered to take a twenty-one-year lease out on the theatre at £300 p.a. and to assume full responsibility for the repair and maintenance of the building. While effectively going against CEMA's constitution, which was for the 'furtherance of the arts, and not for investment in bricks-and-mortar' (Landstone 1953: 44), CEMA was never a corporate body, and such anomalous actions were possible. Citing the 'rare beauty' of the theatre, which had echoed with the voices of 'Siddons, Kemble, Kean, Macready, Irving and Ellen Terry', Keynes wrote a letter to The Times in May 1943, explaining that '[CEMA] is able to do by inadvertence or indiscretion what obviously no one in his official senses would do on purpose...Thus in an undisciplined moment we accidentally slipped into getting mixed up with a theatre building' (CEMA 1943).

Keynes in no way intended this action to undermine the dominance of London, and from its opening in 1943 until the end of the war, the Theatre Royal served as a receiving house for CEMA-sponsored tours of established professional companies. But Keynes was concerned to create 'centres of excellence' and, in fact, only prevented from acquiring a whole string of regional theatres by opposition from other members of the Council who were concerned that money designed for the provision of the arts in deprived areas was going instead towards the acquisition of theatre buildings. Even so, this action foreshadowed one of the more significant schemes of the future Arts Council, the 'Housing the Arts' scheme, which was established in 1965 in order to save provincial drama. More importantly, it brought regional theatre into CEMA's fold and into the system of subsidy.

CEMA's acquisition of the Bristol Theatre Royal was also connected to one other event at this time that was profoundly to affect the later development of the country's regional theatres. Noting the increased interest in regional theatre generated by the Council's involvement with Bristol, the British Drama League requested a meeting with CEMA to discuss its ideas for the creation of a civic theatre scheme. With a view to safeguarding British theatre after the war, the League had drawn up a plan to help sustain and develop the repertory movement. The scheme was based on three major ideals: firstly, that the development and maintenance of civic theatres would require both state and local financial aid; secondly, repertory would best be served if each theatre had its own resident company; and finally, that theatre companies would need to be of a large enough size to undertake a full repertory programme and simultaneously supply a company to tour the surrounding regions.

Keynes was heavily involved in these discussions, most notably with regard to the question of local authority involvement. Despite his personal elitism, he recognized that fostering of the arts could most ideally be realized through a combination of private, state and local support. Under the 1925 Public Health Act, local authorities were strictly forbidden to fund any activities with the primary purpose of entertainment. In response to the Drama League's suggestion about plural funding of theatres, Keynes opened the question of local government's powers to fund such enterprises and what action might be taken to increase these. Although the strictures of this law were not lifted until after his death in 1948, his advocacy of plural funding planted the idea as a central ideology that would function at the heart of Arts Council policy.

What Keynes could not foresee was the potential for contradictory obligations that such various sources of funding might create for a theatre company. Particularly important with regard to the stamp Keynes personally imposed on the Arts Council was the question of how far a 'civic theatre' could simultaneously function as a public amenity and a centre of excellence. Contrary to the culture of excellence emphasized by Keynes, the civic notion of theatres promoted by local authorities, following their increased involvement from the 1950s, focused more on welfare and accessibility. As became all too apparent in later years, in financially restricted circumstances, such broad and disparate obligations could prove almost impossible for regional theatres to reconcile. Under the terms of parity funding in the 1980s and 1990s, such problems became particularly acute when failure to satisfy one public funding body could potentially lead to the loss of a theatre's entire grant and therefore its closure.

By the end of the war, therefore, even before state funding of the arts had been accepted as official government policy, many of the factors that would influence the development of regional theatre in Britain were in place. While the arguments for standards and accessibility offered sufficient grounds for the acceptance of subsidy, and created an environment that would nourish the growth of regional theatres, the failure to resolve priorities equally meant that their development would be conditioned by the contradictions unresolved by CEMA. The importance such issues would play in the development of regional theatres was expedited with the foundation of the Arts Council of Great Britain after the war.

* * *

When the war ended, Keynes moved to get CEMA instituted as a permanent organization with a Royal Charter and a new name. In doing so, he helped create the apparatus that would facilitate the development of Britain's regional theatres on a scale previously only imagined, while simultaneously ensuring that the success of such theatres would be consistently fragile.

As with CEMA, the creation of the Arts Council was almost inadvertent. In the words of one secretary-general, CEMA had substituted a 'demonstration for discussion' (Sinclair 1995: 48). While Keynes' strong leadership and opinions ensured that the Royal Charter establishing the Arts Council of Great Britain was less paradoxical than CEMA's constitution, it still presented aims that without adequate funding to achieve them could prove mutually exclusive in practice. The charter accepted by the post-war Labour government on 9 August 1946 read:

> For the purpose of developing a greater knowledge, understanding and practice of the fine arts exclusively, and in particular to increase the accessibility of the fine arts to the public throughout Our Realm, to improve the standard of execution of the fine arts, and to advise and co-operate with Our Government Departments, local authorities and other bodies on any matters concerned directly or indirectly with those objects.[11]

Despite the experiences of CEMA, it is unlikely that there was a full awareness of the potential implications of leaving drama policy unqualified. So when the Arts Council was incorporated, its charter served as *the* artistic policy for all art forms, and a specific national policy for drama was not drawn up until 2001. The lack of a national policy ultimately meant that, from the outset, regional theatres were subject to the vagaries of the Arts Council at any given moment, and, until forced to make changes under financially straitened circumstances in the 1980s, the funding body reacted to the needs of the arts community as they arose. While complaints about the confusing criteria became common amongst regional theatres, particularly in times of short supply, in the early years the accent was clearly on excellence.

Although Keynes died before the Arts Council was incorporated, he had mapped out a framework to ensure it would concentrate its efforts on the high arts as produced by the professional artist, with a presumption that much of the Council's work would be for an already knowledgeable audience rather than for the development of new ones.

In its first annual report, the Arts Council stated:

> It has been the task of the drama department to begin building up a permanent theatre organization on the basis of the work done during the war...The object is to achieve better productions by getting away from the system which makes it necessary to present a new play every week.
>
> (ACGB 1945/6: 12)

Despite this, while professing its concern for the 'standard of the smaller repertory theatres' (ACGB 1945/6: 12) in the regions and encouraging them to raise production standards by forming small circuits or federations, the Arts Council's official involvement with regional theatres immediately after the war was on a small scale. The first annual report mentions financial aid for only a handful of producing houses: companies in Bristol, Salisbury and the Midlands were directly managed, with a couple more in the West Riding of Yorkshire and Swansea being added to the list over the next few years. Small sums in the form of grant-in-aid were given to theatres in Colchester, Ipswich and Glasgow that the Arts Council had inherited from CEMA. Officially, these were the first examples of the Arts Council's efforts to answer its dual obligations of standards and accessibility – commonly described as 'the best for the most' under CEMA – as outlined in its charter. Setting the pattern for many years to come however, standards, as defined by the capital, were clearly prioritized in a way that effectively undermined any emphasis on accessibility.

As the Arts Council stated in its first annual report, 'the provision of companies at self-contained centres' (ACGB 1945/6: 12) across the country was intended to gradually replace the wartime tours of the provinces. The tours had been perceived as both costly and of uneven standards and were something the Arts Council was keen to dispense with. Instead, supporting a select few regional theatres was seen as an effective way of providing quality theatre to a wider public. They equally supported the repertory idea as a way of improving production standards through longer rehearsal and performance periods by an ensemble company, with the emphasis placed firmly on 'worthwhile drama'.

In Arts Council terms, worthwhile drama remained undefined. In practice it seemed to refer to traditional text-based work in the form of revived classics together with a smattering of new works. In neither arena was any demonstrable concern for audience taste shown. In fact, the possibility that the Arts Council's preferred drama might not be the popular fare enjoyed by the theatres' traditional audiences was not considered an issue at this time, one of the idealistic arguments offered in favour of subsidy being that it 'gave the right to fail' (Devine in Arts Council of Great Britain 1970: 30).

Given such attitudes, it is perhaps inevitable that the Arts Council's early involvement with regional theatres had mixed results. On the one hand, the introduction of repertory work saw critically acclaimed artistic programmes in most of the associated theatres. The Arts Council's annual reports for the first five years constantly emphasized these theatres' success in overcoming the 'pernicious treadmill of weekly repertory' (Sinclair 1995: 420) and made reference to noteworthy productions in its programmes. In other ways these ventures were less successful, and by 1951 the Arts Council had pulled out of direct management of all but one theatre. In most cases, the Arts Council's withdrawal was primarily explained in terms of the overwhelming costs of maintaining such enterprises, although in certain cases, such as that of the Swansea and West Riding theatre schemes, it was admitted that there had been a lack of local interest. Closer examination of the circumstances reveals that the issues were more complicated, relating as much to the constitution of the funding body, together with its internal divisions and relationship to the state, as to the operations of the theatres themselves.

One factor that seems to have contributed to the limited success of early Arts Council involvement in regional theatres was the relative indifference of the executive committee to its work in the provinces. Following the emphases established by Keynes, the concerns of the council were primarily focused on prestigious London companies that received the greatest part of the Arts Council's budget. Comprised primarily of 'the great and the good', unpaid volunteers taken from the ranks of the country's intellectual aristocracy and gentry, they considered the proper focus of the Arts Council to be nurturing art that would demonstrate Britain's national and international artistic prestige and status, rather than contributing to any more general social or cultural development within society as a whole.[12] Nowhere was this more evident than in the fact that Covent Garden and Sadler's Wells accounted for more than 50 per cent of the 1945/6 grant between them.[13]

Since Keynes concentrated executive power in the hands of the council, drama panels have often had to argue the importance of their art form to individuals with little interest or widely differing opinions. Much to the frustration of the organization's first associate drama director, Charles Landstone, the sixteen-strong council in the immediate post-war years never had more than a 'smattering' of drama representatives, and those who were invested in the theatre were primarily interested in the prestigious London companies. In 1947 the lone member of the council with any interest in the theatre was Sir Bronson Albery. He was managing director of Wyndhams Theatres Ltd., a commercial company that owned three prestigious West End houses. As a consequence, the small amount of interest or understanding the council did display was concentrated firmly on the issues surrounding the metropolitan companies:

> From the moment that the power of the Drama Panel was reduced by Lord Keynes in 1945, each successive Drama Director has had to struggle with a Council of which only a minority had any understanding of theatre problems. Solely taken up with what we termed 'Tennentry' and 'Old Vickery,' they have never really regarded the work in the provinces as anything but window dressing.
> (Landstone 1953: 22)

In 1945, when only two members of the council were drama representatives, regional theatre was considered important only insofar as it could operate as a site for pre-West End try-outs or post-West End tours, or as a training ground for future directors or actors of leading metropolitan companies.

Such indifference to the concerns of regional theatre is pointedly demonstrated by the case of the Arts Theatre in Salisbury. Foreshadowing later problems with the Arts Council, particularly following the notorious *Glory of the Garden* strategy paper, the theatre's short-lived collaboration with the Arts Council from 1945 to 1951 outlines how such attitudes could be both beneficial and destructive to the regions.

Prior to the war, the small rural cathedral city of Salisbury had no theatre. In 1944, however, Southern Command allowed Murray MacDonald, a captain on Salisbury Plain and a producer before the war, to convert an old cinema into a garrison theatre seating 400. At the end of the war, the Arts Council took over the lease of the theatre and management of the resident company. While officially justified as part of Keynes' public drive to 'decentralise and disperse the dramatic, musical and artistic life of the country' (Keynes 1945: 32), the decision was probably more heavily motivated by limited opportunities to establish 'centres of excellence' elsewhere. Not least, this was due to a dearth of decent buildings in the regions, many having been ravaged by the spoils of war, or converted for other purposes following the cinema craze in the 1920s and 1930s.

The idea was to create a resident company based at Salisbury that would rehearse and run a play for three weeks, serving both the local community and the surrounding environs. The problem was that, as a resident company, the Salisbury troupe remained responsible for its base theatre even when it was left empty during the company's absences touring the regional towns – for two weeks out of every three-week run, or when rehearsing. It didn't help that the surrounding countryside, rather than being home to heavy industry, was a sparsely populated agricultural area and had a limited box office.

The enterprise was a great artistic and popular success, but still cost the Arts Council £12,000 annually, a heavy toll that continued to rise despite efforts to reduce the amount of time the theatre went black by introducing a second company in 1948. Under this scheme, one company would be in rehearsal while the other performed at home for two weeks and went touring on the third.

If the financial burden caused serious grievances in the Arts Council, it was doubly painful because such sums were being spent on Salisbury. Although, by 1951, the two companies were playing to 4,000 people a week, Salisbury was considered too much of a backwater by the Arts Council to warrant the expense. In the seven years of direct management, only two members of the executive committee – Sir Ernest Pooley and Albery – ever visited the company after opening night. And the latter did so only under duress. In 1949, when Albery was still the only drama representative on the council, he was reluctantly persuaded by Landstone to visit

Salisbury. Albery was duly impressed with the production of Noel Coward's *Tonight at 8:30*. However, his 'ingrained outlook as a leading figure of the West End theatre made it very hard for him…to have full sympathy with the Arts Council's provincial theatre schemes' (Landstone 1953: 110). As he commented to his host during the performance: 'This is magnificent. But it's much too good for Salisbury' (Landstone 1953: 112). In 1951, the Arts Council ended its direct management of the Salisbury Arts Theatre on the grounds of the overwhelming burden to its budget. Despite offering an annual grant of £3,000 to be combined with £1,100 from the Salisbury Corporation and £500 from other local authorities, by 1953 the theatre had fallen back on a programme of weekly repertory.[14]

The prioritization of capital over regional concerns has continued to affect the development of regional theatre, with the larger, primarily London-based national companies continuing to take a disproportionately large percentage of the drama budget in the years since. In the two decades after the war, concern for work in the provinces never seemed more than nominal. This was the case to the extent that the 1949 All-Party Enquiry by the House of Commons Select Committee on Estimates explicitly criticized the Arts Council for its preoccupation with a few prestigious companies in the capital and recommended they should 'turn their energies to making the arts more accessible, being content at first, if necessary, with less ambitious standards'.[15] In particular, the Select Committee suggested that 'the provinces, where the arts are not so readily available to the public, provide a more valuable field than the metropolitan area for the activities of the Council'.[16] The Arts Council responded to this recommendation by pursuing a diametrically opposite policy. Only two years after the results of the enquiry were published, it began closing down its regional offices. Given that the Arts Council was enjoined by its charter '*in particular* to increase the accessibility of the fine arts to the public throughout Our Realm' (added emphasis), it is pertinent to ask why the principle was worded in such a way as to make it sound like a primary consideration, when in fact questions of accessibility, particularly as they related to work in the regions, have historically occupied a secondary position.

The answer to this may well lie in the fact that Keynes was obliged to include the clause as a concession to the welfare state under which the Arts Council was incorporated, rather than to fulfil any deeply felt belief about the importance of widespread provision of the arts for the people. It should be noted that although the Arts Council was established in 1946, it was not a Labour or a socialist creation. The organization grew out of an ad hoc wartime institution, and the decision to perpetuate CEMA as the Arts Council of Great Britain was actually one of the last decisions made by the short-lived caretaker Conservative administration that ran the country following Labour's withdrawal from the wartime coalition prior to the 1945 election. Its capacity as an organization simply inherited by Labour from the wartime consensus provides one reason why the post-war Arts Council should have initially proven a force for cultural conservatism.

The consensus politics governing the policies of successive Labour and Conservative administrations through the 1950s further buttressed this cultural conservatism. The idea of consensus politics, in which Antonio Gramsci's theories of hegemony have been applied to Britain in the war and post-war years, have come to be the accepted explanation for the perpetuation of the socio-political status quo at this time. This particularly relates to the maintenance of the values and power of the British ruling/upper classes. According to Gramsci:

> The life of the state is conceived of as a continuous process of formation and superseding of unstable equilibria (on the juridical plane) between the interests of the fundamental group and those of subordinate groups – equilibria in which the interests of the dominant group prevail, but only up to a certain point.
>
> (Forgacs 1988: 205–6)

In other words, hegemony is achieved 'though a certain compromise equilibrium' (Forgacs 1988: 211). After the war, by maintaining a consensus of agreement on certain key issues, opposing political parties were able to maintain the oligarchy of the great and the good by adjusting the equilibrium of power without provoking so much resistance that consent was withdrawn. Paul Addison's account of British wartime politics, *The Road to 1945*, argues that,

> The new consensus of the war years was positive and purposeful. Naturally the parties displayed differences of emphasis, and they still disagreed strongly on the question of nationalisation. At the hustings the rhetorical debate between state socialism and laissez-faire capitalism was renewed with acrimony. In practice, the Conservative and Labour leaders had by-passed most of it in favour of 'pragmatic' reform in a mixed economy.
>
> (Addison 1994: 14)

Considered from this angle, the patrician make-up and conservative outlook of the Council, particularly in its relationship to the state, begins to make sense. As the social critic Raymond Williams, who served on the Council's executive committee between 1975 and 1978, commented:

> The British State has been able to delegate some of its official functions to a whole complex of semi-official or nominally independent bodies because it has been able to rely on an unusually compact and organic ruling class. Thus it can give Lord X or Lady Y both public money and apparent freedom of decision in some confidence, subject to normal procedures or report and accounting, that they will act as if they are indeed state officials.
>
> (Williams 1989: 44)

In other words, 'the true social process of such bodies as the Arts Council is one of administered consensus by co-option' (Williams 1989: 44).

Post-war consensus politics offers one explanation for the perpetuation of a system at the Arts Council whereby the reins of power continue to be held by individuals with similar preoccupations and standards.[17] Reiterating this point, a survey conducted in 1970 by the sociologist John Harris concluded that there were

strikingly few differences in the social background of Labour and Conservative appointees to the council – except that Labour tended to appoint more from the top twenty state schools. Almost none were working-class in origin, only two were below the age of forty, and only a quarter of the 68 appointees surveyed had earned their living as artists.
(Hewison 1995: 140)

And the power structure implemented by Keynes augmented this situation. The Arts Council has never operated as a democratic body and executive committee members have always been appointed either internally or by government.[18] Since they have never been elected, no individual with executive power has ever derived any part of their authority from the artists or the public. As such, according to Richard Hoggart, the left-wing cultural theorist, it was not unusual for members of the executive committee to owe their nomination 'more to their membership of a quite small, upper bourgeois "cultivated" in-group than to their likely grasp of council matters' (Hutchison 1982: 39). In this context, it is perhaps possible to understand why regional representation on the executive committee has historically been disproportionately low and that, in recommending the Arts Council should provide a better balance of regional membership, a 1980 Arts Council/Regional Arts Association working group noted that 'similar recommendations have been made in the past and have apparently been accepted by those concerned. But in practice there has been very little change' (ACGB 1980: 17)

A second important issue brought up by the Arts Council's early involvement with regional theatres is the question of what constituted standards. Despite the lack of a specific written policy for drama, from the outset the Arts Council has been recognized as espousing overwhelmingly patrician values (Hutchison 1982: 124).

Its initial dealings with regional theatres established the tradition of patronage and excellence. Here, excellence was assumed to be achieved through an emphasis on 'text-based drama produced through a network of playhouses building on the old rep structure' (Peter Boyden Associates 2000). In other words, standards were imposed, from London, based on what the great and the good deemed 'worthwhile theatre', rather than through any concern about what people might like to see. Certainly this seemed to be the only way of becoming a 'non-profit-distributing company' and of receiving exemption from Entertainments Tax, the official requirement of the Arts Council outlined in the Standard Drama Agreement. And it could be argued from this perspective that any efforts the Arts Council made to answer its obligation of making the arts more accessible translated straightforwardly into increased access, rather than any attempt to examine the nature of that access. Fortunately, 'worthwhile theatre' was in tune with the government's own vision at the time. An important part of Labour's plan for reconstructing post-war Britain was the creation of a responsible society. In particular, the new leisure 'threat' of escapist Hollywood films, detective novels, fun fairs and dog tracks should be tackled with interests more in keeping with the construction of a civilized, socially democratic society. The dominant popular culture represented in such commercial activities was seen as threatening the development of fully rounded members of society. An agenda for improving the people, therefore, was broadly shared by many on the political left who aimed to encourage a greater interest in educational activities and enlightenment. Keynes' notion of making 'the theatre and the concert hall and the art gallery…a living element in everyone's upbringing' (Sinclair 1995: 46) complemented these aspirations. The standards set by the Arts Council were therefore endorsed and carried through by both the post-war Labour government and the Conservative governments of 1951, 1955 and 1959.[19]

These lofty ideals have consistently posed a challenge to the box office of regional theatres associated with the Arts Council. And, as with the metropolitan bias, this was evident from the outset. Of the handful of theatres with which the Arts Council was involved in its first five years, two were admitted to be unmitigated failures. Management of theatres in West Riding and Swansea lasted for one and two seasons respectively, and the problems in both were officially blamed in Arts Council reports on a lack of local interest. If true, this, in turn, related heavily to the imposition of standards from afar. The 1946 West Riding Theatre scheme saw a regional company set up and closed down by the Arts Council in the space of a year, not least from the collapse of an approved programme deemed attractive to the local audience. The opening production, a highbrow, morally pious production of Pinero's *Trelawny of the 'Wells'* set the tone. Also including a modern-dress production of *The Taming of the Shrew*, a play simultaneously being performed by the Arts Council-funded Old Vic company in London, a serious piece called *Shabby Tiger* adapted from a Howard Spring novel and George Bernard Shaw's *The Apple Cart*, the season left little room for any humour or light-hearted entertainment. More to the point, this highbrow 'programme bore no relation to the likely popular response' (Landstone 1953: 125). Only one play was offered as a concession to popular taste, but this was not enough to win audiences. The Arts Council didn't help its cause by patronizing the local public in its dealings over the theatre. During the post-mortem of events, it was admitted that there had been no attempt to gauge local opinion about the scheme. Even the Arts Council's regional director was perfunctorily notified rather than consulted about any decisions. It was perhaps inevitable that any chance of raising local interest in the project was lost when 'likely supporters were notified and more or less commanded, instead of wooed tactfully' (Landstone 1953: 125) to give their backing. Even the Arts Council press conference announcing the scheme was held in Leeds, a town miles away from the theatre and its catchment area. The cost of the scheme to the Arts Council was £26,000 in six months, more than a quarter of the entire drama department's budget.

As with the Salisbury Arts Theatre, the specifics of this case are unique to a particular theatre. However, it should be noted that the criterion of excellence, as first embodied in the repertory idea, has remained an unwritten requirement of subsidy since this time, continuing even when access began to be more heavily emphasized under Jennie Lee in 1965. It has continued to remain important, even being upheld as an explanation for cutting grants to certain companies that failed to meet such ambiguous standards during times of economic hardship in the 1980s. Numerous playhouses, such as the Harrogate Theatre, lost their funding for this reason under *The Glory of the Garden*, the Arts Council's radical 1984 strategy paper, and similarly saw it radically reduced for such reasons in 2007. In fact, over the years, subsidy has contributed to the creation of something of a vicious circle for regional theatres. Its emphasis on excellence inevitably raises production costs and typically involves minority programming that has consistently reduced the potential box office. As such, regional theatres' reliance on subsidy has increased. But a good box office has continued to be a vital condition of both subsidy and survival. The Arts Council's inquest report into the failure of the Swansea Theatre scheme in 1950 began, 'Among factors which emerged during the post mortem on this enterprise were: there must be an active preliminary interest among local citizens and a solid centre of box-office support' (ACGB 1950/51: 6). When, twenty years later, the Arts Council launched another major enquiry into the state of Britain's theatres, most of those theatres could also expect substantial contributions from other funding bodies, principally the local authorities. Even so, the Arts Council noted that regional theatres were still expected to gain 75 per cent of their income through the box office to break even (ACGB 1970).

A perennial challenge to regional theatres has been the consistent failure of public funding to keep pace with the increasing demands placed on them as a condition of that subsidy, a challenge similarly faced by the Arts Council itself. From its advent, the size of the grant-in-aid voted by Parliament was considered wholly inadequate to fulfil the role the Arts Council was asked to play. Given the extent of the national debt at the end of the war, the major concern about the arts within the post-war Labour party was that they shouldn't become yet another burden to add to what Keynes termed the 'financial Dunkirk' threatening the country.[20] This concern was clearly indicated by the party's decision to move responsibility for the Arts Council from the Ministry of Education to the Treasury. In other words, moving it from a spending ministry to its opposite.[21] Keynes had been against such a move and raised questions over whether the Chancellor of the Exchequer was the best minister to exercise the power of appointing the members of the national funding body and answer for the Council in Parliament. Such a concern was reinforced by the surprise appointment of the businessman and former Warden of the Drapers' Company, Pooley, to the chair after Keynes' death in 1946.[22] Despite his position as vice-chairman of Sadler's Wells and the Old Vic, Pooley had little history of arts patronage. Sir Kenneth Clark, a founding member of CEMA and revered arts enthusiast and patron, had expected to be offered the position and was outraged at the appointment of someone he considered 'a man of bottom' (Clark in Sinclair 1995: 57). Given the scarce government resources however, Clark understood the decision: 'Having no interests in the arts, [Pooley] could be relied on not to press their claims too strongly' (Sinclair 1995: 57). Clark himself succeeded Pooley seven years later. Perhaps having learnt his lesson, he made sure Whitehall was aware that he too could be relied on not to press the claims of the arts, or the Arts Council too strongly. 'I am not in favour of giving the Arts Council a very much larger grant because I think it will simply get itself into trouble', he told the House of Commons Select Committee on Estimates in 1949.[23]

To try to show the Labour government that state funding of the arts would not be a burden, the Arts Council initiated the pattern of asking for less money than it needed to complete the tasks outlined in its manifesto. The budget for the Arts Council's first year of operation was £235,000 – a sum equivalent to less than 1 per cent of its budget today, after inflation is taken into account, and negligible when considered in light of government spending in other areas and when compared with public spending on leisure: 'In that same period, as a critic of the new arts body noted, the British public spent nearly one hundred million pounds on dog racing and football pools, and half that sum on going to the cinema. Obviously, state expenditure on the arts was a drop in the ocean of popular expenditure on recreation' (Sinclair 1995: 54). Although the budget grew to £500,000 by 1950, this sum was still trifling when considered in terms of the Arts Council's chartered obligations. As its work developed, it inevitably found it needed more than it was being given to raise subsidy to adequate levels to support established companies and take on deserving new applicants, not to mention counteract the insidious effects of inflation. Unfortunately, after its modest start, it never received enough to do all three. During the 1950s, the Arts Council felt itself to be incredibly restricted by the reluctant pace at which its grant was suffered to rise and used its annual reports to make an increasingly desperate and angry case for further government subvention. The titles of many of the annual reports testify to this problem: *The Arts in Great Britain* (1951/2), *The Public and the Arts* (1952/3), *Public Responsibility for the Arts* (1953/4), *Art in the Red* (1956/7), *The Struggle for Survival* (1958/9) and *The Priorities of Patronage* (1959/60).

Initially at least, the impact of any shortfall in the required subsidy was not quite as significant to the regional theatre movement as in subsequent years. One obvious reason for this is that in the first five years of state funding only a handful of theatres received aid through the Arts Council. The fifth annual report, for example, mentioned seven regional theatres that were receiving funding. But over the next five years the figure rose significantly, with the Arts Council's review of *The First Ten Years* in 1955/6 stating that twenty-three of the country's estimated one hundred provincial repertory theatres were being granted subsidy.

This figure continued to grow and place greater strains on Arts Council support, particularly after two major changes in the cultural environment ensured that for the regional theatre subsidy very quickly became a condition of survival. The first problem was the steadily diminishing size of audiences for regional theatre. Continued support from a small percentage of wartime audiences had 'proved, in the post-war years, to be the backbone of support for the Repertory Theatre movement' (Landstone 1953: 60). The changes to leisure-time activities in the 1950s saw this audience starting to shrink at an alarming rate. Following the coronation of Queen Elizabeth II in 1953 and the introduction of commercial television in 1955, two-thirds of the country's households had television sets. From this point, the cheaper comforts of home, combined with television's higher production standards, ensured that theatre became a more attractive proposition to many when watched on television. As the Arts Council 1970 enquiry, *The Theatre Today*, commented, 'Far more people in this country than ever before regularly watch plays but most of them seldom, if ever, go to a theatre, the traditional home of drama. They watch plays on television' (ACGB 1970: 11).

In addition, the pool of actors willing to leave London for any length of time was continually declining. While wanting to remain near the market that offered larger and easier rewards, the relative comforts of working in television combined with improved standards of living also ensured that the upcoming generation of actors were not prepared to tolerate the inconveniences of touring or the poor backstage conditions of most old theatres. As *The Theatre Today* also noted, 'Stars are exceptionally allergic to touring' (ACGB 1970: 11).

While the growing popularity of television increased the difficulties of attracting respected or celebrated actors to the provinces, something that could have later helped attract back flagging audiences or made theatres a more attractive proposition for business sponsorship, it also marked the beginning of the move away from the practice of maintaining an ensemble company. Until this time, the popular practice of building-based producing theatres was to maintain a permanent or semi-permanent ensemble company for the duration of a season. In the 1960s, dissatisfaction with this system began to increase in regional theatres, particularly with respect to the limits it placed on perfect casting and the choice of programming. Many directors saw the practice of casting on a play-by-play basis as more conducive to artistic excellence. But even its most vocal critics conceded that there were other benefits to the ensemble system. It provided job security, eased restrictions on rehearsal periods, and ensured a theatre was burdened with only one set of salaries for actors at any given time. For audiences, there was also the question of familiarity and ownership. Many regional theatres established after the war were built with substantial help from local communities' fund-raising efforts. Employing a resident company who would socialize and live within the community, and presenting the audience with an array of familiar faces on stage week after week, often provided theatres with an effective way of maintaining local loyalty. Peter Cheeseman, a huge advocate of this system, continued the practice throughout his thirty-five years as artistic director at the Victoria Theatre, Stoke-on-Trent. The theatre was established in 1962, and Cheeseman's emphasis on community often involved the ensemble company devising pieces around local events. It is interesting to note that the Victoria Theatre was one of the few regional houses that did not experience a significant decline in audience figures during the hardship years of the 1980s and 1990s, nor did it find itself with such a huge financial deficit as to threaten closure.

Despite the respective arguments for and against the resident company system, from the mid-1950s onwards declining audiences and reluctant actors increased the financial stresses already straining regional theatres. Less money for actors' salaries meant the number of actors that could be employed by theatres at any given time dropped, and with it fell the viability of the resident company. In accordance with the Arts Council's emphasis on excellence and innovation, regional theatres typically tried to present a wide range of drama each season. As the number of actors in a company dwindled, it became increasingly difficult to cast a variety of shows with any degree of credibility. With a few exceptions, this situation led to the gradual disappearance of permanent ensemble companies. By the end of the 1970s, the resident company was primarily a thing of the past. It was predominantly replaced by the system of casting actors on a play-by-play basis. While preferred by many because it provided no obstacle to artistic freedom and ideal casting, this was rarely achieved in practice. Rather, the two sets of salaries necessitated by this system – one for actors in performance and another for those in rehearsal – increased the theatres' financial outlay and under progressively difficult financial circumstances caused them to move steadily towards the practice of safe programming of small-scale productions. By the 1980s, it was the exception for regional theatres to present plays with more than six actors, and *Shirley Valentine* was a staple in almost all programmes. Under these circumstances, this practice, along with the programming restrictions that accompanied it, was widely considered to be a betrayal of the theatres' artistic standards, a failure on the part of audiences and destructive to the acting and writing professions alike.

Compounding this problem in the 1950s were the diminishing resources available from private benefactors. Prior to the war, the repertory movement had been largely supported by wealthy individuals. But the incentive to be a private benefactor was greatly reduced after 1945 when the welfare state brought about a dramatic redistribution of wealth, and theatres were unable to offer their increasingly hard-up sponsors even the enticement of tax relief to continue their donations. The opening statement of the Arts Council report 1952/3, *The Public and the Arts*, expressed alarm at the rate private munificence was waning:

> Private patrons of the arts are not extinct in modern society, but they become scarcer every year. They are diminishing not only in numbers but also in their capacity to subscribe more than token support to art collections, orchestral societies or theatre projects.
>
> (ACGB 1952/3: 3)

The direct result of this was increased hardship for British theatre. The 1950s saw inflation raise production costs at a far greater rate than seat prices. This, combined with disappearing audiences and higher production standards, conspired to make theatre an increasingly unprofitable business and, over the course of the decade, commercial managements began to sell off their provincial holdings for development at an increasingly alarming rate. Discussion in the Arts Council's annual report for 1956/7 focused on 'The Plight of the Living Theatre', where it acknowledged that 'Many theatres have lately been shut down or demolished, and… the process is bound to continue' (ACGB 1958/9: 12). By 1970, the 130 commercial theatres that had existed forty years previously had dwindled to approximately thirty, and the Arts Council was loudly predicting that if the trend were to continue, ultimately only twelve would survive. Perhaps foreseeing this possibility, increasing numbers of regional theatres achieved non-profit-distributing status and turned to the Arts Council for assistance in the 1950s.

By this time, regional theatres found themselves relying increasingly heavily on subsidy to stay afloat. The Arts Council's 1951/2 annual report stated: 'In its patronage of the arts the State has reached a "point of no return", and it cannot now diminish the scale on which it has fostered those developments which have occurred since the Arts Council was set up in 1946' (ACGB 1951/2: 9). In 1956, the funding body reported that, 'during the Arts Council's first 10 years there has been a steady increase in the number of provincial repertory theatres. It is estimated that there are now 100 such theatres, of which perhaps 40 are non-profit distributing, and of these 23 now receive grants from the Arts Council ranging from £250 to £5000' (ACGB 1955/6: 40).

The distortion of the market brought about by the increasing role of subsidy did not help the commercial sector at this time. Forced into competition not only with the cheaper, more accessible media such as television and film, commercial theatres found themselves increasingly pitched against subsidized theatres in a way that found them at a disadvantage. The financial benefits afforded to subsidized theatres often meant they could pay practitioners more generously, provide higher production standards and offer reduced ticket prices. The consequences for many commercial companies were devastating. Numerous touring companies and smaller repertory companies suffered fates similar to that of the D'Oyly Carte Opera Company, whose attempts to compete with the newly subsidized market meant that by the time it was forced to apply for state funding to survive its application was rejected on the grounds of low standards.

After a century of commercial success following its establishment in 1876, the touring company was forced to reduce production costs because the popular venues at which it played charged increasingly lower entry fees. Deflated ticket prices were acceptable to the subsidized companies that from the 1960s dominated such venues. However, for D'Oyly Carte, such ticket prices meant that even full houses would not cover expenses. The company's reduced production costs inevitably translated into a drop in standards and thus D'Oyly Carte's performances compared poorly in the public eye to the higher standards of the company's subsidized colleagues. This proved particularly devastating for the company after its copyright for Gilbert and Sullivan ran out. When attendances subsequently declined, D'Oyly Carte was forced to apply for state funding in order to continue. The company was rejected on the grounds of low standards, with its scenery and costumes singled out as being particularly outmoded. It subsequently closed in 1982. Many smaller commercial repertory theatres, caught in the same vicious circle, suffered much the same fate when waning audiences showed a preference for the better product offered at nearby publicly funded theatres. These dangers had been predicted by CEMA's drama panel in their wartime resistance to the Council's association with Tennents. And this situation arguably led to an increasingly bureaucratic theatre, something anticipated by opponents of state funding of the arts a century before.

The regional theatres that were successful in their attempts to achieve non-profit-distributing status and receive subsidy, however, did not find that all their financial troubles immediately disappeared. The problem of the shortage of funds available to the Arts Council, spread increasingly thin as their client base expanded, was further exacerbated by the continued prioritization of metropolitan interests.

The conflict between London and the regions had been a contentious issue since the Arts Council's establishment. The increase in the provincial client base gave rise to escalating criticism from the regions over the amount of money the Arts Council spent in London, with provincial theatres increasingly indignant at the way they were treated as the poor relations. If the metropolitan bias reflected the concerns of the post-war Council, the shortage of funds only intensified the situation. In answering the charge of prioritizing London's interests, in 1951 Arts Council secretary-general William Emrys Williams observed that the level of funding from the government simply did not allow the Arts Council to fund the arts as generously as it would wish.

> In reconsidering the exhortation of its charter to 'Raise and Spread', the Council may decide, for the time being, to emphasise the first more than the second word, and to devote itself to the support of two or three exemplary theatres which might reaffirm the supremacy of standards in our national theatre. The motto for the Arts Council in the next few straitened years...might be 'Few, but roses,' including, of course, regional roses.
> (ACGB 1949/50: 29)

In fact, with the clear emphasis on 'raise', regional considerations seemed to become increasingly secondary as the Arts Council's regional offices were gradually wound up and the national funding body withdrew from directly managing regional theatres and theatre tours. Most of the 'roses', moreover, seemed to be in the metropolis and non-dramatic roses at that, as an examination of Arts Council funding during these years reveals. In 1950/1, the Council spent more than half of its £314,000 grant on music, opera and ballet, with only £142,500 on drama and the visual arts (ACGB 1950/1). Ten years later this had risen to two-thirds, and in 1960/1 it spent over one million of its £1.5 million grant on music, opera and ballet, with under £200,000 being spent on drama and the visual arts. Throughout this period, Covent Garden alone consistently absorbed over half the Arts Council's budget to support the Royal Opera House and Sadler's Wells.

To help work within the limits of its budget, the regional theatres that the Arts Council subsequently took on as clients were given subsidy primarily in the form of grant-in-aid or guarantee-against-loss.[24] However, grant-in-aid, while reducing the costs to the Arts Council, increased the financial risks to theatre companies, as Williams noted in the Arts Council's 1956/7 annual report, significantly entitled *Arts in the Red*.

> [Grant-in-aid] guarantees that all money allocated is subject to annual control by Parliament; it is, theoretically, based upon a calculation of actual need; and by its short-term nature it restrains its beneficiaries from developing grandiose ambitions. Its disadvantages are equally apparent: it inhibits long-term planning, allows no margin for accidents, discourages any accumulation of reserves for rainy days.
> (ACGB 1956/7)

Subsidy thus by no means guaranteed the survival of all recipients. There are few examples of Arts Council annual reports that do not mention a regional theatre experiencing serious financial difficulties, a problem that mushroomed in the 1980s and 1990s when the Conservatives insisted that theatres be subjected to the blast of market forces. In the interim, however, the situation was further complicated by the involvement of new public funding bodies and a changing cultural policy in central government.

Notes
1. Hugh Jenkins was Minister for the Arts from 1974 to 1976.
2. The British Museum was created by an Act of Parliament in 1753 and then funded by a national lottery. Similar provisions allowed for the erection and maintenance of the National Gallery in 1924, the National Portrait Gallery in 1856 and the Tate Gallery in 1896. The 1855 Public Library Act

allowed local authorities to spend up to a penny rate on building and maintaining public libraries in their area.

3. For more information on the development of repertory theatre in England, see Jackson and Rowell 1984 and Chisholm 1934.
4. It is difficult to quantify the actual number of resident companies at any given time based on the fact that no official statistics have ever been collected and published, and with regard to the constantly differing accounts offered by theatre managers and the national press.
5. It should be noted that the original name of the organization was the Committee for the Encouragement of Music and the Arts (CEMA), the committee being made up of six individuals under the chairmanship of Lord Macmillan. The name was changed when the Board of Education became more heavily involved and set up a council with two additional members under its own auspices.
6. CEMA's original executive committee consisted of nine appointed officials: Lord Macmillan (chairman), Dr Thomas Jones (vice-chairman), Sir Kenneth Clark, Sir Henry Walford Davies, William Emrys Williams, Dr Lawrence du Garde Peach and Dr Reginald Jacques. Mary Glasgow was appointed secretary.
7. These include the Market Theatre Company, which was specially suited to serve the needs of the villages, The Travelling Repertory Company, two teams of The Pilgrim Players and the Perth Repertory Company, which toured the west and north of Scotland.
8. Keynes was offered the chair of CEMA in December 1941. He accepted the appointment along with a peerage and officially became chairman on 1 April 1942.
9. Alan Peacock, chairman of the Scottish Arts Council, quoted in Sinclair 1995: 39.
10. 1916 Entertainments Act, section I, subsection 5.
11. NB. This charter was amended in the 1960s to read as follows:
    To develop and improve the knowledge, understanding and practice of the arts;
    To increase the accessibility of the arts to the public throughout Great Britain; and
    To advise and cooperate [as above].
12. 'The great and the good', also known as 'the Establishment', or 'the intellectual aristocracy', refers to the institution of a certain class of people, originally largely taken from the aristocracy or gentry, thought suitable for the 40,000 voluntary and part-time public appointments in Britain. The power of this aristocratic formation, which, until Thatcher came to office, was largely responsible for maintaining the consensus politics of post-war Britain, extends beyond the official centres of power to include the whole matrix of official social relations within which power is exercised, primarily socially.

    The official existence of the institution can be traced to the Ministry of Labour's register of 80,000 people whose 'brains might be useful' in wartime, and a similar list kept by the Treasury.
13. In his essay "The Intellectual Aristocracy", historian Noel Annan accounted for the continuation of Establishment values in British society in terms of the the nineteenth century rise to power of an administrative class which replaced the traditional aristocracy in government without ever challenging it socially. In this context, it is interesting to note that when the National Lottery was introduced in 1992, it was informally, but widely acknowledged, that it was an attempt by John Major to help the troubled Royal Opera House solve its financial problems.
14. Prior to local government reorganization in 1972, 'corporation' was a term used to refer to the municipal authorities of a British town, borough or city.

15. Nineteenth Report of the Select Committee on Estimates, Session 1948–9, para.39.
16. Nineteenth Report of the Select Committee on Estimates, Session 1948–9, para.39.
17. The composition and attitudes of the Arts Council in the post-war years, and its relationship to the state, certainly reinforces such a theory. To illustrate: at the time of his arrival at CEMA, Keynes was also chairman of Covent Garden Opera House. He was offered the position at CEMA by the Conservative minister for education, R. A. Butler, who was the son-in-law of Samuel Courtauld, a great benefactor of the visual arts and for fifteen years a trustee of the National Gallery. Courtauld's work for the National Gallery coincided with Clark's time as director, and Clark himself was both a founding member of CEMA and chairman of the Arts Council 1950–7. Courtauld was also one of the first trustees of the Royal Opera House, alongside Keynes, and also a member of the Arts Council's art panel. Moreover, the Conservative chancellor of the wartime government who announced the incorporation of the Arts Council, Sir John Anderson (later Lord Waverley), was Keynes' successor as the chairman of Covent Garden Trust.
18. Initially by the Chancellor of the Exchequer, and after the Arts Council was moved to the Department of Education and Science in 1964, by the minister for education.
19. The Conservative Cabinet of 1951 comprised largely the same personnel as the Conservative caretaker government at the end of the war that made the decision to incorporate CEMA.
20. The British national debt in 1945 was £21.3 billion, making the nation one of the world's biggest debtors and effectively bankrupt.
21. The official reason behind the movement of the Arts Council to the Treasury was the fact that its jurisdiction already covered a number of other cultural and scientific organizations. See Hutchison 1982: 160.
22. Although recognized as the first chairman, Keynes actually died nine months after the creation of the Arts Council and before it was incorporated.
23. Minutes of Evidence Taken before the Select Committee on Estimates (Sub-Committee C), 'The Arts Council', House of Commons Paper 315 (HMSO 1949), 54, para. 5328.
24. Between 1945 and 1950, the Arts Council withdrew as lessee of Bristol Theatre Royal in favour of a trust on which it, the theatre and local interests were all represented. The vice chancellor of Bristol University, Philip Morris, became chair of the management committee, and in February 1946 the theatre opened with a new name (in association with the London company – a satellite), the Bristol Old Vic.

2

PLURAL FUNDING, MULTIPLE PROBLEMS

> *One Clerk of the [local] Council wrote to the director of the local playhouse that a grant was being made to it, and 'he accordingly enclosed a cheque for one guinea.'*
> (Sinclair 1995: 153)

Aware that the work of the Arts Council would be constrained by a tight budget but was still required to answer the dictates of 'the best for the most', Keynes had anticipated that his vision for a national culture could best be realized through collaboration with local government. Before 1948, such a collaboration would hardly have been possible since public spending of money collected from the rates, the forerunner of the council tax, had been severely limited. In particular, the 1925 Public Health Act prohibited local authorities from financing 'entertainments which involve...costumes and scenery...[and] performances in the nature of a variety of entertainment'.[1] In other words, it prohibited local authority support for theatre. A growing awareness among politicians of the need to control leisure, combined with the principles of the welfare state, conspired to change this situation. In 1948 the Local Government Act was passed, allowing local authorities other than county and parish councils to levy anything up to the equivalent of a sixpenny rate (6d, today's equivalent of 2½ pence) to support the arts in that region and lifting all restrictions on how that money should be spent.[2] In theory, this legislation should have allowed culture to develop in the way Keynes had envisioned. However, for the arts in Britain, and for regional theatres in particular, the Local Government Act proved to be a 'mitigated disaster' (Elsom 1971: 75).

In part, the problem was simply a financial one. Despite providing the opportunity and incentive for better local patronage, the levy remained discretionary and did not qualify for supplementary support from central government as part of its support for authority budgets.[3] In 1948, up to £50 million could be spent by local authorities on the arts. Nowhere near even half this sum was raised. And right from the start, local authority support was erratic, varying from generous to non-existent, and was always hard to quantify.[4] Complicating the matter was the fact that authorities that did choose to patronize local arts had the right to decide which art forms should benefit. Thus, while contributions to regional theatres increased following the 1948 act, typically the amounts they received were far from generous. In regions where a levy was added for the arts, the funds raised would primarily go to music festivals or orchestras, such as Manchester's acclaimed Hallé Orchestra and Liverpool's Philharmonic Orchestra. Apparently, local councils could more easily accept these as civic amenities than they could a theatre. Two years after the act was passed, the Arts Council made little attempt to hide its dismay at the poor response, commenting that 'the examples of civic aid to local theatres remain a disappointing drop in the ocean of need' (ACGB 1950/1: 25). As early as 1950, the Council was noting lack of sufficient support from the town council as contributing to the failure of regional theatre at Swansea.

The local authorities proved to be uneasy bedfellows in more ways than one. Not only were they less forthcoming with their money than might have been wished, but few local authorities were interested in taking advice from the Arts Council on how they should spend any money they raised. In return, the Arts Council did not act as diplomatically as it might have in this matter. Despite announcing that it set the provision of advice to local authorities 'as one of its most urgent tasks', alongside the creation of a new post 'to concentrate on new regional experiments, particularly those sponsored by local authorities' (ACGB 1948/9: 5), it undermined its commitment by cancelling the appointment after only a year. The ending of this short-lived position also saw the introduction of plans to close the regional offices, the bases from which the Arts Council could most effectively work with the majority of local authorities. So while outwardly the desire to work with local authorities did not weaken in the early 1950s, the practical apparatus through which to do so did. Consequently, in addition to comments on local authorities' stinginess, after 1948, the Arts Council's annual reports constantly called for a change in attitude. The report for 1951/2 adopted a system of naming and shaming when it included a list of selected subsidies by certain cities to highlight the disproportionate contrast between local authority contributions and those of the Arts Council. The highest rate was provided by Canterbury, which had committed a 4d levy, although other city councils were noted for contributions towards maintaining their regional theatres.[5] The very comment, 'there is no need to be disappointed with the volume of municipal patronage of the arts since the 1948 act was passed. But there is every reason to press for further realization by the Local Authorities of the nature of their powers and responsibilities under the Act' (ACGB 1951/2: 6) illustrates the extent of the Arts Council's frustration at such low levels of municipal support.

In contrast to such meagre beginnings, a period of economic prosperity and urban renewal brought about a change in the situation in the late 1950s and 1960s. As the hardships of the post-war years began to ease with increased employment, an end to rationing and extensive building projects across the country, many local authorities saw the construction of new theatres as a way of giving physical expression to civic self-confidence. But rather than straightforwardly relieving the problems of the regional theatres as the Arts Council had so ardently hoped, the increased involvement by local authorities complicated matters further.

The Arts Council's early plans to raise the standards of regional theatres had been hampered by a lack of adequate housing. In 1945/6, the funding body had noted: 'the small town work presents...very serious problems. The first is the lack of adequate halls or theatres. Most public halls have been built without any regard to proper stage facilities' (ACGB 1945/6: 13). A shortage of funds meant there had been no money to improve this situation, and in 1959 and 1961 two surveys conducted by the Arts Council deemed the majority of buildings uneconomic and inadequate to meet the demands of directors, actors and audiences for better working conditions and more comfortable surroundings. In 1965, extra government aid earmarked for capital purposes allowed the Arts Council to follow up its 1961 report. In *The Needs of the English Provinces*, it argued that every town with a population of 200,000 should have at least one theatre, but that 'in the housing programme of this country the arts are still right at the end of the queue and have as low a priority as prisons' (ACGB 1961: 9). Increased government aid enabled the Arts Council to offer local authorities a financial incentive to help improve the situation through a new scheme called Housing the Arts. Challenge funding offered through this scheme, whereby the Arts Council would provide help conditional on their sum being matched by the local council, received an overwhelming response from local authorities, and new theatres were built across the country at a rate not matched since the Frank Matcham boom of the 1890s.

Increasing post-war prosperity, accompanied by a widely shared faith in the necessary and inevitable improvement of the country's standards of living, facilitated a change in people's perception of the arts, and theatres were seen as one possible way of contributing to this improved lifestyle. In such an atmosphere there was greater public support for the notion of the arts as a valuable part of a healthy and progressive society, and they came to be considered a necessary complement to the technological transformations. Support was bolstered by the element of competition, whereby a good incentive for one city to erect a new theatre was if the next town built one. The first post-war theatre, the Belgrade in Coventry, so-called because it was constructed with wood donated by the Yugoslav government, was built in a city that had been devastated by fire and bombing during the war, and it was seen as offering an exemplary programme of urban renewal. Within six years of its construction, two new theatres had been built in the neighbouring towns of Leicester and Nottingham, and several more were planned nearby.

Between 1938 and 1958, the year the Belgrade opened, no new theatres had been built in Britain. By 1970, twenty-one new theatres had been opened across the country. Twenty of these were in the provinces, and fifteen were specifically designed for regional repertory purposes. Although often supplemented by contributions from local community fund-raising, they were primarily funded by donations from local authorities who then typically became the proprietors of the new buildings. In most cases, the developments took the shape of new or substantially rebuilt theatres with a marked increase in auditorium size and technical capabilities. Proven repertory companies were often beneficiaries. Coventry, Nottingham, Sheffield, Birmingham, Bristol, Billingham, Bolton, Chester, Exeter, Farnham, Greenwich, Guildford, Salisbury, Worcester and Leatherhead all benefited, with, for example, Sheffield's new Crucible Theatre, seating 1000, replacing an older building with 547 seats. The new Nottingham Playhouse, seating 760, replaced an older building seating 433. There were also numerous new ventures embarked on and buildings constructed in such major cities as Liverpool (Everyman), Manchester (Forum, Contact and Royal Exchange), Newcastle (University Theatre) and Leicester (Phoenix), as well as new theatres in Stoke-on-Trent, Mold, Scarborough, Chichester and Pitlochry.

While general enthusiasm and increased financial subvention in many ways gave the regional theatre movement a new lease of life, a lack of forward planning meant that, for many theatres, the long-term effects of local authority investment provided as many problems as benefits. Rather than providing and maintaining a theatre at no charge to the resident company, in many towns a situation arose whereby regional theatres were using the subsidy they received from the local authority to pay that same authority back the mortgage, lease or rates tax on the building. In some cases, this was more than the annual subsidy provided by the local council. In 1970, seven years after it was built, the Nottingham Playhouse was being given an annual subsidy of £22,000 by the city council. Meanwhile, the resident company was repaying the council the total original cost of the building to the tune of £27,000 a year. The Arts Council commented angrily:

> This figure is more than some West End theatres ask for rent – and they are able to charge much higher prices for seats than the reps can – although the reps seem to flinch too easily from their obligation to consider price increases. These heavy mortgages... make a very big hole in Arts Council subsidies...Why should a civic theatre not be considered an amenity comparable with a municipal library or art gallery?
> (ACGB 1961: 9)

Local authority involvement brought other problems for regional theatres. The increased expense of running much larger, more technologically advanced buildings immediately put a further strain on most companies' already overstretched budgets. Maintenance costs are something particularly vulnerable to outside variables such as escalating inflation and recession, two factors unforeseen during the economic boom of the 1960s, but which effectively characterized the 1970s. Designed and built primarily in an era of expansion and development, the new buildings needed considerable sums just to stay in working order. The international oil crisis saw heating costs quadruple in price between 1973 and 1974. And when this coincided with a substantial rise in the salaries of actors and staff, the spaciousness and technical capabilities of these theatres could be viewed as a burden rather than a benefit.

The Birmingham Repertory is a good case in point. In 1974/5, the theatre's maintenance costs before salaries, set and costume expenses accounted for 66 per cent of the theatre's total budget, something not untypical in regional theatres at the time. Ideally, part of the elevated costs should have been covered by a better box office from the new, spacious auditorium. But as audiences became choosier about what they wanted to see, particularly following the rapid rise in ticket prices in the inflationary 1970s, Birmingham's large auditorium could sometimes look bleak and deserted, even with several hundred people inside. The same could be said of Leatherhead, Coventry, Sheffield and many others.

Such challenges were not helped by the continuing disputes between the Arts Council and the local authorities concerning the roles and functions of the regional theatres. Civic support meant increased civic interference. Since many of these theatres were built as much for the popularity and prestige of city councils as out of any concern for the arts, it is perhaps understandable that a certain municipal aura became attached to many provincial houses. Local authorities were often less keen on the highbrow, minority programmes that excluded a large part of the community, or the exploratory, risk-taking ventures the Arts Council began to emphasize in the 1960s as a vital part of a healthy arts scene. 'Populist' was not anathema to local authorities in the way it was to the Arts Council, and many city corporations, concerned primarily with accessibility, encouraged the view that regional theatres should be seen as community-oriented arts centres. While drama remained at the hub of their activities, local councils also expected the theatres to function as multipurpose arts centres, presenting a variety of activities such as art exhibitions, screenings, youth programmes and public amenities. They had, after all, been officially erected by local authorities as part of the welfare state's social democratic ethos; in other words, they were built to provide a social service.

Local authority funding also required accessibility be maintained in terms of affordability, and theatres were expected to keep tickets at reasonably low prices such that they would be available to all. Early post-war intervention by the Arts Council had unquestionably helped artificially depress ticket prices in associated theatres. By the 1960s, however, such a concern largely took second place to the national funding body's emphasis on standards, whereby subsidy was primarily given to improve artistic quality and allow for an adventurous programme. While the Arts Council was suggesting that regional theatres should raise seat prices to make up the shortfall in income, from the 1960s, keeping the cost of tickets down was seen by the regional theatres as necessary to fill the large new auditoriums and to maintain funding from local authorities. Such conflicting demands escalated in times of financial shortage, particularly contributing to a whole series of difficulties under Thatcher. As we shall see, the history of artificially deflated ticket prices placed increased restrictions on the amount of revenue theatres could generate to compensate for falling levels of subsidy. At the same time, retaining even small amounts of state support was conditional on offering a broad range of costly social utility programmes.

The theatres' continuing problems of pairing local authority and Arts Council objectives further fuelled antagonism over questions of responsibility. The Arts Council had initially encouraged local authority investment partly to relieve its own burden. Certainly, city corporations bore the lion's share of the construction costs of building and renovations in the 1960s and 1970s, and started providing more substantial annual subsidies than they had previously. Even so, the proportional increase in their funding from this time consistently failed to keep up with the rising costs of the increased number of companies on the Arts Council's books. And local authority contributions rarely matched the grant-in-aid provided by the central funding body. Although matching or parity funding was not officially adopted until 1986, from the 1960s it existed as an unofficial condition of Arts Council grants. Under these terms, as will be seen, increased intervention by local authorities often made their support something of a double-edged sword for regional theatres.

Historically, serious difficulties in ensuring local authority funding has kept pace with that of the Arts Council stems from the fact that local authority funding has always been subject to the vagaries of local politics. Their continued support depends on municipal decisions made on an annual basis. These, in turn, are subject to variations in the economy and the political affiliation of the local authority. Elections for local government are held every four years, and many councillors' support for the theatres has traditionally been undermined by the belief that the arts are not a high priority in the local public's mind. To complicate matters further, over the past fifty years, local government in Britain has been reorganized on numerous occasions.[6] Most importantly for arts funding, the Local Government Act of 1972 altered the system to establish two tiers of local government, each with 'comprehensive powers enabling them to provide or assist cultural activities' (Devlin and Hoyle 2000: 44).[7] But their geographical jurisdictions often overlapped, and the division of their responsibilities with regards to arts funding has often been seen as ambiguous. And as separate bodies, county councils and district or city councils could also have different party political affiliations, something that has led on numerous occasions to enormous confusion and hostility over the question of who should be responsible for the local theatre.

The case of the Bristol Old Vic in the 1980s serves as a good example. Britain's oldest continually-running theatre spent most of the decade with a deficit so large as to put it constantly on the brink of closure. Many of its problems related to the tense relationship between Bristol City Council and Avon County Council. Since the reorganization in local government, the two had famously failed to get along and refused to coordinate responsibility for grants. The situation deteriorated further when Bristol City Council's discretionary grant was restricted by central government after rate-capping was introduced in 1984. The local authorities' failure to agree over questions of responsibility meant that between them they consistently failed to provide enough funding to raise the Old Vic's subsidy to a level equal to that of the Arts Council's. In turn, the central funding body retaliated by effectively holding the theatre to ransom and consistently refusing to raise its grant unless the local authorities reached a matching level. In the ten years from 1981 to 1991, Arts Council funding only rose by a meagre £30,000, far behind inflation. And at the end of this period, when the Arts Council's grant to the Bristol Old Vic was £520,000, well below the needs of a playhouse of its size and scale, the theatre still only received £120,000 from the City Council and £115,000 from Avon County Council.

In other cases, the consequences have been even more extreme, particularly after parity funding was adopted as official Arts Council policy in 1986. Under the Conservatives in the 1980s, the Arts Council offered parity funding as an official reason for withdrawing grants from a number of theatres. While promoted as a way of safeguarding theatres, critics often countered that it offered a convenient scapegoat and means of relieving the central body's own financial burden. The earliest victims to suffer in this respect were Canterbury's Marlowe Theatre and the Lyceum Theatre at Crewe, which both lost their entire Arts Council grants on these grounds in 1981. The policy of parity funding was also instrumental in the bankruptcy of the Liverpool Playhouse in 1990 and the closure of the Merseyside Everyman in 1993, as documented in chapter nine. To this day, plural funding remains an important principle and one supported by theatre boards and artistic directors alike as theoretically minimizing the vulnerability of theatres to the changing political priorities of national and local government. In practice, the multiple and conflicting demands placed on theatres by their numerous support systems have often undermined the benefits and made regional theatres' dependency on public funding more and more problematic.

Local authority investment and the increasingly vital role theatres were subsequently expected to play in their communities brought up further questions about the organization and control of regional theatres. A series of crises afflicting various theatres as they tried to find a way to balance questions of artistic integrity and financial accountability can be seen as precursors to the more serious problems posed to theatre management during the later Conservative administration.

Subsidized regional theatres founded after the war have typically been governed by trusts or limited companies. Many of these non-profit-distributing companies were originally formed by local theatre enthusiasts and managed by a board of directors comprised of elected representatives from the community. From the 1960s, these representatives were joined by local councillors, with local government funding often conditional on a number of seats on the board being reserved for their members.

By law, the board has historically held overall responsibility for the conduct of a theatre's affairs. However, as the Arts Council noted in its 1970 theatre enquiry, 'artistic control of a theatre should be vested in the Artistic Director. As long as he keeps within the budget, and retains the confidence of the public, the choice of plays and all that is implied in the choice should be his' (ACGB 1970: 51). While the divisions of responsibility have generally been clear and respected, increasing and often conflicting demands on the boards and funding bodies have occasionally seen boards encroach on the artistic director's territory. The first notable incidents of this took place between 1966 and 1969, when a spate of disagreements on policy led to the departures of artistic directors in Stoke, Glasgow and Nottingham. Most notorious of all was the 'Neville Affair' at the Nottingham Playhouse.

In 1967, Nottingham's popular director, John Neville, had tendered his resignation, more nominally than anything else, in protest at the low levels of subsidy being offered by the Arts Council. A strange situation then transpired when the board asked him to withdraw his resignation, but then refused to accept that withdrawal. Behind the board's change of heart was mounting indignation at the independent manner in which Neville had conducted the theatre's business. Apparently embarrassed by his refusal to remove a 'tasteless' art exhibition from the Playhouse's foyer, the board's support for their artistic director had then further waned following a personal crusade by Neville to visit the Arts Council chairman, Lord Goodman, to ask for an increased grant. Threatened by a director encroaching on what they perceived to be the board's territory, their frustration escalated at reports of an 'angry' Goodman and turned to anxiety lest Neville had put the theatre's funding in jeopardy. In their decision to let Neville go, they were also almost certainly influenced by advice from Joe Hodgkinson, a member of both the Playhouse's board of directors and the Arts Council's drama panel, whose official line at that time recommended changing artistic directors every five years. Consequently, it was widely believed that getting rid of Neville was a means for the board to increase their control of theatre policy. Ignoring the outcry from the local community at their refusal to allow Neville to withdraw his resignation, the board announced the name of the new artistic director. Four hours later they told Neville's support group that it was too late to accept the 14,000-name petition for the director's reinstatement despite the fact that the group had been attempting to submit it for the previous two days.

In *The Repertory Movement*, George Rowell and Anthony Jackson note that, with hindsight, such problems were 'almost inevitable teething troubles brought about by new circumstances' (Jackson and Rowell 1984: 116) of expanded activities and responsibilities for the theatres. This may have some validity, but the relationship between the board and the artistic director has always offered scope for abuse, a situation that increased tenfold with the introduction of local councillors at board level.

The distinct interests of the various groups comprising theatre boards since the 1960s have inevitably complicated the task of reconciling artistic and financial responsibilities. Prominent amongst them, for instance, are the local representatives, unpaid volunteers who largely tend to be drawn from populations with generous amounts of leisure time and disposable income. As such, local representatives have historically been drawn largely from the wealthy bourgeoisie and gentry, or from amongst local pensioners. Not surprisingly, then, there has been 'some class bias in interpreting artistic endeavour' (Sinclair 1995: 126) and the traditionally conservative outlook of elected volunteers has tended to align itself with the intellectual emphasis of the Arts Council. Such priorities, of course, typically differ from those of local councillors, who are primarily concerned with financial accountability, social utility and accessibility. In times of affluence, such as in the late 1960s, such disparate groups were, for the most part, able to coexist harmoniously. Under circumstances of financial hardship, as in the 1980s and 1990s, the different, often contradictory emphases could easily lead to damaging internal divisions within the board, which had the potential to effectively debilitate a theatre, a fact demonstrated to alarming effect in the case of the Salisbury Playhouse during the 1990s (see chapter five). And as will be discussed in more detail later, the added strain on financial accountability that came with the introduction of the 1988 Insolvency Act made increased board interference in artistic policy virtually inevitable, and made working in regional theatre an increasingly untenable proposition for many artistic directors.

The challenge of trying to please several masters – the Arts Council, the local authorities, the boards of directors and the audiences – became even more complicated when a third string of funding bodies was added to the equation. The creation of the regional arts associations was first initiated by local individuals and organizations as a way of asserting the importance of devolution, or rather the importance of maintaining regional control over local concerns. Even so, for Britain's regional theatres, they too have proved a mixed blessing.

Ironically, the regional arts associations were a direct result of the Arts Council's efforts to assert and consolidate control in London. The years 1952 to 1956 saw the Arts Council close down all nine of its regional offices across the country.[8] Grant-in-aid was replacing direct promotion as the primary form of funding, and the funding body had withdrawn from direct management of all provincial companies. Consequently, from the Arts Council's point of view, the regional offices had become obsolete middlemen and eliminating them would save the Arts Council £20,000 annually, approximately 5 per cent of its total grant at that time. The decision, however, did not go down well in the provinces, particularly when it coincided with the announcement that additional annual grants of £80,000 were to be made to Sadler's Wells and the Royal Opera House, Covent Garden. The changes were largely the work of the new secretary-general, William Emrys Williams, who had taken up the post in 1951 and, with a background in adult education, might have been suspected of leaning more towards the interests of the ordinary man in the provinces. As secretary-general, however, Williams firmly joined the ranks of the patriarchal and the centralists. The man infamous for coining the epithet 'Raise and spread', it was he more than anyone who was responsible for putting the emphasis on 'Raise'. Closing the regional offices was, he argued, was a policy of consolidation in preference to further diffusion; the Arts Council's job was to consolidate standards in London.

The regional offices had been highly valued by local arts organizations for an expertise that spanned both Arts Council policies and the specific needs of the local population. The south west, for instance, had few theatres or council halls and had relied on the Arts Council's Bristol office to help coordinate small tours and book artists. The declaration that the Bristol office was to be closed in 1956 so angered local representatives and arts practitioners that a six-strong delegation set off to London to confront Williams. They were, in many ways, successful. In his obituary, another member of the delegation described how the Cornishman Perry Morgan, the first chairman of the first regional arts association, South West Arts, effectively intimidated Williams into agreeing to a grant to help fund a new local arts administration:

> It was Trelawney's day, entirely appropriate for a Cornish-led rebellion. Undaunted by the fading décor of the ballroom at 4 St James's Square, and equally unresponsive to Sir Williams's voluble blandishments, Perry rapped the table...and said with quiet authority, 'Sir William, please be silent; we have come to do the talking.' We reeled out an hour later with a few thousand pounds in our pockets and the agreement to set up a regional arts association.
> (South West Arts 1980: 3)

Two years later a similar association was established in the Midlands, and over the course of the following two decades ten other regional arts associations were founded across the country. By 1973, when the final association, South East Arts, was created, almost every part of Britain was covered by a regional body.

From the outset, the regional arts associations' collective relationship with the Arts Council was patchy. Certainly, the Arts Council was always ambiguous about and suspicious of the regional arts associations, which it traditionally saw as junior partners, existing to take responsibility for smaller, less 'important' art forms such as rural and folk activities – 'amateur theatricals, the crafts and the like', Lord Goodman described them in a House of Lords debate in 1972 – and as marketing officers to develop audiences for existing subsidized companies. In turn, for their part, the regional arts associations constantly asked for more substantial expressions of confidence in terms of money and power from the Arts Council. Lord Feversham, the first chairman of the Standing Conference of Regional Arts Associations (CoRAA), told a regional studies conference in 1974:

> During the five years in which I have been involved with this business I have been constantly baffled by the expression of mystification which comes into the eyes of Arts Council mandarins at the mention of the regional arts associations. I cannot remember a time when I have had the feeling of being received at the Arts Council as a colleague involved in the same business. Rather one is given the feeling that one is some kind of orange three-headed martian with antennae sprouting from the forehead who has just landed by flying saucer in Green Park.
>
> (Feversham 1974: 8)

The circumstances surrounding the creation of the associations didn't help the situation. Each individual association was formed by its local community in circumstances unique to the particular region, developed its own artistic policy and had its own constitution. Although autonomous bodies as opposed to regional outposts of the Arts Council, the regional arts associations nevertheless received varying levels of funding from the central body. The alternative would have been direct provision by Whitehall, something the Arts Council was keen to avoid, officially because it would undermine the sacred arm's length principle, unofficially because it might have rendered the Arts Council redundant in much of the country and reduced it to nothing more than a regional association in its own right. Unfortunately, the administrative costs of running such agencies took up vital funds that it was widely thought could have gone directly to the theatres themselves. While undermining Williams' official reason for closing the regional offices in the first place, this perception meant the inflated administrative costs later caused enormous resentment and strained relations between many theatres and their regional funding bodies, something that reached its peak under the Conservatives in the 1980s.[9] Certainly, such tensions were not helped by the fact that each association had its own constitution. They never operated collectively as more than a loose federation of funding bodies, with individual artistic policies often not only differing from each other's, but from the Arts Council's as well.

Many of the regional arts associations were created and funded partly through matching grants provided by local authorities, with the condition of such funding being local authority representation on the executive board. With representatives from the district and county councils often holding different political affiliations, following local government reorganization in 1972 the ambiguous question of local government responsibility for arts funding has, on occasion, seen representative officials using their positions on the boards to exercise their political ideals and the regional arts associations subject to the vagaries of local politics.[10]

Regional arts association income from local authorities has never exceeded 30 per cent. Despite this, it has often been argued that their involvement in supporting the regional arts associations has led local authorities to believe themselves relieved of the burden of directly supporting arts organizations such as the provincial playhouses, particularly after responsibility for the theatres was increasingly devolved during the 1980s and 1990s. Given that matching funding by local authorities remained an unwritten condition of receiving Arts Council funding following the introduction of the first regional arts association, precariousness as well as patchiness was characteristic of regional patronage.

On their side, the regional theatres were not happy that responsibility for their care was being passed to second-tier disbursement agencies with less power and money than the Arts Council. Such delegation has alternatively been perceived as designating provincial theatres as secondary considerations, or, worse, passing the buck. As Robert Hutchison, a former senior research and information officer for the Arts Council and later chief executive of South West Arts, commented: 'Government in practice depends on the devolution of unpopular tasks, and it is to the regional arts associations that responsibility for some of the stickier questions of arts subsidy...has been passed' (Hutchison 1982: 150). Such a comment proved particularly astute under the Conservative government with regard, for instance, to the Arts Council's 1984 strategy of devolution, *The Glory of the Garden*. Here, devolving certain 'troubled' regional theatres to the regional associations was widely perceived as a way of shifting responsibility, and thereby criticism, one step further from the equally troubled national funding body. Whether tactical manoeuvring or not, what made such delegation particularly difficult for regional theatres was the fact that the regional arts associations have historically had very little money. Despite having much wider responsibilities than the Arts Council, in the five years between 1974/5 and 1979/80, for example, the total expenditure of the twelve regional arts associations increased from £2.5 million to £8.4 million. During the same period, the total expenditure of the Arts Council increased from £16.5 million to £49.4 million.

* * *

The increasing emphasis on plural funding in part resulted from the election of a new Labour government in Britain in 1964, a change that opened a completely new chapter on the arts in Britain. The election of Harold Wilson's party to office ended an uninterrupted thirteen-year Conservative rule and reflected a move away from the largely paternalist society of the early post-war years. Changes in the socio-economic situation in Britain, varying from the increasing affluence that stemmed from the 1950s and 1960s post-war economic boom to the expansion of higher education following the 1944 Butler Education Act and the growth of the consumer culture, saw a significant change in the national mood. This was marked most clearly by a notable liberalizing of social and moral attitudes.[11]

The 1960s witnessed a sense of optimism and increasing personal freedom that resulted in a greater questioning of authority and tradition, a new sense of confidence amongst the young and sections of the working classes and the belief in the real possibility of change in British society as a whole. Included in this change were new ideas about the significance of culture and the forms it should take. But, in retrospect, this period of expansion and change only added to regional theatres' long-term difficulties.

Prior to the 1964 election, the Labour Party had shown an indifferent record of support in the field of culture and communications. In February 1965 however, four months after the election, it became the first British government to produce a White Paper discussing official policy on the arts.[12] *A Policy for the Arts: The First Steps* was the first official government document to recognize the increasing importance of culture in people's lives and the broad sense in which it existed. As part of this, it noted and condemned the post-war period's failure to acknowledge and value culture in any terms other than the narrow patrician definition of the fine arts. It pledged to 'bridge the gap between what have come to be called the 'higher' forms of entertainment and the traditional sources – the brass band, the amateur concert party, the entertainer, the music hall and the pop group – and to challenge the fact that a gap exists' (Lee 1965: para. 71). To facilitate such a change, Labour accompanied *A Policy for the Arts* with the appointment of the energetic Jennie Lee as the first minister for the arts. At the same time, it moved responsibility for the arts from the Treasury, where the emphasis had always been on good housekeeping and probity, to the more generous Department of Education and Science. The following years saw substantial increases in the size of government subvention to the arts, which almost trebled in four years, rising to more than £7 million in 1967/68.[13]

The significant increase in arts funding allowed the Arts Council to experience a period of extraordinarily energetic growth and, almost for the first time, financially support its clients above subsistence levels. This allowed the funding body to 'contemplate the most revolutionary change of all, namely a transition from the poor-law technique of limiting our assistance to a bare subsistence level, with stringent means tests, towards a system of planned subsidies for improvement and growth' (ACGB 1965/6: 9).

Such generosity did not come without strings. Despite the Arts Council's history of complaints about the size of its annual grant, the consistent shortage of funds had afforded the funding body one advantage – it had avoided attracting attention from Parliament. The astute Keynes had once said to an employee, 'As long as the Arts Council doesn't get too much money, the Government won't start interfering' (Sinclair 1995: 123). And not without reason, as with increased money came increased intervention. From this point on, there was no question but that Arts Council policies should reflect those of the government – a situation the organization has since been unable to escape.

In 1965, Arnold Goodman was appointed to succeed Kenneth Clark as chairman of the Arts Council. Goodman was a solicitor who had represented several prominent members of the Labour Party. He was also an unofficial adviser to Harold Wilson and a close friend of Jennie Lee. He shared the government's liberal tastes, and, under his leadership, the policies of the Arts Council shifted to embrace the broad-minded and expansive ideals of the Labour party. A year after he arrived, the shift in policy was clearly visible, with Goodman noting that if the role of the Arts Council 'is to improve the working conditions of artists and to preserve and enlarge their public...it is this latter function that constitutes our major activity' (ACGB 1967: 2). A flurry of new schemes were developed by the Arts Council, whose attempts to 'bridge the gap' included more grants for individuals, bursaries for development work and assistance to enable the inexperienced to acquire greater knowledge in their field. A new emphasis on community arts, meanwhile, saw increased awareness of the importance of the arts for young people. A Young People's Theatre Panel was set up in 1967 and funding given to found the National Youth Theatre in 1969. The Arts Council also created a New Activities Committee in 1968, created to support forms that did not respect traditional cultural categories and which found new creativity in mixing media in the shape of 'installations', 'environments' and 'happenings'.

In the theatre, laboratory work, alternative drama – which began to develop following the abolition of the Lord Chamberlain's role in theatre censorship in 1968 – community arts, young people's theatre and educational theatre were all given financial incentives. Such was the liberal attitude and the relatively generous funding of Wilson's government and its intermediary body the Arts Council, that, by the end of the 1970s, the half-a-dozen 'fringe' groups that had existed in the mid-1960s had mushroomed to over a hundred 'alternative' theatre companies receiving subsidy of various levels from the Arts Council or local sources.

Despite the fact that no national policy for theatre was produced outlining the Arts Council's ideas, the radical change in the outlook of its main funding body meant that Britain's provincial playhouses had to re-examine and alter the scope of their programmes. Thus, for example, the Arts Council report on *Theatre for Young People*, published in 1966, criticized the regional theatres for their negligible efforts to reach young people. While recognition of this gap in provision and the subsequent funds offered to redress the balance were welcomed by many regional theatres, it was also generally recognized that including activities for young people in the programme would help secure the theatres' subsidies. Consequently, the late 1960s saw a proliferation of programmes for young people produced through the regional theatres. This is both true of Young People's Theatre (YPT) and Theatre-in-Education (TIE) teams, who took educational programmes into local schools, using theatre techniques and exploring new ways of using the theatrical medium for social gain. Following initiatives at the Coventry Belgrade Theatre in 1965, other TIE troupes were introduced at the Bolton Octagon (1967), Leeds Playhouse (1969), Greenwich Theatre (1970) and at Nottingham, Glasgow, Watford and Lancaster, amongst others, in the early 1970s.

Competition from newly funded, alternative theatres increased the urgency with which the regional theatres had to expand their programmes. As John Pick comments:

> The fashionable language used by this newly subsidized realm – they were 'committed', doing 'relevant' work, 'reaching out' to the 'community', was aped by some of the more traditional repertory theatres, which suddenly saw merit (listening to the newly-adopted jargon in Arts Council circles) in holding workshops, running TIE troupes that 'reached

> out' amongst the young, and in putting on the occasional 'committed' play at a point in the season when the inevitable box office drop would do least harm.
>
> (Pick 1986: 11)

The new, alternative and fringe companies embodied in the work of artists such as Jim Haynes at the Edinburgh Traverse Theatre Club presented a direct threat to the 'establishment theatres' in the provinces. Many such companies actually proclaimed their primary objective to be the destruction of all establishment theatres whose operations and programmes they considered elitist and obsolete.

To keep up with the times, compete for new, younger and socially eclectic audiences and fulfil the undefined criteria required for Arts Council subsidy, from the 1960s, regional directors were confronted with the task of bringing such new work and new trends into their theatres as well. But the largely experimental theatre work was, for most provincial playhouses, entirely unsuitable for the main auditoria. This type of work tended to require smaller, more intimate spaces. Moreover, the subversive nature of much of the material threatened to alienate large sections of regional theatres' older, more conservative audiences. The same problem applied to the major funding bodies outside the Arts Council, most specifically the more welfare-oriented local authorities, if performed as part of the main stage programme. Given the continued emphasis on good box office, and the increasing weight on plural funding already discussed, it subsequently became essential for many regional theatres to find alternative playing spaces to mount such work. Taking their cue from some of the more prestigious London or national companies, such as the Royal Court, which added its Theatre Upstairs in 1969, or the Royal Shakespeare Company, which opened The Other Place in 1974, by the end of the 1960s many provincial theatres were planning or had already built studio theatres on the premises to accommodate such work.[14]

In a similar vein, the regional theatres were forced to respond to the challenge from the alternative sector and address the problems of the direct relevance of theatre to the masses by reassessing certain traditionally held preconceptions of what theatre was. To do this, many theatres started introducing outreach community work into their programmes, often forming individual travelling units that would take socially relevant work directly to the local people in the streets, pubs, clubs and community centres. In this way they were able simultaneously to play a part in the community and reach new audiences.

'Bridging the gap' applied to the diffusion of culture on a geographical as much as social level and similarly underlined Labour's concern that the nation should be more a community where elite cultures were not separated from popular tastes. Responding to the concern over the privileging of metropolitan high art in previous years, the White Paper emphasized that the arts should occupy a central place in every region and encouraged increased 'local artistic activity and the enrichment and diversification of regional cultures' (Lee 1965: para. 66). To help with this, the government earmarked a quarter of a million pounds to fund the Housing the Arts scheme, administered through the Arts Council with the intention of saving the impoverished regional theatres, emphasizing that such investment should be matched by both the local authorities and the private sector.

It was also under Lee's leadership that the regional arts associations were built up. Prior to taking power, Labour had produced a document called *The Quality of Living*, which recommended that a network of regional arts associations should be instituted to bring in local authority and business support for the arts through the Arts Council. This report had formed the basis of the White Paper, which directly stated that the Arts Council was expected to use the increased government funding to 'make a larger contribution to regional associations' (Lee 1965: para. 66). By appointing a former civil servant, Nigel Abercrombie, as secretary-general, Lee was able to put a new emphasis on devolution in the Arts Council and increase the concern for regional provision. Abercrombie, who succeeded Williams on his retirement, was the major influence behind the dramatic growth of the regional arts associations, which increased in number from four in 1965, to ten by the time Labour was voted out of office in 1970. During Abercrombie's term in office, from 1963 to 1968, there was something of a change in the allocation of Arts Council grants, with the funding body's spending gradually shifting from an almost exclusive concentration on high culture and the four national, primarily London-based companies, to a higher proportion of funds being directed to the regions to fund both the regional arts associations and regional companies directly.

This period, marked by an extraordinarily energetic growth and vitality, is often considered the high point in the subsidized regional theatres' history. Yet it could also be argued that in the long run such expansion added to the provincial playhouses' problems. In times of prosperity, under a liberal government whose annual arts subvention increased at a rate above inflation and allowed the continued funding of a wide-range of activities on a level above subsistence, there were few problems. But by the end of the 1960s, the mood of the country was changing. There were signs that Middle England was growing less tolerant of the activities of political radicals and the counter-culture, and economic confidence and faith in the Labour Party was undermined following the government's decision to devalue sterling in 1967 and an international monetary crisis in 1968. The return of the Conservatives in 1970 marked the change of the national mood and signalled the beginning of a new era in which political difficulties and economic depression translated into a devaluation of the arts.

Most significantly, the unexpected rise in oil prices, the battles over industrial relations and trade unions' power that resulted in the 1972 and 1974 miners' strikes, the three-day working week and the 'winter of discontent' in 1978/9 almost crippled the economy and caused inflation to escalate.[15] So while the Treasury grant-in-aid to the Arts Council continued to grow steadily, by 1973/4 even a substantial increase of £3.5 million, which raised the annual grant to £17.4 million, was not enough to keep up with a hefty inflation rate of 14.3 per cent. From the next few years, the value of the annual Arts Council grant continued to decrease in real terms. Such a diminution in the value of the organization's funding necessitated a tightening of the reins, and once again the Arts Council had to prioritize.

Despite the liberal attitude it displayed when funds were forthcoming, when the backlash came as the economy faltered in the 1970s, the response of the Arts Council was reactionary; a return to the traditional emphasis on the high arts focused on the metropolis rather than continued expansionary support for emerging alternative cultures. The New Activities Committee for instance, which had turned out to be a rebellious cuckoo and spent a lot of energy criticising the Arts Council for being elitist and old fashioned, was wound up in 1970. Similarly, the Young People's Theatre Panel lasted only five years. Writing in the 1975/6 annual report, entitled *The Arts in Hard Times*, the new and conservative chairman, Lord Gibson, commented:

> Inevitably and rightly, most of our new money has gone to the traditional arts. This is not due to any desire on the part of the Arts Council to dam the flood of change. It is due to a belief that each generation has a right to enjoy its cultural heritage.
> (ACGB 1975/6: 12).

If ideas about the social hierarchy of culture remained largely unchanged in the Arts Council, this was perhaps even more true of the body's attitude towards the geographical hierarchy. Despite Abercrombie's proactive attempts to bridge the gap by devolving more power and money to regional arts, the Arts Council as a whole remained avowedly wary of moving away from its traditional metropolitan emphasis. The three successive chairmen who straddled the 'years of opportunity' and its backlash in the 1970s, Lords Cottesloe, Goodman and Gibson, were all firmly centralist. Goodman was certainly concerned to take the civilizing influence of the high arts to the regions, but in acquiring culture, he believed, the provinces should take their cue from London. The capital, in his view, should continue to set the standard for the rest of the country and, as such, should remain the seat of power of the omnipotent primary funding body. During a search for upgraded premises for the Council, Goodman had responded to a suggestion from Lee that the Arts Council might consider moving its headquarters outside London by saying, '[I]t is idiotic that the regions, which are pretty barren of talent, should run the show. You can't find that in Wigan or Warrington' (Sinclair 1995: 149). The Arts Council eventually found new premises – at 105 Piccadilly.

Goodman's attitude was reflected by the majority of those working with him at the Arts Council, with one notable exception. In his attempts to devolve, Abercrombie was largely carrying out the will of the government, and resentment within the Arts Council at Whitehall's encroachment through the appointment of a former civil servant as secretary-general was only fuelled by what was perceived as his further attempt to undermine the autonomy of the national funding body. Anthony Field, the Arts Council's finance director from 1971 to 1984, was once overheard telling Abercrombie, 'What you're doing, you realize, will leave us all without jobs' (Sinclair 1995: 134). Thus, despite all Abercrombie's attempts to the contrary, devolution was never as far reaching as official statements might have implied. As with the funding of alternative art forms, larger grants to the regions could be offered, but only if administered and assessed from London with a substantial increase from Whitehall. By the end of the 1960s, when two-thirds of the total grant-in-aid was spent outside London, 90 per cent of local activities were funded by direct grant from the Arts Council with only 10 per cent filtered through the regional arts associations. When his contract ran out, Abercrombie was booted upstairs into the newly created position of chief regional arts adviser. This new appointment was outwardly portrayed as an indication of the Arts Council's positive attitude towards regional development. In reality, the position was never that important, and Abercrombie's attempts to promote the provinces were rewarded by his exile to them.

Given the extent of the expansionist activities undergone by the majority of regional theatres during the late 1960s, including the capital projects undertaken through the Housing the Arts scheme, the reduction of subsidy in the 1970s was a disaster. If reliance on outside funding had already been increased by such factors as the move away from weekly repertory in the decades after the war and depreciated ticket prices, the new, welfare-oriented activities greatly increased regional theatres' dependence. Expensive to run, none of the socially committed operations ever had the potential of breaking even, much less making a profit. In a similar vein, the small audience capacity of the studio theatres meant that even a full house, with spectators all paying full ticket prices, would still result in a net loss for most companies. Despite the Arts Council's positive assertion that in 1970 the majority of the country's regional theatres recovered an average of 75 per cent of expenditure at the box office, by the late 1970s this figure had dropped to under 50 per cent. When, for example, in 1963/4, the Bristol Old Vic was still operating in premises untouched since the war, total earned income had been £51,466, while its total subsidy of £16,500 came to less than a third of that. In 1979/80, however, following the renovation of the main building and the addition of the New Vic and the Little Theatre, two studio theatres, the picture looked somewhat different. At this time, total earned income came to £317,034, while subsidy from all sources totalled £428,477. Such an increased reliance on subsidy amongst regional theatres by this point was the norm.

The Arts Council's return to a more conservative policy during the financially difficult 1970s only aggravated the situation. Although there was no question that the national funding body had ever lost its emphasis on a classical repertoire, the diminishing funds and concurrent disappearance of budgets specifically assigned for 'education', 'youth work' or 'new activities' during this period did not allow the regional theatres to adjust the scope of their operations to accommodate the reduction of their subsidies and increasing operating costs.[16] Although the exact criteria for Arts Council funding remained vague, the increasing return to a traditional policy, whereby standards once again took priority over accessibility, meant the organization's ideals, once again, were often diametrically opposed to those of the regional theatres' other funding bodies.

One of the ideas behind the move to increase plural funding had been the protection it would afford the arts. If a theatre was subsidized from more than one source, then theoretically the effects of a reduction in subsidy from one funding body would not be as devastating. This idea, of course, was based on the premise that other funding bodies would not be affected. In times of recession this theory does not apply. The economic hardships of the 1970s affected local authorities just as much as government intermediary bodies such as the Arts Council. Given the fact that the Arts Council and local authorities together formed the primary source of funds to the regional arts associations – which many practitioners believed were just taking up vital funds for administration – subsidy diminished on all sides.

Such a premise was also based on the idea that the collective funding bodies would have clear ideas about shared responsibilities and objectives. For civic theatres that were owned and subsidized in part by local authorities, municipal emphasis in the 1970s continued to focus on the social welfare benefits of the theatres' programmes. Under the Housing the Arts scheme, during which many local authorities had begun to play a much more significant role in the support and policy of regional theatres, the idea of a civic theatre had caused many regional producing houses to be conceived in terms that extended beyond mere playhouses. Many were designed to function effectively as arts centres, with 'regular art exhibitions, lunchtime concerts, lectures and poetry recitals, post-performance discussions, educational programmes on examination texts for school children' (Jackson and Rowell 1984: 32), and not least as community forums for social gatherings based around the inevitable bar and restaurant. Given this philosophy, it is perhaps understandable that local authorities continued to prioritize the welfare elements of the regional theatres' programmes, sometimes privileging educational or youth work over the repertory work performed in the main house. Such an attitude often extended to the regular audiences, many of whom became involved in regional theatres through their children and who, unaware of the behind-the-scenes difficulties of running a theatre, could be outraged at the privileging of elitist art over the concerns of the local community. Such a situation, for instance, was instrumental in the closure of the Salisbury Playhouse in 1995. Under such circumstances, trying to break even by cutting any welfare activities risked the loss of subsidy from one source or another for the regional theatres. But by this point, elevated costs, the unofficial principle of parity funding, decades of deflated ticket prices and the practice of repertory meant that risking subsidy from even one source could prove potentially fatal to a provincial company.

One final change that can be traced back to this period of expansion served to ensure that the regional theatres were set up for a crisis under the Conservative regime of the 1980s and 1990s. While an increased grant from Whitehall translated into increased government interference in Arts Council policy, it also meant more accountability. Under the leadership of the autocratic Williams, Arts Council claims for higher funding had been based on the 'quality of life' argument. Together with the combined government munificence, following Williams' retirement in 1963, the arrival of Abercrombie, a new, less indomitable leader, caused the Arts Council to rethink its line of argument in order to sustain a higher level of funding. It was at this point that the arts began to be valued in monetary terms, as finance director Anthony Field recalled:

> I said that we must change the argument to get more funds. We must say that money spent on the Arts was not subsidy but investment. I produced statistics showing that for each one million pounds invested, the Treasury received three million from foreign tours and tourism, royalties and employment taxes. I led the Arts Council into its sad decline of quantifying the arts in material terms.
>
> (Sinclair 1995: 129)

This attitude backfired when the Conservatives, led by Thatcher, took the Arts Council at face value and summarily started perceiving the regional theatres as businesses operating in a market economy whose worth could be discerned by their ability to earn their keep. If regional theatres had once had that ability, the advent of subsidy following the war, and the fluctuating and contradictory manoeuvrings of the funding bodies in the intermediate decades, combined to make subsidy a necessity of survival for the theatres and compromised the possibility of self-sufficiency being achieved in the future. By the time Thatcher entered 10 Downing Street in 1979, a crisis in Britain's regional theatres was virtually inevitable.

Notes

1. Prior to the Local Government Act, local authorities had been allowed to use money gained through the rates to support 'the provision of concerts only in corporation buildings or parks;... the maintenance of bands only for out-of-door performances and of orchestras only by "spas and public resorts," and...entertainments which involve no costumes and scenery, no performances in the nature of a variety of entertainment', and no films 'other than those illustrative of questions relating to health or disease'.
2. Section 132, Local Government Act, 1948.
3. County councils gained this power in 1963 when authorities were also allowed to support ventures outside their administrative boundaries.
4. The Institute of Municipal Entertainment in Great Britain carried out two surveys of expenditure on municipal entertainment 1961/2 and 1968/9. Although not all authorities concerned replied to the questionnaire sent out, it was considered that the returns gave an almost complete picture of municipal expenditure on arts and entertainment. In 1961/2, the gross expenditure of 535 authorities was £7,432,568, with a net of £2,549,186, the figures for 1968/9 showed the gross expenditure of 511 authorities as £11,911,234 with a net expenditure of £5,269,612. The Arts Council's grants-in-aid for those two years were £1,745,000 and £7,750,000 respectively.
5. Included in this list were Bristol, Birmingham, Chesterfield, Coventry, Salisbury, Dudley, Nuneaton, Guildford, Winchester and Chippenham.
6. It is about to change again. Unitary authorities, supplanting the two tiers of local government established in the 1970s, will come into being in 2009. In Scotland and Wales, unitary authorities replaced two-tier authorities in 1995.
7. Increasing problems with the system of local government, whereby increased power of central government combined with an outmoded structure that no longer reflected the social geography of the nation and where there were increasing disparities in the size, income and requirements for different authorities that should have had the same responsibilities, led Conservative Prime Minister Edward Heath, who ousted Harold Wilson in 1970, to implement a new system. The 1972 Local Government Act established a two-tier structure throughout the country: county councils were given responsibility for planning, protective and personal services such as education, social services, highways and public libraries. District councils became responsible for housing, environmental health and amenities.
8. The nine regional offices had been placed in Newcastle, Leeds, Manchester, Cambridge, Birmingham, Nottingham, London, Southampton and Bristol.

9. See, in particular, chapters six, seven and eight on The Surrey Cluster, the Thorndike Theatre, the Redgrave Theatre and the Yvonne Arnaud Theatre, and their relationship with South East Arts for specific examples of such problems.
10. See the chapters on the Salisbury Playhouse and The Surrey Cluster for examples of this.
11. Several pieces of new legislation that underlined the increasingly liberal national attitude included the Obscene Publications Act of 1959, the legalization of gambling in 1960, the abolition of the death penalty in 1965, homosexual law reform and easier access to abortion in 1967, the abolition of the Lord Chamberlain's censorship of theatre in 1968 and the Divorce Act of 1969.
12. White Paper: 'An official report which describes the policy of the Government on a particular subject' (*Collins Advanced Learner's English Dictionary*).
13. Funding rose from £2,730,000 to £3,205,000 in Labour's first year in office, to £3,910,000 in 1965/6, £5,700,000 in 1966/67 and £7,200,000 in 1967/68. The increases in the last two years were 45 per cent and 26 per cent respectively. Increasing government munificence was reflected in the titles of Arts Council annual reports during these years: *Policy into Practice* (1964/5); *Key Year* (1965/6); *A New Charter* (1966/7); *Changes and Moves* (1967/8).
14. The Belgrade Theatre's studio opened in 1968; Bolton Octagon's in 1967; and plans for studio theatres were also incorporated into designs for the Sheffield Crucible, the new Birmingham Rep, the soon-to-be-rebuilt Bristol Old Vic and the expanded Liverpool Playhouse.
15. The 1978–9 'winter of discontent' saw an outbreak of trade union strikes predominantly in the public sector – including ambulance drivers and council cemetery workers, who in one case refused to bury the dead – as a response to the Conservative government's attempt to limit wage increases to 5 per cent. Days lost through industrial action during this fiscal year totalled thirty million.
16. 'Community arts' continued to be funded on a smaller scale until responsibility was entirely devolved to the regional arts associations in 1981; 'amateur companies' like the National Youth Theatre lost funding in 1981.

PART TWO: THE CRISIS

3

THATCHER GETS DOWN TO BUSINESS

Everything is costed; nothing is valued.

(Peacock 1999: 33)

When Margaret Thatcher became prime minister following her election victory in 1979, four decades of state funding had ensured that the operations of Britain's regional theatres effectively revolved around subsidy. This had become both the reason for and condition of their survival, and the ideological persuasions of the Arts Council ensured that, as things stood, other potential avenues of support had been closed to them. Keynes' belief that subsidy existed to protect high art from the insidious effects of commerce had originally been mitigated by his parallel confidence in what one nineteenth-century civil servant had coined the 'trickle down theory' – the idea that 'a drop in the ocean of our expenditure would sufficiently impregnate the powers of taste, in a country nationally prolific in every department of genius' (Sinclair 1995: 311). Had this succeeded, the regional theatres should have ultimately increased their audiences to the point that they could be self-sufficient and operate without subsidy. However, the increasing pressure to include typically loss-making social welfare programmes as part of their activities made this an all but impossible task for many theatres, and with theatre-going an increasingly elitist activity following the arrival of commercial television, the box office itself was never developed in the manner desired by Keynes:

> The puritan influence of the followers of F. R. Leavis and his disciples had influenced a generation into a Manichean division of culture – mass culture, which was low and commercial and often based on electronics, and minority culture, which was high and unaffected by new technology and set in theatres and concert-halls, galleries and libraries.
>
> (Sinclair 1995: 311)

After years of high inflation and funding shortages in the 1970s, many regional producing houses were already operating on a shoestring budget when the Conservatives came to power. At this point, their reliance on state funding was such that any further cuts or changes in the conditions of subsidy could potentially prove catastrophic.

The 1979 victory of the Conservative Party ushered in just such a change. The subsequent eighteen years of Tory rule, ending in 1997, saw a determined move away from state support in favour of an arts system that would operate within the consumer market. As we have seen, the regional theatres were constitutionally not set up to deal with such a shift. Consequently, the gradual erosion in the producing houses' traditional funding base, accompanied by increasingly complex and problematic requirements in management, saw theatres plummet into a spiral of decline. The increased pressure to maintain an equitable, plural-funding base of public support, while maximizing income from the private sector and the box office, put Britain's regional theatres in the position of having to answer an escalating number and variety of demands that were often out of proportion to their budgets and occasionally in polar opposition to one another. At the same time, the lack of capital with which to answer the expanded requirements meant that many companies increasingly struggled to operate effectively in a competitive market. In 1994, the number of regional theatres that had either gone dark or were facing closure caused the chairman of the Arts Council, Lord Gowrie, to liken his job to 'staffing an increasingly crowded casualty ward' (Gowrie 1994). By 1995, changes made under the Conservative government's enterprise culture had created such a widespread crisis that the Arts Council was commenting, 'One of the nation's greatest cultural assets, its provincial theatres, remains on the brink of an irreversible spiral of decline...repertory theatres must evolve or die' (ACE 1995: 4).

A line of the 1979 Conservative Party manifesto declares: 'The years of make-believe and false optimism are over. It is time for a new beginning' (Thatcher 1993: 9). By the end of the 1970s, years of high inflation, unemployment and civil unrest had left Britain in a cloud of despair. In attempting to locate the root cause of the national malaise, Thatcher pinpointed the post-war consensus that she believed had crippled the state and created a 'dependency culture', in which a paternalistic government had created an apathetic nation and stifled initiative:

> To me, consensus seems to be: the process of abandoning all beliefs, principles, values and policies in search of something in which no one believes, but to which no one objects; the process of avoiding the very issues that have to be solved, merely because you cannot get agreement on the way ahead. What great cause would have been fought and won under the banner: 'I stand for consensus?'
> (Hewison 1995: 209)

From her perspective, the potential for change could only come through dispensing with this approach and electing a determined leader with strong views that appealed to the majority of the electorate. As Thatcher emphasized before taking office, she was neither a consensus nor pragmatic politician, but a *conviction* politician.

In 1984, Thatcher told parliamentary lobby journalists that she wanted to lead a government that 'decisively broke with a debilitating consensus of a paternalistic government and a dependent people; which rejected the notion that the state is all powerful and the citizen is merely its beneficiary; which shattered the illusion that Government could somehow substitute for individual performance' (Kavanagh 1987: 247). According to Thatcher, Britain's decline was both economic and moral, with the health of the economy being the lens through which national anxiety was reflected. In her attempts to better the situation, she saw a new approach to economics as the vehicle through which to improve the spiritual as well as material health of the nation. As she commented in *The Sunday Times* in 1988, 'Economics are the method. The object is to change the soul' (Hewison 1995: 212).

The key to this new approach lay in market liberalism. Distancing herself from the Conservatives' historic role, Thatcher, and her colleague Sir Keith Joseph, came up with a new philosophy that set out to release new energies and produce cultural change. Thatcherism, a term coined by the Marxist sociologist Stuart Hall before Thatcher even took office, replaced the old social democratic beliefs of community and collectivism with a neo-liberal ideology that emphasized economic individualism, anti-statism and competition. These ideals all complemented the traditional Tory emphasis on family, nation, duty, authority, standards and traditionalism. The old dependency culture would be replaced by a new enterprise culture, in which 'the individual, empowered through the sovereignty of the consumer, was to be liberated by the freedom of the market not only from the dependency culture of collectivism, but the old hierarchies of deference, status and taste' (Hewison 1995: 212).

Under the terms of the enterprise culture, attempts to achieve full employment and the primary reliance on a manufacturing economy were to be discarded in favour of an expanded service industry, with state control of the money supply to achieve zero inflation. Such methods drew heavily on the ideas of right-wing think-tanks and economists such as Friedrich August von Hayek and Milton Friedman, who emphasized the political dangers and economic inefficiency of central planning and instead advocated a free market economy. Pivotal to this New Right philosophy was Friedman's concept of monetarism. Unsupported by any empirical evidence, Friedman's theory argued that inflation occurred when the money supply exceeded the gross domestic product. Through government restraint, theoretically, zero inflation could be achieved.[1] This might initially result in a rise in unemployment, but, in contrast to Keynesian economics, which advocated government interference to ensure as near full employment as possible, monetarism argued that there might be a natural wage level and concomitantly a natural level of unemployment. As such, some unemployment would be acceptable. Unemployment, which reached a record high of 3.2 million in 1985 following the reductions to the manufacturing industry, was what Major's chancellor, Norman Lamont, would call 'a price worth paying'. However, the cost of unemployment benefits meant there was no reduction in public spending as a proportion of the gross domestic product, even though that was one of the founding principles of supply-side economics, which argued that public spending undermined private initiative.

The emphasis of monetarism lay in its belief in a free market. Hayek argued that individual freedom meant the liberty to make choices. A vital part of political freedom therefore translated into the economic freedom of capitalism in terms of voluntary buying and selling. Thus monetarism advocated freeing the market by removing the interference of inefficient government, reducing levels of taxation, privatizing and deregulating industry and commerce, and abolishing protective legislation such as rent control, minimum wage levels, employment legislation, regional and industrial subsidies, and constitutional limitation of taxation and spending. In adopting these ideas, the New Right argued that monetarism would lead to a strong nation freed from government intervention.

Ironically, given that the terms 'freedom' and 'choice' became slogans for the new Conservative government, the means through which Thatcherism planned to free the economy was by employing the authority of the state. The New Right used the weight of government to remove any centres of opposition to the new regime. As a conviction politician, Thatcher emphasized the fact that she 'could not waste time having any internal arguments' (Thatcher 1993: 634). Once in government, she quickly consolidated her position by purging her cabinet of any oppositional 'wets', a definition she applied to liberal Conservatives not entirely in agreement with her politics. Outside government, this translated into systematically attacking the last bastions of the post-war consensus that represented collectivist, 'permissive' ideals and traditions. The years between 1979 and 1997 witnessed a sustained assault on all institutions that, to the New Right, reflected the ideologies of the post-war consensus and the social democratic ideals of the welfare state. Beginning with Keynesian economics, the nationalized industries and the trade unions, the Thatcher administration extended its assault to reduce the powers of local government and, similarly, public services such as the National Health Service (NHS) and the education system. Culturally, it targeted the old institutions of the consensus era, such as the BBC and the Arts Council.

The Arts Council has traditionally been classified as a quango (quasi-autonomous non-governmental organization), an institution that carries out a wide range of administrative and regulatory functions on behalf of the government but operates at arm's length, with appointed council members and advisory panels working on a voluntary basis. At the time Thatcher took office, the non-elected officials who sat on the Council were largely drawn from the great and the good and as such represented more than just the inherited values of consensus politics. As Richard Hoggart wrote, '[quangos] emerged from and could only work where there was an assumed pattern of values about the nature of the good society and the good life' (Hoggart 1992: 271–2). Examined from a different angle, a more insidious motive could be attached to this model. Through quangos such as the Arts Council, support was sustained to uphold the vested interests of a particular group whose values were represented in terms of the public good.

This inherited tradition of privilege was anathema to the enterprise culture. Thatcher was deeply suspicious of the great and the good and their supposed unassailable right to public funds to support their needs. To her, the idea of the establishment conjured up images of 'favouritism, injustice and propping up the status quo' (Thatcher 1993:634), which stifled rather than encouraged initiative. As she wrote in her chronicle of her years in office, *The Downing Street Years*:

> I was not convinced that the state should play Maecenas. Artistic talent – let alone artistic genius – is unplanned, unpredictable, eccentrically individual. Regimented, subsidised, owned and determined by the state, it withers. Moreover the 'state' in these cases comes to mean the vested interests of the arts lobby. I wanted to see the private sector raising more money and bringing business acumen and efficiency to bear on the administration of cultural institutions.
>
> (Thatcher 1993: 634)

The utilitarianism of the free market rejected aristocratic entitlement, instead offering access to power to anyone who could make money. In locating freedom in the realm of economics, the enterprise culture gave the individual the right to profit and thrive, but also to sink and drown. In New Right terminology, quangos such as the Arts Council perpetuated the collectivist and patrician traditions of the dependency culture while espousing the interests of the arts lobby rather than the popular voice. As such, they were a drain on the public purse and stifled private enterprise. Far preferable in Thatcher's terms was exposing them to the blast of market forces, where the ultimate form of expression was economic and the citizen-turned-consumer could become arbiter and inspiration for initiative and improvement.

In 1979, there were 2,410 quangos, or, in Tory parlance, 'non-departmental bodies'. By 1983, the government had dissolved more than five hundred of them. Although the Arts Council ultimately survived, albeit in a greatly reduced form, at the beginning of the 1980s the funding body found itself under sustained attack from numerous quarters, to the extent that it felt its very existence threatened. As such, it was forced to make extreme changes to secure its position.

Even before Thatcher came to power, the Arts Council had long been on the defensive following years of high inflation and financial restrictions. By 1974/5, the funding body was already complaining that grant-in-aid was falling behind inflation. As the critic Harold Baldry said, 'provision for standstill, always insufficient, plus a minimum allowance for growth in some areas remained the order of the day' (Peacock 1999: 34). Insufficient funds contributed to the continuing debates over the efficacy of subsidy; opposition from the political right denounced the Arts Council for its continued support of performance art and 'left-wing' theatre groups, while the left criticized the insufficient funds allocated to community arts and the national funding body's continued privileging of highbrow art forms. Any degree of optimism that the Arts Council chairman of the time, Sir Kenneth Robinson, professed in the 1978/9 annual report all but disappeared when just months later the first Tory arts minister, Norman St. John Stevas, announced the shape of things to come under the incoming government:[2]

> The Arts World must come to terms with the fact that Government policy in general has decisively tilted away from the expansion of the public to the enlargement of the private

> sector. The Government fully intends to honour its pledge to maintain public support for the arts as a major feature of policy, but we look to the private sphere to meet any shortfall and to provide immediate means of increase.
>
> (St. John Stevas 1979)

In principle, the Thatcher government accepted the consensus settlement of support for the arts and recognized some responsibility towards them, but the first budget immediately made it clear that the arts world could no longer depend on the government to cushion them from economic reality. Although an initial cut of £5 million to the arts grant of £61,275,000 set by the outgoing Labour Party was partially restored during 1980, so that the actual figure was only £1,114,000 less than the previous year's funding, it nevertheless aggravated the already beleaguered position of the arts community and added to a growing insecurity about the future.

In looking back over fifteen years of continued crises in regional theatre, the Arts Council's 1995 consultative paper, *Drama in England,* was clear that public funding, or rather the lack of it, had played a major role.

> Public funding, needing to be spread ever more thinly, is failing to keep pace with the increased demands on regional producing theatres. In every theatre, whatever its scale, the depth of crisis is affected by a number of factors – including, of course, the skills of the director, administrator and board. But one of the major factors is the inability of public funding to support the increased range of work that is now expected of them and which they expect of themselves. Increased emphasis on education, community and outreach work, increased sophistication in fund-raising and marketing, the need to comply with ever more complex legislation and the greater administrative demands created by the funding system itself, have deflected the resources from the creation of productions. During the recession, the problems have been exacerbated by box office shortfalls.
>
> (ACE 1995: 11)

Almost without exception, for every regional theatre that announced it was having difficulties during this period, under-funding was a cited as a primary cause. In 1995, after sixteen years of Conservative rule and just after the introduction of a new source of funding from the National Lottery, Britain's regional theatres were estimated to be carrying a combined deficit of £6 million. The crisis was widely concluded in the media to be 'the result of a long-term decline in Government funding' (Taylor 1995).

Before going any further, it is worthwhile examining this assertion. In *The Downing Street Years*, Thatcher wrote, 'Perhaps nowhere were the proper limits of what the state should do more hotly disputed than in the world of the arts' (Thatcher 1993: 633). Notwithstanding, she contended that during her time in office, government support for the arts 'rose sharply in real terms... though from the chorus of complaints about the "cuts" you would not have known it' (Thatcher 1993: 633). In terms of the straightforward grant-in-aid afforded the Arts Council during the Conservative administration, such a statement is not entirely without validity. However, taking these figures at face value is to ignore numerous factors that tempered the actual value of the increases.

On average, arts funding remained slightly ahead of inflation in most years of the Conservative administration, falling behind in three years only. It leapt by 30 per cent in 1986/7 to £135.6 million, but this figure includes the £25 million post-abolition funding provided to compensate for the arts funding lost by the abolition of the metropolitan authorities, the effects of which will be discussed later in this chapter. When this sum is removed from the grant, the actual increase in funding for that year amounts to 4.29 per cent, only slightly ahead of inflation. After Thatcher left office in 1990, the situation deteriorated somewhat, with several years of standstill funding from 1992/3 and a reduction in the arts budget of £3.2 million in 1994/5. In real terms, this reduction meant a loss of £7 million for that year alone. When the highly labour-intensive nature of the performing arts is also taken into account, the value of the government's increase over this period falls even further.[3]

The level of funding as it pertains to regional theatres would have been further affected by the way in which the Arts Council and regional arts associations divided the government grant. A random example from 1981/2, analysed by D. Keith Peacock in his comprehensive study *Thatcher's Theatre*, demonstrates the difficulties of assessing funding. As he notes, in 1981/2 drama received almost exactly half of the total Arts Council budget. But once the proportion allocated to the national theatres is removed, this figure falls to 16.48 per cent, divided between the Arts Council's metropolitan, touring and regional clients. At the same time, this figure does not take into account the unknown quantity also allocated through other Arts Council sources, such as community project funding and regional arts associations. It also fails to account for the funds allocated by other bodies, such as the British Council or, most significantly, the local authorities, for which there is still no collected cohesive data. It is known that local authority funding did increase significantly over the course of the decade, rising to above £100 million by 1985, at which point it outdid Arts Council spending on the arts. Even so, it is questionable how much of this went towards regional theatres specifically. Moreover, it should be noted that arts expenditure has never been a high priority for local authorities and has always been particularly vulnerable to fluctuations in the economy, as demonstrated during the recession at the beginning of the 1990s and following the problematic introduction of the poll tax.

The final problem in interpreting funding statistics relates to the way the Arts Council allocated its grant. Although the Arts Council's grant-in-aid rose in real terms in certain years under the Conservatives, this did not automatically translate into an increase in its clients' subsidy. In 1984, for example, the Arts Council felt it necessary to hold back funds to create a substantial reserve, and its 6.05 per cent increase in grant-in-aid was reduced to a mere 3 per cent increase by the time it reached certain companies. Inflation during this year averaged 5 per cent. Similarly, in 1985 the grant-in-aid increase of 4.04 per cent was reduced to 2 per cent for numerous clients, while others received standstill funding. In other years, specific funds were earmarked for government schemes, similarly reducing the size of the potential grant that could reach theatres. In 1988/9, for example, a much vaunted increase obtained by Arts Minister Richard

Luce was undermined by the fact that 40 per cent of the government's increase was assigned to incentive funding to encourage business sponsorship. Similarly, the direct benefits to regional theatres from the £19 million grant-in-aid rise awarded in 1991/2, when the arts enthusiast David Mellor was minister for the arts, was compromised by the fact that £7.5 million of it was kept back for the Enhancement Funding scheme introduced that year, through which the government allocated extra funding to a few specific 'leading' companies.[4] The Arts Council kept back a further £5 million of the extra funding to boost its contingency fund.

Although such considerations make it impossible to chart accurately the exact changes in funding to regional theatres over the course of the Conservative administration, there is a strongly accepted opinion that when all sources of subsidy, both direct and indirect, are taken into account, there was a significant decline in the levels of arts funding over the years. For example, in 1985/6 the Arts Council disputed the government's claim that arts funding had increased by 18 per cent since 1979 by pointing out that a large proportion of this increase had been put towards other activities, such as libraries, most notably the £450 million that went towards building the new British Library. Once funding for these activities had been removed, the increase in arts funding was reduced to only 6 per cent. Moreover, the government's figures were compiled using the Retail Price Index. The Arts Council insisted, conversely, that because of the labour-intensive nature of the arts, a more accurate figure could be gained by applying the increases to the Average Earnings Index. In this case, funding of the arts would have fallen by 6 per cent. In line with these considerations, statistics supplied by the Arts Council for the years from 1986/7 to 1994/5 recorded a further drop in the real value of government spending on the arts of close to 10 per cent, a situation that was subsequently exacerbated by the reduction in funding of £3.2 million in 1994/5. In 1996/7, the last year of the Conservative administration, the Theatrical Management Association put the total loss of spending on regional theatres in the previous eight years at £12 million.

At the beginning of the 1980s, the initial government cuts made to the arts budget were seen as a harbinger of things to come. The anxiety this caused was added to by other changes in the socio-economic situation. While severe reductions to local authority spending put their non-statutory contributions to the arts in serious jeopardy, problems were compounded by a world recession prompted by a further rise in oil prices. In 1980, this resulted in inflation rising to 21.9 per cent, the minimum lending rate climbing to 17 per cent and unemployment exceeding two million for the first time in Britain since the 1930s.

Government cuts and inflation were serious enough to immediately cause severe problems for Britain's regional theatres, particularly given the shoestring budget on which they had traditionally operated and the extensive demands of managing the houses. The situation was exacerbated by the government's concomitant decision to increase Value Added Tax (VAT) from 7 per cent to 15 per cent. Complementing the Conservatives' emphasis on creating a free market economy, VAT places the tax on spending rather than earning, 'in order to restore incentives and increase the freedom of choice of the individual' (*The Stage* 1979d). The Tories argued that the simultaneous reduction in direct taxes such as income tax would facilitate increased personal wealth and therefore 'enable many private citizens to contribute to the arts' (*The Stage* 1979c). However, the typical operation of regional theatres at the beginning of the 1980s meant that they were unlikely to gain from this new form of taxation. By 1979, the effects of increased dependence on subsidy and the technological revolution had evolved to ensure that subsidized regional theatres not only catered to, but were already perceived as representing, the interests of an increasingly exclusive market. VAT was considered to be a class tax in one regard, because the cuts to income tax for which it partly compensated hugely favoured the wealthy middle and upper classes that already constituted the majority of theatregoers.[5] While savings on income tax therefore largely benefited the wealthier sections of society who could already afford to go to the theatre, the 8 per cent increase on ticket prices put access to the theatre out of the range of many social groups and may have acted as a deterrent for some of the existing audience. Although certain subsidized regional theatres, such as the Cheltenham Everyman, tried to absorb the increase in ticket prices to save the box office, years of standstill funding meant that many theatres were in no position to do the same. The 28 per cent drop in audience figures subsequently recorded by the Merseyside Everyman, a theatre which was situated in a depressed area and had to raise ticket prices by 30 per cent to also compensate for a reduction in local authority funding, was perhaps amongst the most severe. The national press, and theatre trade paper *The Stage*, reported significant drops in attendances in regional theatres across the country at this time.

Panicked by such events, in 1981 the Arts Council responded to the new circumstances by cutting funding, without warning or explanation, to 41 of its clients. The decision, publically announced on Christmas Eve 1980, affected eighteen theatre companies. The list included two regional theatres, the Marlowe Theatre, Canterbury, and the Lyceum Theatre, Crewe, both of which were officially dropped as clients because of the low levels of funding supplied by their local authorities. Apart from these two, building-based regional producing houses largely escaped the cuts, with the Arts Council preference being to withdraw funding from touring companies such as Prospect Theatre and Broadside Mobile Workers Theatre. They had comparatively fewer connections with their local communities and the cuts were therefore less likely to attract publicity. Also targeted were certain left-wing political groups and youth organizations, such as the National Youth Theatre, with the Arts Council's traditional emphasis on high arts and professional work being prioritized over educational and amateur activities. Although the regional theatres escaped relatively unscathed from these 'Christmas Cuts', the announcement fostered a growing insecurity amongst the theatres. Not least, their unease related to a concern that the Arts Council was simply doing the government's bidding in reducing public expenditure and removing companies whose work reflected deep-seated antipathy towards the Conservative administration. Such fears, it could be argued, were not without some justification. While reduced subsidy and increased VAT appeared to confirm the theatres' concerns that they would be in for difficult times under the new government, simultaneous changes in the system of public administration made the situation increasingly precarious.

In October 1982, the first of many official reports criticizing the Arts Council was released. The All-Party House of Commons Select Committee on Education, Science and the Arts had been set up to investigate the balance between private and public funding of the arts in 1981/2. The report presented serious concerns about the operations of the Arts Council, with many of the twelve recommendations perceived as little more than veiled criticisms of the organization. Sadly, this was something fuelled by the fallout from the Christmas Cuts, where the high-handed manner in which the Arts Council had made decisions, lacking any warning, explanation or right of appeal, had resulted in accusations of arrogance and incompetence being levelled at the funding body. For some time afterwards, the Arts Council became known as 'the Sweeney Todd of Piccadilly' by those affected. Certain of the recommendations made by the Select Committee, such as the call for greater devolution, government earmarking of funds to certain companies and the suggestion that a ministry for arts, heritage and tourism be created, were largely seen as a vote of no confidence in the Arts Council and a call for it to play a significantly reduced role.

The report did recognize that the arts were 'irresponsibly under-funded'. But in the case of subsidized theatres, rather than building a case for increased state support, it suggested that companies should turn to the private sector to increase their income. It acknowledged that a large untapped source of potential in the lower income groups, who did not normally patronize the theatres, would be difficult to target since 'access-pricing' would inevitably result in an immediate loss of income that could only be alleviated by increased subvention. A more hopeful possibility, in the Select Committee's eyes, lay in the potential of business sponsorship. In particular, the report recognized the growing influence of the Association for Business Sponsorship of the Arts (ABSA), set up by a group of professionals in 1976. The suggestion that more energy should be spent on broadening this source of income was a precursor of the government's, and later the Arts Council's, attitude, but failed to acknowledge that the difficulty of securing sponsorship could and would occupy time and money that many theatres felt would have been better spent on artistic activity.

While the Arts Council vehemently rejected such recommendations, the government appeared to give the Select Committee's findings a little more credibility. The threat posed by the report became increasingly imminent the following year when Thatcher persuaded the Arts Council to allow a civil servant, Clive Priestley, to enquire into the operations of the then financially troubled Royal Shakespeare Company and Royal Opera House in exchange for a one-time grant of £5 million that the funding body could use to clear its accumulated deficit.[6] Such an incursion by government was a clear breach of the arm's length principle and suggested little confidence in the Arts Council's own abilities to assess its clients. This factor was particularly galling given that the investigation effectively singled out the national companies that were experiencing difficulties. In so doing, it elevated them in importance over other Arts Council clients such as the regional theatres and ignored the other two national companies, the National Theatre and Sadler's Wells, whose good housekeeping skills had kept them out of the spotlight. While the isolated assessment of two troubled clients could be said to have reflected unfairly on the Arts Council, on whose affairs Priestley concentrated almost as intensely, the focus displayed a clear bias in the government's attitude to the arts. This so dismayed the director of the National Theatre, Peter Hall, that the following year he commissioned a report into the affairs of the National by way of attempting to avoid loss of subsidy as a penalty for good housekeeping (Rayner 1995).

The Priestley Report, published in November 1983, appeared to confirm the Arts Council's worst fears. Although he emphasized that the two companies were under-funded to the extent of 20 per cent, Priestley also suggested that they should be removed as Arts Council clients and funded directly by central government. Such a recommendation threatened the authority of the Arts Council, suggesting a demotion to the rank of second-tier disbursement agency with responsibility for less important arts organizations. 'Direct funding would divorce the national companies from the rest of the arts world which they are meant to inspire, and a class system would be developed in which the Arts Council is left with "second class organizations"' (Sinclair 1995: 249), declared the Council's concerned chairman, William Rees-Mogg. Following the publication of the Priestley Report, the arts budget for 1984/5 was raised to £101.9 million, providing a real increase of 6 per cent. But in line with Priestley's suggestions, the grant earmarked specific funds to be passed on to the Royal Shakespeare Company and Royal Opera House to raise their basic funding levels. Another £1.3 million was similarly earmarked for two other major metropolitan opera companies. The manner in which this allocation was structured prompted a fierce outcry, particularly from the regional arts associations and provincial theatres, who were upset at the way the government appeared to favour high-prestige organizations. This is understandable, given that the tagging of large grants for specific clients meant that, despite the rise in the Arts Council's grant, the increase for other companies fell well below inflation rates to a mere 2.9 per cent. The rate of inflation in 1984/5 averaged 5 per cent.

The Priestley Report was a second blow to the Arts Council, coming almost immediately on the back of the government's announcement of its plan to abolish the metropolitan authorities in 1986. Since local government reorganization in 1972, the Greater London Council (GLC) and five metropolitan county councils had been primary sources of arts funding amongst local authorities, a system that had become particularly prominent as government spending on the arts fell with the arrival of the Thatcher administration. In part, this related to the fact that the metropolitan councils were a source of significant opposition to central government. In the local elections in 1981, when the Conservative government had been experiencing a period of extreme unpopularity, the councils had come under Labour control. They had subsequently been amongst central government's most strident critics and the least agreeable to the Conservatives' attempts to curb public spending. Increasing arts funding was one way the metropolitan authorities could compensate for the impact of government cuts in their local districts. It simultaneously offered a way of launching an ideological resistance through subsidizing an alternative, politicized culture. 'GLC funded' became a slogan commonly attached to arts events around the Greater London area during the five years of Labour control from 1981 to 1986, and the GLC consciously politicized the arts, redefining the term 'community arts' to refer to communities of interest or minority groups, rather than using the term in its traditional sense of referring to geographical areas.

In the face of such opposition, it is not surprising that the Thatcher government decided that such a threat should be neutralized. Unfortunately, the impending loss of the GLC and five other metropolitan councils, announced in the White Paper *Streamlining the Cities*, in October 1983, would mean the loss of an estimated £46 million for the arts in Britain. Recognizing the devastation this could cause in the already troubled arts community, the government simultaneously issued a consultation paper on the effects of abolition on the funding of the arts. Here, the double threat posed by increased government interference already suggested by Priestley and reduced subsidy was reiterated. Amongst the suggestions put forward by the paper to lessen the potential damage were that nine larger producing theatres be designated as of national importance and funded directly by the government. Other theatres would have to get what money they could to make up the shortfall from local authorities, businesses and the box office.

Responding to the threat posed by government interference, Arts Council chair Rees-Mogg vehemently defended the arm's length principle: 'Direct state funding of an artistic company is as unacceptable as direct state funding of a newspaper. Like the Governors of the B.B.C., the Arts Council exists to protect the independence of creative people' (Rees-Mogg 1983). Such an argument was based on the concern that direct funding of the arts by political authorities would force organizations to take political factors into consideration when planning artistic policy and thus restrict the freedom of creativity. Although the effectiveness of the arm's length principle had been questioned in the past, there is no doubt that there was a significant shortening in the length of the arm under the Conservative administration. The threats from perennial under-funding, constant attacks on its operation, and changes to local government, were compounded by the lack of support the Arts Council received, even from those who should theoretically have championed it.

Thatcher's determination that there should be no room for dissent in her cabinet, and her view that cabinet ministers 'were there to do her bidding' (Sinclair 1995: 249), quickly resulted in a move to get rid of any opposition within government. The first to go was St. John Stevas, Thatcher's first minister for the arts. A One Nation Tory, St. John Stevas' public criticisms of the new monetarist policy, and his attempts to defend the arts budget in the face of government cuts, put him out of favour with the leadership.[7] Following his outburst at the Arts Council's failure to consult him over the Christmas Cuts, St. John Stevas was dismissed by Thatcher in her government re-shuffle in January 1981. Subsequent arts ministers were, at least outwardly, far more loyal to the ideology and methods of the New Right. As such, rather than battling for a better share of the budget, successive appointees made it clear that arts funding should take its place in the general context of government spending. St. John Stevas' replacement, Paul Channon, for example, was responsible for starting the increased intrusion of government into Arts Council affairs, expressing pride in the fact that, 'I invented Clive Priestley' (Sinclair 1995: 252). Despite this, he was somewhat selective in his acknowledgement of the report's findings. Priestley was only one of many officials emphasizing the inadequacy of government support for the arts at this time. Despite this, Channon did not fight for increased funding and gave evidence before the Select Committee in 1982 that the arts were 'managing to survive' (Sinclair 1995: 252).

His replacement in 1983, the Earl of Gowrie, was in the compromising position of also being Treasury spokesman in the House of Lords and was widely viewed as more committed to government spending policy in this capacity than he was to the arts. His comments in the House of Lords following the Tories' second election victory in 1983 made it clear to the arts community that he 'wasn't the sought-after buccaneer making hit-and-run raids on Government spending policy' (*The Stage* 1983). Rather, he informed their Lordships, 'As Culture Minister it is, I am afraid, also my duty to administer something of a culture shock. The party is not over, but the limits of hospitality have been reached. From now on, central government funding will remain broadly level in real terms' (Hewison 1995: 251).

After passively accepting the chancellor's cuts in the arts budget for the fiscal year 1983/4, which fell below inflation, Gowrie also failed to secure guarantees that metropolitan authority funding for the arts would be fully replaced following the planned abolition of the councils in 1986. His most decisive action was to introduce the Business Sponsorship Incentive scheme in 1984, whereby, through ABSA, the government offered to match selected new sponsorship deals obtained by arts organizations at a 25 per cent to 75 per cent ratio. To initiate this incentive for companies to increase efforts to obtain funding from the private sector, Gowrie kept back £1 million of the arts budget for 1984/5. While he argued that this money could potentially produce three times as much for motivated companies, he received enormous criticism from the vast majority of provincial theatres, who found their Arts Council grants had been reduced or withdrawn completely that year.

Given Gowrie's confirmed monetarist politics and suspicion of 'no-strings' subsidy, it is somewhat ironic that he was later appointed chairman of the Arts Council.[8] But, in addition to applying financial pressure, the Thatcher government methodically brought the old consensus institutions into line by populating them with their own people. Gowrie was by no means the first political appointment. In 1982, when the five-year tenure of the then Arts Council chairman, Gerry Robinson, came to an end, the tradition of appointing non-elected individuals to the highest posts allowed the Tories to replace him with an individual sympathetic to their ideals. Although the new chairman, William Rees-Mogg (later Lord), emphasized that he had not had any formal connection with the Conservative Party for two decades, he was, according to Peter Hall, 'seemingly content to dismantle the subsidy structure of the previous twenty years and allow the Council to dwindle from an independent agency fighting the cause of artists into a tool of government policy' (Peacock 1999: 47).

Rees-Mogg was very much of the establishment, but his sympathies with the New Right were such that he was someone Thatcher would have termed 'one of us'. As a former editor of *The Times*, he believed in the arm's length principle, but was equally aware of the importance of keeping the proprietor happy. Similarly, his appointment as vice-chairman of the BBC in 1981 had been a deliberate move to rectify the fact that the broadcasting corporation was 'not an enterprise culture, but a spending culture' (*The Stage* 1986b).

Arriving at the Arts Council in 1982, Rees-Mogg set about changing the structure of the institution to fit government policy more closely. He accepted that state support for the arts was not going to expand and believed strongly that the arts should be able to operate independently. Deeply suspicious of the tradition of collectivism that he believed had created a dependency culture and caused many artists to become trapped in a dated and provincial set of attitudes, he emphasized his intentions to lower arts organizations' expectations about state funding and push them to find alternative sources of income. Prominent amongst these was the allegedly untapped potential of business sponsorship. He also elevated the needs of the consumer to a privileged position over the artist. In a controversial interview in *The Times*, Rees-Mogg likened the Arts Council to the NHS, asking, 'Ought the health service to exist for the medical and administrative staff, or for the patients? Ought arts funding to be for the artists or for the audiences?' His personal opinion was clear. As he continued, 'Arts grants should be primarily a consumer and not a producer subsidy' (*The Times* 1993).

To facilitate the reform of the Arts Council to fit his agenda more closely, Rees-Mogg followed the government's lead of initiating political appointments to the Arts Council. Most significant was the replacement of the secretary-general, Roy Shaw, whose emphasis on arts education and hatred of business sponsorship put him in diametric opposition to the new chairman. Instead, almost by stealth, Rees-Mogg instigated the appointment of Luke Rittner, the 36-year-old director of ABSA, as his new deputy, managing to secure Rittner's position despite enormous internal opposition. The subsequent years under Rees-Mogg and Rittner marked a clear move to bring the Arts Council's activities and ideals more closely in line with the Thatcher government. This may have saved the organization from extinction, but, if so, it was at the expense of turning it into an instrument of government. As clients of the newly restructured organization, whether capable or not, regional theatres were increasingly forced to alter their operations to coincide with the New Right philosophy in order to retain any state support. The first Arts Council initiative that marked a clear move towards this end was the announcement in 1984 of its 'strategy for a decade', *The Glory of the Garden*.

The Arts Council's attempts to fight off the threats to its position resulted in a letter, sent to 250 of its major clients in 1984, asking what would happen if their subsidies were cut, substantially reduced or significantly increased. In the 'Ilkley Letter', named after the location of the meeting at which the idea was coined, Rittner continued the tradition of employing horticultural metaphors historically used by the Arts Council and explained the rationale behind the questions by quoting Rudyard Kipling:

> Our England is a garden, and such gardens are not made
> By singing: 'Oh how beautiful!' and sitting in the shade,
> While better men than we go out and start their working lives
> At grubbing weeds from gravel-paths with broken dinner knives.

In March 1984, three months after the Ilkley Letter was sent out, the Arts Council produced *The Glory of the Garden*, which outlined some of the most radical structural and policy reforms in the funding body's forty-year history. Named for Kipling's poem, the strategy paper 'announce[d] the largest single programme of devolution in the history of the Arts Council' (ACGB 1984: iii).

It also built on suggestions made in *Towards a New Relationship*, an Arts Council study produced two years earlier that had recommended the regional arts associations be developed and given more responsibility based on 'whether a particular activity is better assessed by the regional or national body' (*The Stage* 1982). The Arts Council's traditional emphasis on the capital had always meant that London had been privileged at the expense of the regions. Although the Arts Council had typically justified this imbalance by elevating London as the artistic centre of excellence that set the national standard, examined in the context of the consistent shortage of funds, such prioritizing had contributed to long-term under-funding in the provinces. In 1984, no theatre company outside London, including the larger companies in the major cities, enjoyed an Arts Council subsidy equal to even a tenth of that given to either the National Theatre or the Royal Shakespeare Company. Emphasizing the fact that the first aim of the Arts Council's original charter, 'to decentralise and disperse the dramatic and musical and artistic life of this country', had not yet been adequately realized, *The Glory of the Garden* announced an accelerated programme of devolution of assessment and funding to the regional arts associations. It proposed an arts-funding network based in thirteen major cities with an emphasis in the following decade on art, dance, drama, music and education. Theoretically, subsidy would be increased to regional clients by making cuts in funds to larger, prestigious London companies and through fostering local government patronage and private sponsorship.

Although the strategy should have provided clear benefits for the regional theatres, in some ways it increased their problems. Commenting on the strategy of devolution, the Arts Council claimed, 'It is a genuine and major act of administrative decentralization, a step back from centralized bureaucracy as a mode of administering the arts in Great Britain. We are not people who believe that London always knows best' (Sinclair 1995: 269). But contradicting such a statement were four decades of putting London first and of resistance to government pressure for further devolution of power to the provinces. Rather than reflecting any heartfelt change in the organization, the strategy was widely perceived as a sop to a government that recognized that there were more votes to be had from a decentralized system of arts administration, particularly at a time of severe economic depression in the old industrial centres in the north. While the proposals did entail some diminution of the national funding body's power, they could be seen primarily as strategies implemented to secure the Arts Council's position. The Arts Council always intended to keep control of the purse strings, failed to clarify how far the power to make independent regional policy accompanied the shift in responsibility to the regional arts associations and ultimately retained responsibility for four times as many organizations as its devolution plan had forecast. Under such circumstances, few regional theatres found the strategy to be beneficial.

Under the terms of *The Glory of the Garden,* six regional building-based theatres were devolved to regional arts associations, while another six had their subsidy withdrawn completely.[9] Nor did the money saved from their subsidies, or from the other arts organizations that lost their grants, translate into substantially increased funds for other regional clients. The independent Cork Report, *Theatre IS for All,* commissioned by the Arts Council out of a concern for the state of theatre in Britain and published in 1986, found that, with two exceptions, *The Glory of the Garden* produced no significant improvements in the situation of provincial theatres:

> In real terms, the effect of the *Glory of the Garden* has been to restore theatres in Leicester and Sheffield to their 1978/9 levels of Arts Council funding, and to leave most other theatres slightly less well off.
>
> (Brannen and Brown 1986: 9)

Moreover, it noted a failure to rectify the imbalance in funding between London and the regions. According to the statistics presented in the Cork Report, the combined share of drama funding allocated to the National Theatre and Royal Shakespeare Company had increased from 30 per cent to 47 per cent of the Arts Council's budget between 1970/1 and 1985/6, while the proportion given to regional theatres had dropped from 62 per cent to 39 per cent over the same period.[10]

Rather than bringing the power and the money to make decisions to the people on the ground, an immediate problem that arose from selective devolution was that the 'arrangements under which regional arts associations are responsible for some of these theatres and the Arts Council for others militate against the development of [coherent] strategies' (Brannen and Brown 1986: 21). For the devolved theatres, this was not just a question of increasingly ambiguous criteria for funding. Many were unhappy because they were afraid they would lose their national status if funds came from a regional body rather than from London where the power, influence and European connections lay. Adding to this anxiety was the fear that the regional arts associations' traditional concern with local rural and folk arts might not expand to allow room for the newly devolved theatres. While the Arts Council did manage to secure guarantees from the regional bodies to continue funding the devolved theatres at at least current levels for three years, there was no obligation to increase grants during this time, or to continue funding the companies when the three years were up.

The Arts Council had decided which theatres would be devolved without any consultation with the theatres themselves, or any public explanation for its decision. The fragile financial situation of many of those devolved led to a perception amongst the theatres that devolution was an indication of their reduced significance, a belief intensified by the fact that the Arts Council was simultaneously streamlining its own regional department in the interests of efficiency and stressing its advisory role. Similarly, the lack of any official criteria to explain why only certain theatres were chosen contributed to a growing belief that it was a way of removing responsibility for impending casualties from the central funding body. While the question of where to lay the blame for their problems did not necessarily add to the troubles of devolved theatres, the decline in morale and the significantly smaller funds available to their new primary funding bodies, the regional arts associations, did.

Although the Arts Council never conceded that *The Glory of the Garden* was a means of ridding itself of troublesome clients, the strategy was undoubtedly an attempt to restructure the funding body to fit more closely the mould of efficient business operation advocated by the Conservative government. In its 1983 White Paper *Streamlining the Cities,* the government had promised that in the coming decade Britain would become a 'chillier, bumpier, less cosy place – but infinitely more invigorating' (*The Stage* 1984a). Thinning out the seedbed was the Arts Council's attempt to prove that it too was capable of ruthless selection in the name of efficiency. The new Arts Council would be leaner, fitter and cheaper. Explaining the proposals in the introduction to the document, Rees-Mogg adopted the jargon and sentiments of the New Right:

> Care for real excellence, encouragement of variety for the audience, support of freedom for the artist, are the foundation of liberty for the arts. The counterpart of liberty is responsibility. An Arts Council which stands back to respect liberty, puts the responsibility for the art on the artists, and the responsibility for practical success on the managers of companies…The task of the Arts Council and, more broadly, the community of the arts will be to make better use of limited resources and to try to continue effective expansion of the quality and availability of the arts in Britain by making the best possible use of such resources as can be made available.
> (ACGB 1984: iv)

Such a comment squarely aligned the Arts Council's new attitude to state funding of the arts with that of the government. The freedom from political interference afforded by indirect state subsidy could not be allowed to 'also mean freedom from "responsibility" and "accountability", "quality" and "marketing" and the dangerous "liberty" of being able to do what one liked' (Peacock 1999: 42). *The Glory of the Garden* afforded the Arts Council the opportunity to divest itself of responsibility for potential liabilities that might reflect poorly on their own system of administration and saw 'an end to the tradition of response in favour of ruthless selection' (Sinclair 1995: 271).

The lack of any public explanation or apparent strategy for the decision to withdraw funding from several theatres fed into the growing insecurity of the Arts Council's remaining clients, particularly when the reasons offered privately varied widely. The Yvonne Arnaud Theatre in Guildford, for instance, officially had its funding withdrawn at this time because it had an overly commercial policy; Harrogate Theatre lost its grant due to the poor quality of its programme; and support for the Queen's Theatre, Hornchurch, was cut because of its falling box office figures. Without a national policy outlining the criteria regional theatres should have been fulfilling to meet the requirements for subsidy, the theatres were also denied solid grounds on which to appeal such decisions.

Although *The Glory of the Garden* was never realized to the extent outlined in the original proposals, the document itself, and the political climate that had led to its creation, signalled a clear change in the operations and thinking of the Arts Council and, in turn, behind state funding of the arts. Expectations that Britain's regional theatres would adjust their operations accordingly led to increasing difficulties for the companies and the continuation of their troubled relationship with the Arts Council.

Notes

1. The money supply ultimately proved impossible to control and all attempts were abandoned by Chancellor Nigel Lawson in 1985. Inflation reached a high of 21 per cent in 1981, but was brought down and held steady at around 5 per cent for the rest of the decade following the increase to Value Added Tax and the recession, which had been brought on by the increase in house prices and reductions to the manufacturing industry.
2. Sir Kenneth Robinson, Arts Council chairman, 1977–82. See Arts Council of Great Britain, *Annual Report 1979/80* (ACGB 1980).
3. The economist Alan Peacock argued that the elevated inflation rate for drama was exaggerated and that it was only slightly ahead of the other arts, at a rate of 0.5–1 per cent. See Peacock, 'Inflation and the performing arts', in H. Baumol and W. J. Baumol, *Inflation and the Performing Arts* 1994: 71–85.
4. The Enhancement Funding Scheme introduced in 1991 earmarked specific companies for extra funding and awarded 'selective additional assistance' with the aim of: (a) enhancing and maintaining the company's work; (b) improving financial management; (c) levering additional funds from the private sector via 'matching funding'.
5. In 1979/80, the basic rate of income tax was cut from 33 per cent to 30 per cent and the top rate from 83 per cent to 60 per cent on 'earned income'.
6. Priestley was a civil servant who led the government's Efficiency Unit and reported directly to the prime minister.
7. The idea of One Nation Conservatism dates back to Disraeli's credo in the nineteenth century, which sought to reconfigure the Conservatives as a party who would temper the social depredations of capitalism and politically represent the idea of a socially just, economically prosperous nation.
8. Lord Gowrie, chairman of the Arts Council England, 1994–8.
9. The regional theatres that lost their subsidy were Basingstoke Horseshoe Theatre, Chester Gateway, Yvonne Arnaud Theatre, Guildford, Queen's Theatre, Hornchurch, Harrogate Theatre and Connaught Theatre, Worthing. Funding was restored to both Chester Gateway and Harrogate Theatre four months later, following appeals. The Horseshoe had partial funding restored. Devolved regional theatres included Derby Playhouse, Watford Palace, Theatre Royal, Stratford East, Redgrave Theatre, Farnham, Thorndike Theatre, Leatherhead, Hull Truck Theatre.
10. See Brannen and Brown 1986, tables 11–14 and table 19.

4

Major Dramas

> *'If the policy isn't hurting, it isn't working.'*
> (Major 1989)¹

The Glory of the Garden marked the first significant step in the move towards an increasingly heavy emphasis on accountability in the Arts Council and its clients. Financially troubled and low in morale, to survive in Thatcher's enterprise culture, both the central funding body and the regional theatres now also had to prove that they could function as efficient businesses in the economic market. For the Arts Council, the need to prove its good business sense translated into increased time and money spent producing constant self-appraisals. As Sinclair pointed out:

> In terms of the survival of the species, [the Arts Council] was no longer hunting for new prey, but spoiling its own nest. The demand for financial scrutinies and management studies was the favoured guerilla tactic of Whitehall, which compelled a body to decline into self-analysis and haemorrhage through dozens of internal inquiries. There was precious little time left for the officers of the Council to administer the arts countrywide when most of their days were spent examining their backfiles to justify their existence.
> (Sinclair 1995: 271–2)

Such an attitude was a precursor of the growing emphasis on management and administration, a preoccupation that subsequently reached fever pitch in the subsidized sector as arts organizations were forced to justify their value in an attempt to hold on to state funding. As Sue Beardon, the administrator of the feminist theatre group Monstrous Regiment from 1976 to 1978, later commented of the 1980s mindset: 'Why fund an arts festival when you can fund a feasibility study on an arts festival? Why pay an artist when you can pay a consultant?' (Peacock 1999: 50).

In the political climate of the time, value increasingly came to be associated with financial efficiency and material benefits. In September 1985, the Arts Council published a prospectus of its achievements called *A Great British Success Story*. Subtitled *An Invitation to the Nation to Invest in the Arts*, the funding body's bid to the government for an increased grant for 1986/7 took the form of a sixteen-page glossy colour brochure advertising the benefits of investing in the arts. If *The Glory of the Garden* signalled the first major efforts to remodel the Arts Council into a more efficient and industrious institution that could function in the new market economy, then the completion of its reform was realized in *A Great British Success Story*. Here the funding body adopted the discourse of the New Right and attempted to sell the arts to the government by evaluating them in purely commercial terms. As the Arts Council finance director, Anthony Blackstock, commented, 'You have to talk to this government in a language it understands' (Sinclair 1995: 282). Featuring photographs of over 50 examples of successful British art and culture, from composer Michael Tippett and the Hallé Orchestra to the Richard Attenborough film *Gandhi*, the prospectus highlighted the benefits of a booming arts industry for the taxpayer, for employment and for Britain's prestige abroad. It also provided a section on the growing investment in the arts by businesses through sponsorship. As the document concluded:

> The money spent from the public purse is a first rate investment since it buys not only the cultural and educational elements, never more necessary at a time when work and leisure patterns are rapidly changing, but also a product with which we compete on equal or superior terms with the rest of the world. The arts are both at the heart of the tourist industry, and a major diplomatic and cultural aid…To provide job opportunities, invest in business expansion, and stimulate production and export, the Government could do no better than put our money into the arts.
>
> (ACGB 1985a: 7)

The material benefits of supporting the arts were becoming increasingly emphasized as the major concern in the Arts Council's operation. In a lecture given earlier the same year, the funding body's chairman Rees-Mogg had gone so far as to place a dollar value on the arts:

> In 1984/5…the Arts Council grant of £100 million was used to finance some £250 million of arts turnover. The £250 million includes some vital local authority support, some private funding and over £100 million from the box office. Approximately £200 million of the £250 million was spent in salaries. That means that about 25,000 jobs were provided…though many more than that were employed in the subsidised arts for part of the year. They paid some £60 million in national insurance contributions and taxes. Of the £100 million of box office receipts, £15 million of VAT was paid, making a return of £75 million in direct revenue to the Exchequer.
>
> (Rees-Mogg 1985: 3)

Presenting the arts as an investment that generated money for the Treasury, Rees-Mogg finished by emphasizing that the cost to the Exchequer of failing to subsidize the arts would have been '£75 million of lost revenue and £50 million of additional expenditure. The public sector borrowing requirement would have gone up by £25 million if the Arts Council had not received a penny' (Rees-Mogg 1985: 3). As this shift in language demonstrates, in the enterprise culture of the 1980s, it was no longer enough simply to emphasize the intrinsic value of the arts. Nor could subsidy continue to be taken as an unqualified right. It had to be justified in terms of an investment that would offer a substantial increase over the outlay in material returns. Thus, the traditional focus on aesthetic beauty and personal and spiritual fulfillment was discarded in favour of advertising the arts industry primarily as a commercial entity.

Inevitably, Britain's regional theatres were forced to follow the Arts Council's lead in subjecting themselves to the business methods of self-appraisal and analysis that would demonstrate the cost-efficiency and material benefits of their operations. In the early 1980s, the central funding body started to apply its newly acquired methods to its clients, asking them to report on staffing levels, financial practices and how far they had been able to match the Arts Council's funding with income from business sponsorship and local authorities. As playwright Howard Brenton commented, 'an Orwellian "artspeak" developed: theatre companies had to deliver "assessments of achievement of financial performance targets" and attend brain-melting seminars on subjects such as "the development of a donor constituency"' (Peacock 1999: 50).

In the latter part of the decade, the Arts Council expanded its efforts to demonstrate the value of the arts by emphasizing their social utility. Reductions in the manufacturing industries had had a severe effect on many of the old industrial cities, and by the end of the 1980s severe urban decay added to the widespread demoralization caused by increased crime, homelessness and unemployment. A chance remark of Thatcher's indicating that there was a job to be done in the inner cities following her third election victory in 1987 was the cue for a flurry of activity relating to urban regeneration, not least in providing the Arts Council with another way of demonstrating the material value of the arts. From highlighting their economic benefits it was just a short step to presenting the arts as a vital element in social and economic regeneration, urban renaissance and job creation. In 1988, the Arts Council produced a pamphlet, *An Urban Renaissance: The Role of the Arts in Urban Regeneration*. This claimed that 'the arts create a climate of optimism… the 'can do' attitude essential in developing the 'enterprise culture' this government hopes to bring to deprived areas…The arts provide a means of breaking this spiral [of economic and moral decline] and helping people believe in themselves and their community again' (Sinclair 1995: 284). Such new possibilities appealed to the prime minister. 'The city was not a real true city merely by industry and commerce and services. It was only a real true city when it also had libraries, art galleries, music, orchestras, choirs,' she opined (Sinclair 1995: 289).

In response to this new stress on social efficacy, the old social welfare emphasis of the post-war era of consensus politics was once again accentuated at the end of the 1980s. Thus regional theatres were expected to continue presenting an education policy and provide extended opportunities and employment for members of minority groups such as women, ethnic minorities and the disabled. In other words, under circumstances of increasingly severe poverty, regional theatres were expected to retain high standards and answer traditional social obligations in their programmes, while spending increasing amounts of time and resources on improving and demonstrating the efficacy of their operation.

This new emphasis on good housekeeping forced many regional theatres to reconstruct their system of management and radically expand their administrative departments, often at the expense of production values. This frequently meant introducing new positions specifically to deal with grant applications to the Arts Council and local authorities and to handle the increased requirement of obtaining business sponsorship. As Peacock notes:

> Throughout the theatre the features of capitalist business management – accounting, cost analysis and cost-saving, measurable objectives, marketing, appraisal, efficiency, resources (human and material), the apparently ubiquitous consultants, together with expensive training courses on fund-raising – represented a discourse hitherto unfamiliar even in the subsidised sector.
>
> (Peacock 1999: 49–50)

The imposition of such a new method of operations met with a varied response at management level. Some artistic directors became increasingly dispirited. Bill Morrison, artistic director of Liverpool Playhouse, resigned in the wake of *The Glory of the Garden*, saying 'This never-ending struggle to defend the arts really saps the creative energy. It really is a matter of directors wanting to direct and not become bureaucrats' (*The Stage* 1984c). Others, such as Richard Digby-Day, artistic director of Nottingham Playhouse, at first found incentive in the prospective reward of an increased subsidy. 'I found it a very exciting process and we had a wonderful team, but what I reach at the end of the day is – was it all worth it?' he questioned. 'We have a beautifully typed report containing endless things we want to take up and then we turn round and find we have a standstill grant' (Sinclair 1995: 306).

As Digby-Day discovered, successfully reorganizing and marketing a regional theatre as a cost-efficient operation could be a pyrrhic victory. In the enterprise culture, accepting the capitalist discourse of the 'real world' and adopting the business methods and artspeak advocated by the Arts Council were the only ways for regional theatres to ensure any chance of retaining funding. But if the government's annual grant-in-aid remained static or was cut, no amount of good housekeeping could guarantee a raise. Moreover, in such circumstances, certain theatres felt themselves penalized for their success: demonstrating their efficiency and independence could just as easily provide the Arts Council with an excuse to reduce the theatre's grant-in-aid, just as its own had been. The government's reward to the slimmed-down, more efficient Arts Council, in the wake of the purges made through *The Glory of the Garden*, was to offer a below-inflation grant for the following year. As Blackstock said, 'when you prove you are more efficient, you need less public money' (Sinclair 1995: 274).

The other way of demonstrating good business sense was through increasing the income earned from the private sector. Gowrie's incentive funding scheme was succeeded by challenge funding in the Arts Council, which offered matching funds for money earned by arts organizations from business sponsorship equal to or above a certain sum. As a result of such efforts, increasing amounts did come to be raised from this source. By 1986/7, ABSA was claiming income generated from arts sponsorship lay between £20 and £25 million, a sum that had risen to over £60 million by the beginning of the 1990s. However, such figures need qualification. In the theatre, the bulk of sponsorship went to the more 'prestigious' companies, such as the Royal Shakespeare Company's £3.3 million deal with Royal Insurance between 1988 and 1994. Alternatively, it focused on the more commercial arts activities or relatively uncontroversial mainstream arts in the main metropolitan centres, where audiences were largest. In contrast, smaller regional theatres did not offer such an attractive proposition. As the artistic director of the Manchester Royal Exchange pointed out in 1979, 'Industry is only willing to sponsor companies which are well known or have well-known people in them' (*The Stage* 1979b). But celebrated actors became increasingly reluctant to appear at regional theatres, and other potential benefits for businesses to invest in provincial producing houses were minimal. This relates to the limited scope of regional theatre's audience, a consideration compounded by the fact that theatre, by nature, can be politically and socially contentious. In turn, the public status of subsidized theatres restricted the type of sponsorship they could negotiate. So where sponsorship was obtained for regional theatres, it tended to be on a project basis and only in relatively small quantities. It was, moreover, an uncertain source of income, given that business sponsorship is particularly susceptible to fluctuations in the economy. Accordingly, while business sponsorship of the arts rose to £65 million in 1992, it fell back to £58 million in 1993 following the national recession and to £51 million in 1994. Since ABSA's foundation in 1976, it has never accounted for more than 13 per cent of the combined total spent on the arts by local and central government.

Under such circumstances, many regional theatres became increasingly resentful at what they considered the wasteful amounts of time and money spent on a futile bid to increase funds from this source. The Theatre Royal, Stratford East, had hired a professional fund-raiser in 1983 to help obtain sponsorship, but abandoned all attempts the following year because the costs were far exceeding the benefits. Similarly, in 1985/6, Birmingham Repertory, one of the large-scale regional theatres in Britain, raised £44,800 in sponsorship, a 'result of hard effort by a prestigious regional theatre' (Brannen and Brown 1986: 50). This accounted for 3 per cent of its total revenue. The fact that the effort put into raising sponsorship could actually cost theatres more than it returned caused the arts lobby group, the National Campaign for the Arts, to comment, 'We think it worth drawing to the [government's] attention the disappointing reality of the situation. We are deeply concerned that theatres may be spending considerable time, energy and money in pursuit of business sponsorship, which is turning out to be something much less than a golden goose' (*The Stage* 1988b).

Such warnings failed to deter the Thatcher administration, and the government earmarked increasingly large portions of the annual arts grants to be kept back for challenge funding when it could have gone directly to the theatres. Following the government's lead, the Arts Council produced the pamphlet *Better Business for the Arts* in 1988 to help 'foster a more businesslike approach among clients and award those groups which boost income by means other than subsidy' (ACGB 1988). While many theatres became frustrated because they believed they were being judged on their fund-raising rather than artistic abilities, the business world became increasingly wary of having to bear the brunt of support for the arts. As the financial crisis in regional theatres escalated over the course of the decade, the small pool of potential sponsors diminished further, with businesses scared off at the potential of bad publicity that would be generated if they became associated with a theatre that closed after sponsorship was pulled out.

Given the limitations on gaining private sponsorship, the pressure to run a financially efficient operation ultimately resulted in poorer working conditions and a severely restricted programme of activities in regional theatres, where artistic questions increasingly took second place to administrative requirements. In order to remain solvent during this period, most regional subsidized theatres found it necessary to compromise on one or more activities. Perhaps most significantly, the decade following *The Glory of the Garden* saw production values reduced and the scope of the activities and repertoire dramatically narrowed in all but the large municipal regional producing theatres.

The first to go in many theatres were the fringe activities, such as educational programmes, young people's theatre groups and studio theatres. In attempting to retain Arts Council funding, these traditionally loss-making activities could be perceived as peripheral to the primary activity of the theatre. The Arts Council's own cuts to the National Youth Theatre in the Christmas Cuts of 1981 had clearly demonstrated its own bias and its clear preference for professional companies. The TIE and YPT programmes were particularly vulnerable to such cuts, following the increased tendency to consider them as the educational responsibility of the county councils. A recommendation made by the Cork Report in 1986 suggested that 'a more systematic approach to funding of TIE and YPT companies be established, derived from the funding bodies locally recognized as most appropriate' (Brannen and Brown 1986: 37). This would have lifted the onus from the regional theatres, but problems in realizing such a suggestion arose from the increased restrictions the Conservatives placed on local authority spending. Moreover, changes to the school administration system under the 1988 Education Reform Act left state schools in charge of managing their own grants. Equally affected by long-term cuts in public expenditure, many schools were subsequently left in no position to sustain regular engagements with TIE companies, particularly with the inclusion of a clause that prevented parents from being asked to cover the costs of education-associated activities. Following initial closures at the beginning of the Conservative administration, such as Nottingham Playhouse's closure of its TIE programme, Roundabout Theatre, in 1979, there was a clear decline in the number of TIE and YPT programmes attached to regional theatres. Between 1986 and 1995, following the Cork Report, the number of TIE companies operated through regional theatres reduced from twenty-three to seven, while the number of YPT schemes fell from twenty-four to eighteen (Brannen and Brown 1996: 380).

While cutting these programmes may not have directly affected the central business of the main theatres, such decisions were particularly unpopular with local authorities, specifically the county councils, many of whom provided grants unofficially earmarked to fund such activities. Furthermore, the nature of youth programmes made them an extremely sensitive issue for many audience members ignorant of the true extent of the problems being experienced by the theatres. Amongst small and mid-scale theatres operating in smaller communities, many of the children and young people affected were typically related to the theatre's loyal audience. As at Salisbury Playhouse, under such circumstances, poor handling of the cuts could directly affect the goodwill of the town and thereby the box office.

Cutting costs by reducing the main programme was, at least on the surface, potentially less problematic for the theatres. After the 1970s, when the old repertory system that employed a resident ensemble cast had largely died out, regional theatres typically cast actors on a play-by-play basis. From the early 1980s, most theatres found it preferable to alter seasons to include shows that typically involved reduced casts in small-scale productions, rather than make redundancies amongst other permanent staff. The Arts Council's bid for greater funds from the government, *A Great British Success Story*, used the example of the Theatre Royal, Stratford East, to demonstrate how damaging inadequate support for the arts could be. In its thirty-year history, beginning with Joan Littlewood's Theatre Workshop, the Theatre Royal had produced over thirteen West End transfers and film adaptations. But the Arts Council noted that the theatre could not hope to continue such a trend, owing to the fact that its budget permitted an average of only six actors per show. This situation was so widespread across the country that it caused Peter Hall to comment in 1985, 'Every regional theatre is saying, well, we can't employ enough actors to do Shakespeare, we've had to cut down the number of actors we employ. And a writer will tell you, I daren't put more than six characters in a play because I know there's no chance of it being put on' (Hall 1985: 6).

Limiting in themselves, these restrictions were increased by the reduction in provincial theatres' output. The gradual replacement of weekly rep with two-week and then three-week runs in the 1950s and 1960s had inevitably resulted in fewer productions, less choice for audiences and an increasing reluctance amongst regional theatres to risk alienating spectators by presenting any work that was new or challenging on the main stage. For some theatres, this problem had been alleviated by the widespread building of studio theatres in the 1960s and 1970s, but with many such spaces going dark for increasing periods of time, that option was closed to many. Nevertheless, the serious decline in the production of new or experimental works during this period caused mounting concern, as much for the audiences as the artists.

Theoretically, the government's insistence on economic returns and social utility should have translated into efforts to expand and diversify the box office. As one of the many documents issued by the Arts Council during this period noted, 'Funding for drama should foster diversity. A diverse creative environment nurtures more life than a monoculture, allows more cross-fertilization and has room for individual voices. Diversity of creativity also fosters diversity of audience' (ACE 1995: 7).

Caught in the subsidy trap, however, the theatres could not afford to risk alienating their loyal audiences by putting on anything considered remotely risky. The actor Timothy West commented in 1992, 'I think what a lot of people don't understand is just how near the edge a lot of regional companies are. A 5% cut can make all the difference between existence and non-existence' (Surrey Advertiser 1992a). As we shall see in the chapters on the Redgrave Theatre and the Salisbury Playhouse, in this climate, a single play performed at an untimely moment in a season could distance a dependable audience and make or break a theatre.

By limiting their repertoire, the theatres also lost an opportunity to increase and expand the size and composition of their audiences. Although, as the Cork Report noted, 'there is still a need in many theatres for further improvement in analysing box office attendance records' (Brannen and Brown 1986: 50), during the 1980s Arts Council annual reports showed mounting concern over the increasingly exclusive profile of audiences. The first year for which officially accepted figures are available by which to analyse national audience trends is 1986/7.[2] Statistics collected by the Target Group Index (TGI) for this year confirm that the largest group who went to the theatre came from higher social grades (ABC1) and were in the older age groups.[3] Trend analysis that compared TGI figures for the first four years for which they were available (1986/7–1989/90) with figures compiled at the end of the following decade (1995/6–1998/99) suggested that this profile had become progressively more exclusive. In particular, by the latter half of the 1990s, only 14 per cent of those attending plays came from social group C2DE (or lower-middle and working class), and the composition of audiences coming from age groups of people over 50 also rose significantly during these periods, from 38.6 per cent to 44.6 per cent. Meanwhile, a fall was recorded in the percentage of the attendance of young people aged fifteen to twenty-four and of adults living in households with at least one child. When considered in terms of increased life expectancy, this implies that largely the same people were going to the theatre in Britain in the late 1990s as had been in the second half of the 1980s. Unfortunately, while loyal audiences were getting older, they were not being replaced by new younger ones.

The fact that audiences for regional theatres had become increasingly exclusive was both an ideological and economic concern. While many theatres were concerned to find new audiences simply because current ones were literally dying off, others were equally concerned that they were not fulfilling their social objectives. But financial restrictions limited the theatres from pursuing effective marketing drives that could target new audiences from different income or social brackets. As much as anything, as we shall see in the case of the Thorndike Theatre, Leatherhead, for instance, this related to the increasing trend for employing under-skilled administrative staff on a casual basis to oversee individual projects and therefore keeping costs down. Under such circumstances, it was almost impossible to carry out any long-term marketing strategies or audience profiling. Those schemes the theatres did introduce, most significantly the widespread introduction of the subscription marketing scheme, based on selling season tickets at reduced rates, were incentives primarily aimed at maintaining the support of the current loyal audiences.

Under these circumstances, regional theatres began to adopt increasingly safe, middle-of-the-road programmes that would theoretically answer both the ambiguous criteria for a diverse, exciting and quality selection of plays and guarantee the 60 per cent box office capacity unofficially approved by the Arts Council. By 1984, this practice had already become so widespread that the critic Steve Gooch was able to identify what he termed an 'identikit' programme common to regional theatres. As he said:

> Identikit seasons of plays emerge from these subsidy-prisons: one Shakespeare, one Restoration comedy, one Chekhov or Ibsen (or possibly Arthur Miller or Tennessee Williams – foreign at any rate), one slightly more obscure classical play (usually one that's been revived by the National or RSC), one 'modern' play (yet another production of *Godot*, or *The Caretaker*, or perhaps a Stoppard or an Ayckbourn), one 'old favourite' like *Charley's Aunt*, a Ben Travers farce, an Agatha Christie or a Priestley, the Christmas panto and one other.
>
> (Gooch 1984: 29)

Gooch's observations were given validity with the publication, in 1986, of the Cork Report, which noted significant changes in the repertoire of British theatre over the previous decade. Updated figures published in 1996 showed that while Shakespeare continued to represent 6 per cent of all plays produced, the previous fifteen years had demonstrated a significant decline in the productions of classics. This was explained in terms of the typically larger casts and therefore costs required to mount such plays. The number of post-war plays fell during this period (1981–5, 46 per cent; 1986–90, 32 per cent; 1990–5, 22 per cent), while musicals increased (1981–5, 8 per cent; 1980–90, 12 per cent; 1990–5, 18 per cent), as did adaptations of popular novels (1981–5, 5 per cent; 1986–90, 20 per cent; 1990–5, 15 per cent), pieces that, Peacock noted, 'provided a product with brand familiarity' (Peacock 1999: 52). During the 1980s, the most significant drop recorded was for productions of new work, which tended 'to sink without trace amongst the brand names on these cultural supermarket shelves' (Gooch 1984: 29). Following recommendations for extra funding made in the Cork Report, after falling from 12 per cent to 7 per cent in the latter half of the 1980s, the proportion of new writing produced rose again to 15 per cent in the 1990s (Brannen and Brown 1996: 381). However, the Arts Council's collated figures include work produced by a number of non-regional building-based theatres, such as the Bush, Soho Theatre and the Royal Court, that are specifically dedicated to new writing.

While Gooch's identikit seasons became the norm in regional theatres, even such adjustments could not guarantee that a company would break even. As such, the 1980s and 1990s saw an increasing rise in the trend for private-and-public partnerships that would reduce a theatre's overheads and, theoretically at least, increase its potential for profit. This was particularly true of partnerships formed with commercial producers who might be attracted to using a regional theatre as a testing ground for possible West End transfers or national tours. As *A Great British Success Story* suggested, by the mid-1980s it appeared that transfers from the subsidized theatre were providing the lifeblood of the West End. But while such partnerships, when successful, could provide temporary financial relief for the regional theatres, they typically presented a band-aid approach to the company's problems, and the long-term effects of such partnerships rarely proved beneficial. As subsidized companies, regional theatres are traditionally charitable trusts that operate on a not-for-profit basis. As such, their agendas are invariably at odds with those of commercial partners. Nevertheless, with the exception of the Arts Council-commissioned 1979 Hawser/Findlater Report and the 1986 Cork Report, which both addressed the question of exploitation of creative products by businesses and offered possible guidelines, no coherent policy addressing this issue has been produced.

In the economic climate of the 1980s, certain administrators in the subsidized sector began to advocate private-and-public partnerships as one possible solution to the funding crisis affecting regional theatres. Yet they often found themselves criticized by the media, the public and even their own colleagues, who were concerned that artistic values were being compromised and public monies improperly used for the commercial gains of certain individuals. As such, it was possible for a situation to arise whereby one theatre might have its funding withdrawn by the Arts Council or regional arts association on the grounds of an overly commercial repertoire, while another client could be given an increased grant to facilitate a partnership with a commercial producer. This was the situation in which the Yvonne Arnaud Theatre, Guildford, found itself (see chapter eight). After losing its funding from the Arts Council under the funding body's *Glory of the Garden* cuts because of its commercial programming, it was subsequently devolved to the regional arts association South East Arts, who upheld the Arts Council's directive and consistently rejected the theatre's requests for support over the course of the following decade. Notwithstanding, the same consideration did not prevent South East Arts giving its highest drama grant to the nearby Thorndike Theatre to allow the Leatherhead theatre to form a six-year partnership with the commercial production company Bill Kenwright Ltd.

Faced with limited creativity, increased bureaucracy and constant cash crises, regional theatres became an increasingly unattractive prospect for talented practitioners. Growing concern was voiced during this period regarding standards of regional theatres being further eroded by the lack of good directors willing to work under such conditions. In 1986, morale was so low that 42 directors from subsidized regional theatres accepted Peter Hall's invitation to meet at the National, where they passed a unanimous vote of no confidence in the Arts Council and officially expressed their frustration over the widespread damage and demoralization being experienced in British theatre.

One of the ideological beliefs that had supported the continuation of subsidy in the regional sector in the post-war years was that the producing houses provided a locus in which potentially talented directors could find the freedom and opportunity to develop their skills and express their ideas. The Arts Council's official policy on the role of directors in regional theatres stated that 'artistic control of a theatre should be vested in the artistic director; as long as he keeps within his budget and retains the confidence of the public, the choice of plays and all that is implied in that choice should be his' (ACGB 1985b: 22). But as the typically limited repertoire demonstrates, the 'one other' play identified by Gooch might be all the latitude artistic directors had to develop an individual vision. Moreover, such restrictions were aggravated by the increased administrative burden.

Speaking of his time as director of the Royal Court during the 1980s, Max Stafford-Clark described his job by saying, 'I now run a commercial business operation that occasionally puts on plays' (Peacock 1999: 50). For some artistic directors of regional theatres, the added emphasis on management made the job itself intolerable. Speaking about her experiences while chief executive of Salisbury Playhouse from 1991 to 1995 – a title created especially for her appointment to underline the fact that she was in overall charge of management as well as artistic policy – Deborah Paige listed her various responsibilities. These included ensuring

> watertight contracts dealing with every eventuality; planning seasons and procuring scripts for as small-an advance payment and as small-a royalty percentage of the box office takings as possible; casting and paying the actors, traditionally less for six to eight hour rehearsal days than for two four hour performance days; keeping set, props, costumes, and the number of actors engaged to an absolute minimum; planning and holding rehearsals; sitting on various committees and meetings; overseeing production, marketing and all fringe activities, and negotiating all decisions with the Board of Directors.[4]

The partial autonomy that artistic directors in regional theatres may have retained under the increased administrative and financial burdens of the early 1980s was further compromised by changes in managerial practice in the latter part of the decade. In 1988, the government introduced the Insolvency Act, making the board directly responsible for any outstanding debts should an organization on which they sat as directors become insolvent. Excepting the fact that the directors of subsidized regional theatres dealt with public monies, following the implementation of this act, managerial practice in producing houses began increasingly to resemble the relationship between management and hired workers in commercial theatres, in that artistic directors were increasingly required to seek the approval of the board for each season's programme. This became particularly problematic as more businessmen, who could better deal with the new administrative burdens than old theatre practitioners, began to staff the boards. Artistic interests were not necessarily their priority. In the wake of years of financial difficulties, the new personal liability to which the board of directors now became subject made them increasingly conscious of the need to protect the balance sheets as well as simply act as guardians of taxpayers' money. In a climate of doubt and anxiety, the pressure to police all decisions and minimize risks rose exponentially. Throughout the 1990s, reports of problems between boards of directors and artistic directors of regional theatres became increasingly common, with many artistic directors claiming that the boards were encroaching on territory traditionally regarded as their prerogative. Two years after the 1988 Insolvency Act was introduced, the artistic directors of five major provincial playhouses – Sheffield Crucible, Derby Playhouse, Nottingham Playhouse, Leicester Haymarket and Lancaster Rep – resigned from their posts.[5] Each cited a decline in working conditions and new trends in theatre management.

In each case, there was disagreement between the board and the artistic directors. As one reporter wrote:

> Boards, usually composed of councillors and businessmen with no direct experience of the arts, fear that sooner or later a theatre will go bankrupt. Artistic directors are under pressure to plan conservatively for big box-office returns and directors who try to insist on bold and controversial programmes find themselves isolated by commercial and administrative restraints. The days when artistic directors were free to pursue creative instincts with the chance of exciting innovation at the end have gone – to be replaced, it seems, by plays seen primarily as product, not art.
> (Sinclair 1995: 328)

Kenneth Alan Taylor blamed his resignation from Nottingham Playhouse on artistic differences with an 'elitist' board with whom he had to fight 'tooth and nail' (*The Stage* 1990b) to get approval for the season's programme. Citing her reasons for leaving the Sheffield Crucible in 1990, Clare Venables said:

> Planning a season is the most difficult job for an artistic director. You are putting your soul down on the stage with the choices you make. But more and more people demand to know why you are doing it and what it will be like when you've finished. Funders, sponsors, administrators, boards, councils, your own publicity people...everyone pushes you into a kind of fruitless endgaming.
> (Meweezen 1990)

Perhaps the changes in job description might have been more bearable had a career in regional theatre offered some compensation in salary or opportunities for career development. But the treadmill created by years of inadequate funding meant that a career committed to working in regional theatre in the 1980s and 1990s was increasingly considered financially unfeasible. In 1990, Philip Hedley, artistic director of the Theatre Royal, Stratford East, noted that he was getting paid an annual salary of £12,000. Comparisons made with the national theatre companies revealed that salaries were disproportionately lower for work in the provincial theatre, even when taking into account considerations of workload, experience and scale of responsibility, as well as the size and renown of the institutions. What was frequently emphasized was that this was a problem of underpayment in regional companies rather than overpayment in the better funded national institutions (ACE 1995). Furthermore, just as lack of resources posed limitations on artistic programming, so the shortage of funds largely restricted career development in this arena to a random movement of professionals from smaller to larger scale activity. Almost a decade after the 42 regional directors met at the National to express their concern at the state of theatre in Britain, the situation showed no signs of having improved. In 1995, the Arts Council reported that working in provincial theatre had become such an unattractive prospect to a new generation of practitioners that many talented artists, directors prominent amongst them, had chosen to either take a different route or avoid the theatre altogether (ACE 1995).

During this same period, working in regional theatre also became increasingly problematic for other theatre personnel. More successful or respected actors who might have improved standards, brought audiences back into the theatres and interested business sponsors, often refused to work outside London because of the higher remuneration from television and film work. Such a reluctance can be understood when examined in terms of the poor financial compensation for work outside London. As the Cork Report noted in 1986:

> In April 1985, the average industrial wage in England was, according to the New Earnings Survey 1985, for all full-time adult employees, £171 per week. In general, actors in the regional theatre in England are now being paid between £120 and £140 per week and very few are fully employed regularly throughout the year. There are examples where actors were being paid even less. From this they must usually pay a 10% commission, plus VAT, to their agent. Most actors in English theatre earn fractionally over two-thirds of the national average wage for those weeks in which they work.
> (Brannen and Brown 1986: 40–1)

By 1990, this figure had dropped to between 57 per cent and 60 per cent of the national average wage, which was reduced to approximately 50 to 55 per cent when the agent's fee was accounted for.[6] As the National Campaign for the Arts argued at this time, the level of pay was so poor in certain theatres that accepting a job in the provinces could actually cost actors money.

The same financial penalty equally applied to other staff. In 1994, Graham Watkins, then artistic director of the Redgrave Theatre, Farnham, complained that skilled and experienced stage hands were working long and unsociable hours for an average of £3.87 an hour – roughly comparable to a part-time student worker in Marks and Spencer. The potential fallout of low pay for technical staff held more serious repercussions for provincial theatres. Despite the theatres' inability to pay actors the desired rates, the size of the pool of actors, and the level of unemployment, meant there continued to be an effective interchange of actors between national and regional companies. The same could not be said for technical staff. In 1995, the Arts Council noted, 'There has been very little interchange in administrative or technical areas, partly because of the comparative levels of financial reward, partly because of the greater creative opportunities that the national companies offer and partly as a result of the increasingly unsatisfactory working conditions in regional theatre' (ACE 1995: 12).

Many of the difficulties being faced by regional theatres at this time were imposed on them via the Arts Council, but government changes to other public institutions further compromised their position. Prior to their abolition in 1986, the combined expenditure on the arts of the metropolitan councils and the GLC was estimated in excess of £46 million. The government provided the Arts Council with £25 million to fill the gap following their abolition. Meanwhile, the local authorities were largely expected to pick up responsibility for the rest.

Over the course of the decade, support for the arts from local authorities increased significantly. Between 1980 and 1985, arts subsidy from this source more than doubled to exceed £100 million and by the end of the decade was outstripping the amount spent by the Arts Council. Even so, it was never enough to make up the shortfall caused by years of below-inflation increases to the government's grant-in-aid and the loss of arts funding from the metropolitan councils. Moreover, arts funding by local authorities remained discretionary, was offered on an annual basis and typically remained a low priority.[7] In the face of curbs on public spending by central government, local authorities had also consistently been forced to choose between social welfare and the arts. The Arts Council's decision to cut 41 clients in 1981 had, in part, been prompted by the combination of central government reductions to both its own and local authority grants. With the responsibility for picking up the tab from the metropolitan counties falling squarely on the local authorities' shoulders, it often came down to a choice between 'Arts versus an old people's home or arts grants versus a centre for the handicapped'.[8] Where local authorities had the inclination to support the arts, their ability was often limited by rate-capping. When funding from central government was reduced, the response from many local authorities, which, like the theatres, found that reduced income by no means meant reduced responsibilities, was to make up the shortfall in their income by raising the local rates. But high taxation was not only unpopular amongst the populace: it was contrary to the Conservatives' economic doctrine and concern with tightening the reins on public spending. Rate-capping was thus introduced by the government in 1984 to bring high-spending municipalities into line by limiting the amount they could raise in local domestic taxes.[9] And if this caused local authorities problems, it was nothing in comparison with the difficulties incurred in collecting the poll tax following its introduction in 1990, which resulted in a massive shortfall in local authority revenue.[10]

In 1990, Thatcher replaced the domestic rates with the poll tax as a theoretically fairer duty that was easier for local authorities to levy and collect. But the new tax was massively unpopular. There was a widespread perception that it was unfair due to the fact that it was levied on every individual without reference to income or property. Such was the hostility with which its introduction was greeted that it was ultimately widely blamed for Thatcher's eventual downfall, and extensive protests against the tax were expressed across the nation by mass non-payment. Given that revenue from such local taxes combined with central government grants to provide the primary source of local authority budgets, following the introduction of the poll tax, the severity of the long-term squeeze on local authority spending became even more acute. As the quarterly periodical *Cultural Trends* noted, in some areas the subsequent shortfall in local authority budgets was partially recovered by reducing arts funding (*Cultural Trends* 1994).

Plural funding of the arts has traditionally been seen as a safeguard for arts organizations in the event of their primary funding body experiencing financial difficulties. As demonstrated by the 1981 Christmas Cuts and *The Glory of the Garden*, both of which saw the Arts Council withdraw its grants to certain theatres and threaten to remove the funding from several more if local authority provision was not improved, tensions had sporadically arisen between the Arts Council/regional arts associations and local authorities over the problem of equitable funding agreements. An increasingly tough line on parity funding pursued by the Arts Council, following the recommendations of the 1986 Cork Report, helped level funding and ease the financial problems of certain theatres. By 1990, the Arts Council was able to claim that this policy was primarily responsible for increasing local authority support to regional theatres by £1.7 million. It maintained that provincial producing houses, such as the New Victoria in Newcastle and the Nuffield Theatre, Southampton, amongst others, would have closed had the national funding body not pursued such a hard line on parity funding. This may very well have been true, but other regional theatres found that their difficulties multiplied under this policy.

The problems caused by the tough line on parity funding after 1986 were particularly severe for theatres located in the areas affected by the abolition of the metropolitan authorities: Sheffield Crucible, Bristol Old Vic, Merseyside Everyman and Liverpool Playhouse, for instance. The Arts Council was given responsibility for administering the government's £25 million replacement arts funding. But this sum was some £20 million less than the metropolitan councils had been spending, and inevitably it left an enormous gap in arts provision. This situation was, in turn, made worse by the fact that the level of replacement funding from central government fell gradually in subsequent years. In the absence of legislation making arts funding statutory, the cash-strapped Arts Council used its position as administrator of the replacement funds to put increased pressure on the local authorities to offer funding at parity levels. Typically, this involved threatening to reduce previous Arts Council grants to stricken organizations rather than offering extra money to make up the gap left by the loss of the local metropolitan council. Thus, for example, abolition of Merseyside Metropolitan Council damaged the system of arts funding to the extent that the area's seven museums and galleries had to be 'nationalized' and directly funded by the government. The successor authorities were too poor to fund Liverpool's theatres properly, and a protracted series of debates with the national funding body saw the Arts Council ultimately make good its threat to slash the grants to the region's two theatres if Liverpool City Council could not provide more funding.[11] In 1988, the Arts Council grants to the Liverpool Playhouse and the Everyman were cut by £29,000 and £16,000 respectively. The Playhouse, whose previous two directors had resigned in 1984 and 1986 because of their frustration at the bureaucratic demands and constant uncertainty of their job, was only saved from bankruptcy in 1990 by a deal with a commercial producer. The Everyman went bankrupt in 1993.

In 1996, a decade after co-authoring the Cork Report, Rob Brannen and Ian Brown looked back at the subsequent ten years in British theatre in 'When theatre was for all: The Cork Report after ten years'. The conclusions they drew here, that many provincial theatres had benefited from the Arts Council's tough negotiations on parity funding, appear justified by the extensive increase witnessed during this period in local authority funding nationwide. What is less easy to quantify with statistics is the increased strain felt by many theatres. As in the case of the Salisbury Playhouse, the pressure and uncertainty of maintaining equitable levels in the face of constant curbs on local authority spending added to an already difficult working climate.

* * *

By the end of the 1980s, the government's attitude to the arts had provoked mounting anger and resentment in the theatre community. Similarly, the Arts Council, perceived as a progressively more politicized organization, also came in for increasingly vocal criticism. Headlines in the national press and trade paper *The Stage* constantly alluded to the crisis, and numerous conferences entitled variously 'Arts in Peril' (Newcastle, January 1984) or 'Theatre in Crisis' (Goldsmith's College, December 1988) were held across the country. In 1986, the Cork Report emphasized that if current conditions continued, regional theatres could potentially wither and die within five years. The report estimated a shortfall of £13.4 million for British theatre in general, recommending that this gap in provision should be made up with increased contributions from both central government and local authorities. In its attempts to safeguard at least a small number of the regional producing houses, the report recommended that six regional companies be given 'national status' and extra funding to allow them to focus on artistic activity and attract international talent.

The arts minister from 1985 to 1990, Richard Luce, did recognize the extent of the problem and tried to make some concessions to the beleaguered arts community. But the problems they were experiencing in no way caused the government to reconsider its approach. Thus, while Luce persuaded a reluctant Thatcher to agree to a three-year funding package for the arts in 1988, guaranteeing a grant rise of 15 per cent by 1991 to end the trend of hand-to-mouth uncertainty in arts organizations and theoretically allow for strategic and forward planning, the benefits of the plan were seriously undermined by the earmarking of funds for government schemes. While always subject to changes in inflation, which rose alarmingly to almost 8 per cent in 1989, the advantages to regional theatres were further compromised because a large proportion of the grant increase was allocated for specific projects to boost touring, international contracts, alternative funding and management improvements. Most significantly, 40 per cent of the increase was earmarked for incentive funding that would encourage a more businesslike approach amongst clients.

Despite the efforts of the Arts Council, and the evidence of widespread demoralization in the arts at the increasing amounts of bureaucracy, Luce was not convinced that the arts funding system was administratively efficient. In a further attempt to obtain better 'value for money', in 1988 he commissioned a former civil servant from the Office of Arts and Libraries, Richard Wilding, to carry out a thorough review of the roles and functions of the Arts Council and the regional arts associations. The Wilding Report, published in September 1989, found that the two-tier funding system was unnecessarily costly and inefficient, with tensions and delays arising from overlap. It recommended reducing the twelve regional arts associations to seven new regional arts boards, merging the Arts Council with the Crafts Council and reducing the 'overstaffed' administrative system, which would supposedly make estimated savings of £2 million. The report also recommended devolving, or in the government's new terminology, delegating responsibility for, along with half the government grant, all but 30 of the Arts Council's clients to the new regional arts boards. As a vote-catching issue, this recommendation complemented Luce's ideals. Because of constant changes in arts ministers who oversaw the process, however, the number of regional arts boards was ultimately increased to ten and delegation was not actually completed until April 1994. But at this time, the Arts Council of Great Britain found itself in a substantially reduced role when it was split to become Arts Council England (ACE), the Arts Council of Wales and the Scottish Arts Council and responsibility for all the regional theatres was delegated to the regional arts boards.[12]

Devolution should have been perceived as beneficial for regional theatres, bringing the money and power to make decisions to the people on the ground, but the memory of *The Glory of the Garden* left many regional theatres understandably nervous. A reporter for *The Times* noted the reactions of the devolved companies:

> Considering how loudly the subsidised institutions have savaged the Arts Council in the past, the decision to delegate their funding downwards might have been received with thanks. Instead, the theatres have almost all howled with anguish and the list is far shorter than was originally envisaged. However philistine they may think the Arts Council and its comrade-in-arms, the Arts Ministry, they fear they are being pushed out of the frying pan into the fire. Regional committees in the past were characterised by favouritism, artistic interference and log-rolling by party politicians. For all its faults, they say, the Arts Council had an expert staff and understood the need for 'arm's length' handling of artistic freedom...The Arts Minister, David Mellor, has said that delegation must wait until he has cleaned up the regional arts boards. The theory is fine, but it raises fears that a new partisanship will replace the old.
>
> (Sinclair 1995: 332)

In many ways there was justification for the theatres' concerns. Previously, regional arts associations had been responsible for smaller activities that had an amateur or community bias and where questions of standards were less of an issue. In part, this related to the Arts Council's historical concern to maintain control over the larger institutions and the concomitant emphasis on standards. London and the Arts Council, by comparison, were where the money and the influence lay, not least through the European Community. Braham Murray, one of the founding directors of Manchester's Royal Exchange Theatre, expressed his concerns over devolution by saying:

> My fear is that the natural bias of local arts associations is toward community-based arts. They will see big companies as establishment, boring leeches and we will become less potent. The danger is that we will become marginalized, which is the opposite of why we came to the regions: to bring national standing here in the north.
>
> (Sinclair 1995: 362)

A similar concern was expressed in 1990 by the local city council with regard to Birmingham Repertory Theatre, whose regional arts association, West Midland Arts, had a long-standing rural bias. Birmingham had invested substantially in cultural renaissance, having received £200 million during the 1980s from the European Community after being marked as an 'assisted area'. By the time of devolution, however, such assistance was focusing more on England's agricultural south than the country's industrial heartlands and north, and arts subsidy from local councils was becoming increasingly hard to sustain at current levels. As such, the city council emphasized the benefits of Birmingham Repertory Theatre remaining an Arts Council client, where it could remain connected to a national and European network with a higher level of status and financing.

Such considerations, together with the provincial locations and traditional rates of pay, which compared poorly with their counterparts in the Arts Council, also caused questions to be periodically raised about the standards and abilities of those staffing the regional associations. Following his experience as the artistic director of Leicester Phoenix Theatre, which had been devolved to the regional arts association East Midlands Arts four years prior to *The Glory of the Garden*, Graham Watkins warned companies earmarked for devolution that, 'There are fundamental inadequacies in the regional arts associations related to the standard of their officers, their assessment procedures, and above all, the standard, accountability and parochial horizons of their panels' (Watkins 1984). These 'inadequacies' were partly related to the fact that many of the people sitting on decision-making panels of the regional arts associations, and, subsequently, regional arts boards, were councillors who also sat on the arts committees of local authorities. While direct subsidy from the independent Arts Council, particularly with its policy of parity funding, had afforded theatres some protection in circumventing political pressure from the local authorities, this safeguard was effectively lost with delegation. As Watkins continued, 'those arts organizations in favour with regional arts association officers will tend to be well received by local authority arts committees, as well as by the Association itself. But, of course, the reverse is also true' (Watkins 1984).

Anxiety over being placed in the hands of a regional arts board, which might not have the appropriate interest or expertise to effectively assess and support the producing houses, was intensified by the concern that devolution could impose a further financial penalty if not carried through as extensively as outlined in the government's plans. Under such circumstances, primary control might continue to reside with the Arts Council in London, as would its financial emphasis on the prestigious metropolitan companies. Such fears proved founded when Luce's successor, the more centralist David Mellor, announced that the Arts Council would retain responsibility for four times as many arts organizations as originally announced: 81 in all, with 92 being devolved. The regional arts boards would receive only a sixth of the government's grant-in-aid, rather than the half originally designated, and these funds would continue to be administered through the Arts Council. Moreover, Mellor proposed increased central control in his decision to personally appoint the chair of the new boards and retain the power of veto over their chosen directors, who would be selected after consultation with the Arts Council. As John Considien, chairman of Humberside County Council's committee on leisure services wrote, such actions were also 'a clear signal to us that the minister intends to take away the autonomy of the regional arts boards and reduce them to regional arms of the Arts Council' (Sinclair 1995: 332).

With the ideological rationale behind devolution removed, the perception grew that the regional arts boards constituted nothing more than another expensive layer of bureaucracy, 'giving regional administrators a politically correct sense of devolution and an illusory sense of independence' (Peter 1995). By their constitution, regional arts boards were very limited in their powers, unable to shift large amounts of money around the country and subject to the major decisions that continued to be made by the Arts Council in London. Further, despite the loss of 54 jobs at the Arts Council, and 330 throughout the regional arts associations, the creation of the new system increased both bureaucracy and inefficiency, making it increasingly difficult for regional theatres to get the help or advice they needed. Drawing on a popular contemporary advertising jingle for one of the nation's major banks, Stratford East artistic director Philip Hedley likened his experience with the regional arts boards to dealing with 'parts of a friendly banking system, each a listening bank branch passing on messages to head office' (Peter 1995). In more concrete terms, Graham Devlin, who was deputy chief executive and acting chief executive of the Arts Council from 1997 to 1999, estimated that following the creation of the regional arts boards, for a new policy or application to be approved it would have to be passed through approximately 85 individuals, taking an average length of eighteen months.

Rather than solving problems for the regional theatres, delegation aggravated them. The two-tier system remained intact, and traditional problems in the national funding body's relationship with its regional counterparts went uncorrected. Thus, for example, imbalances in subsidy levels that were largely the result of historical accident were continued. A constant criticism voiced over the years by the Council of Regional Arts Associations (CoRAA) that the Arts Council's allocation of grants took no account of changing social and population trends and therefore left many regions dangerously under-funded, continued under the regional arts boards. The problems experienced by the trio of theatres known as 'The Surrey Cluster', all funded by South East Arts, bears witness to this (see chapters six, seven and eight).[13] On top of this, delegation created a buffer between the theatres and the money source. Expanded bureaucracy made it ever more challenging for stricken theatres to obtain increased subsidy from the public sector, given that few regional arts boards had any reserves at all. Delegation also helped redirect anger over the increasingly public crisis in the arts away from the Arts Council and Parliament. Antony Fanshawe, chairman of the Salisbury Playhouse Board of Directors at the time of the theatre's closure in 1995, believed that the regional arts boards were created simply as a scapegoat to disguise the government's poor record with the arts and concluded that the problems experienced by the Playhouse were directly related to delegation to Southern Arts in 1992. It is certainly ironic that, once established, the regional arts boards were estimated to be spending a fifth of their own budgets on their administration, while the original cost of setting up the regional arts boards in 1991 was estimated at £6 million – the equivalent of the collective deficit for the country's regional theatres that same year.

By 1990, when Thatcher left office, regional theatres had been proclaiming a national crisis for almost a decade, and the beginning of the new decade, and a new prime minister, John Major, did nothing to relieve the situation. With the exception of a notable rise in government arts funding during the two years the well-known arts buff Mellor was in office, first as minister for the arts in 1990 and then as chief secretary to the Treasury from 1990 to 1992, the government's attitude to the arts and concomitant low levels of state support continued unabated.[14] The problems these caused were exacerbated by deficits in local authority budgets – coffers emptied as people refused to pay the newly introduced poll tax – and the national recession, which began to show its effects on the economy at the beginning of 1991. Meanwhile, the Theatrical Management Association, the national representative body for professional organizations and workers, noted a steady decline in audience figures for regional theatres, which shrank steadily from an estimated 13.4 million in 1990/1 to 10.7 million in 1993/4.[15] While the recession, continued bad publicity and limited repertoire all contributed to these declining audiences, many critics pointed to what the Theatrical Management Association referred to as an epidemic of 'Back Stage Slums', a term which was by no means confined to the backstage area.

Provision for theatre buildings had begun to improve in the latter part of the 1980s with some help from the European Community, which had, for example, provided Birmingham with £200 million in regional development grants. Under the Arts Council's Housing the Arts scheme, a new provincial theatre, the Theatre Royal, opened in Plymouth in 1982, and another opened in Leeds, the West Yorkshire Playhouse, in 1990. But the resources put towards continuation of this scheme had been substantially slashed in the 1970s and shortage of Arts Council funds had meant they were never restored. Consequently, the decision was taken to wind the scheme up in 1988. However, even during the period when the Housing the Arts scheme continued, theatre buildings were often the last area to receive attention. Until the advent of the National Lottery, launched in Britain in November 1994, the lack of funds for the arts meant that little capital investment was made in new buildings, to the extent that 'there was hardly any expenditure even on existing buildings in need of refurbishment' (Devlin and Hoyle 2000: 51). By 1990, the backstage areas of numerous major producing houses, including those in Canterbury, Cheltenham, Northampton and Salisbury, were deemed hazardous by the Arts Council (ACGB 1985b) and exteriors and interiors were in serious need of attention. Many theatres, such as the Belgrade in Coventry, which had been commissioned during the period of urban renewal and civic pride of the 1950s, had in fact been considered outmoded even by the time they had been built. Without the necessary renovations to allow them to adapt to changing audience needs, theatre buildings came to be continually criticized as increasing burdens, in need of renovation, lacking essential features, the wrong size, or in poor locations:

> Several buildings which opened following that of the Coventry Belgrade, show problems of age, and in some cases, including the backstage arrangements of the Belgrade itself, inadequate planning and provision for contemporary use. Older buildings also have renovation problems. Some, such as the Liverpool Playhouse and York Theatre Royal, were partly renovated in the 1960s, but now need more substantial refurbishment, while others, such as the Theatre Royal, Stratford East, have never had substantial renovation having been patched over the last century until they are now in dire need of proper refurbishment.
> (ACGB National Arts and Media Strategy Unit 1991: 11)

The dilapidated state of many buildings added substantially to a number of theatres' accumulated deficits. When the Salisbury Playhouse closed in 1995, its sizeable debt was partially accounted for by the state of the building, which failed to pass official health and safety standards and was deemed dangerous to the public. Equally problematic, such conditions were increasingly linked to poor showings at the box office. The fact that 'these theatres are not built for today's audiences' meant that by the 1990s, the 'good night out' (Wright 1994) factor conducive to making theatre an appealing option for the public was seen as all but impossible to create. The buildings were generally acknowledged as having the potential to put theatres at the centre of local communities. But as Paul Kerryson, artistic director of the Leicester Haymarket from 1993, pointed out, theatres first needed to be places where people would want to go to drink and socializes, 'regardless of whether or not they are going to wash down their Bacardi and Coke with a hefty dose of Brecht or Beckett' (Wright 1994).

The one source of hope offered to the regional theatres under the Conservatives came near the end of the Tory administration, with the introduction of the National Lottery in 1994. Proposals for a national lottery had been put forward several times during the Conservative administration, but were always turned down by the Iron Lady. According to Gowrie, 'Mrs. Thatcher had rejected the idea on several occasions; she disapproved of gambling because of her strict Methodist upbringing'.[16] John Major had no such scruples. Central government was quick to reassure critics of the scheme that revenue generated from the lottery would not be used as a substitute for core-spending programmes. Even so, it was perceived as a potentially effective way of providing some much needed relief to cultural sectors that had been particularly hard hit by over a decade of reductions in public expenditure; certainly national anger at the plight of the arts was contributing to the increasing unpopularity of the Conservatives at this time. Consequently, the government decided that a percentage of lottery profits would be split between five 'good causes', one of which was designated as the arts. As a result of this decision, the funds available to the Arts Council, who were given responsibility for administering arts revenue generated through the lottery, effectively doubled from 1995 onwards. Unfortunately, however, the government completely underestimated the success of the lottery, and thus spending of the hypothecated tax was heavily restricted.

Initially, arts funding from the lottery was limited to capital funding only. While the country's theatre buildings were collectively in dire need of attention, the unprecedented success of the lottery meant that such restrictions created further problems for the companies. The revenue from the lottery added to a climate in which an increased number of theatres continued competing for declining levels of revenue funding, and audiences, while simultaneously a serious imbalance emerged between the luxurious updated theatres that had benefited from lottery funds and those that had not. Equally, those theatres in receipt of lottery grants often found that the modernized facilities underlined the disparity between the standards of the venues themselves and the products on offer. The fear that this might result in a series of white elephants appeared justified with the problematic opening of new venues such as the Norwich Playhouse. The new 310-seat regional theatre opened in November 1995, with a £400,000 contribution from the National Lottery, alongside £2.5 million raised through contributions from private individuals and charitable trusts. Attendances were substantially lower than forecast, and since there was no available support from national or regional funding bodies or local authorities, the theatre had no way of meeting operational costs. By April 1997, the same month a general election brought a new political party to government, the shortage of revenue funding, estimated at £100,000 a year, had caused the theatre to go dark, with an operating deficit of £300,000 and plans to convert it into a theme pub. The theatre was ultimately saved by a loan from Barclays bank, but when it reopened in 2000 it was as a touring venue and conference hall rather than a producing house.

In 1997, widespread feelings of demoralization at the abrasive attitude and individualist ideology that had characterized the Tory approach to government helped end Labour's eighteen years in the political wilderness. A new government under the leadership of Tony Blair finally offered hope that a new cultural policy might bring a reprieve for Britain's regional theatres. However, the need to accept some of the now deeply ingrained changes, such as low taxation and levels of public expenditure, made under Thatcherism saw to it that the first years of the New Labour administration witnessed little change. Certainly, such alterations as were made were neither radical enough nor substantial enough to overcome eighteen years of sustained assault on the theatre community. Most regional theatres continued to experience difficulties, as we shall see (chapters five to ten). Unfortunately for some, by the time New Labour entered government, it was already too late.

Notes

1. John Major, speaking about anti-inflationary measures on his first day as Chancellor of the Exchequer, 27 October 1989.
2. Target Group Index statistics provide information about gender, age, social grade and education of arts attenders for different disciplines.
3. Socio-economic class groupings in England can be broken down as follows:
    A: upper middle class – high managerial/administrative/professional; eg., company director
    B: middle class – intermediate managerial/administrative/professional
    C1: lower middle class – supervisory/clerical/junior managerial
    C2: working class – semi-skilled or unskilled workers
    E: pensioners, casual workers, others.
4. Deborah Paige, chief executive, Salisbury Playhouse, 1992–6. Letter to author, 1996.
5. Clare Venables (Sheffield Crucible theatre); Kenneth Alan Taylor (Nottingham Playhouse); Peter Lichtenfels (Haymarket Leicester); Annie Castledine (Derby Playhouse); Ian Forrest (Duke's Playhouse, Lancaster).
6. In 1990, the average industrial wage for full-time employees was £263.10. Actors in regional theatre were, on average, paid between £135 and £170 for each week they worked.
7. The Chartered Institute of Public Finance and Accountancy (CIPFA), the organization that examines national spending on recreation and leisure, demonstrated the continued low priority given to arts funding by comparing it with the privileged position traditionally given to sports and leisure. For example, in 1993/4, local authorities collectively spent 65.8 per cent of their recreation and leisure budget on sports-related activities, while the arts received only 18.3 per cent. In the following year, 66 per cent was spent on sport against 18 per cent spent on the arts.

8. Councillor Jon Davies, chairman, Committee for Arts and Recreation, Newcastle City Council, 1984 conference in Newcastle, 'Arts in Peril', quoted in *The Stage* 1984b.
9. In the early 1980s, local councils compensated for Conservative reductions in central government grants by making cuts, privatization or raising the rates. When this did not ensure public spending was reduced to the level required by the Thatcher administration, in 1984 the government introduced a new rate-capping law that fined councils if they raised the rates beyond a certain government-set limit.
10. The poll tax, also known as the community charge, was a local tax or levy collected from those listed on the register of residents or electors. It was introduced by central government in 1990 to replace the domestic rates, but widespread hostility caused it to be replaced by a new council tax in 1993 under Major.
11. The Arts Council wanted Liverpool City Council to agree to an additional £200,000 for the theatres in 1988, such that funding levels would be reduced from a ratio of nine to one to three to one.
12. Despite the Arts Council of Great Britains's remit until 1994, Scotland and Wales had always been virtually autonomous and, under the 1967 Charter, the functions of the Arts Council in Scotland and Wales had been carried out by two committees known as the Scottish and Welsh Arts Councils.
13. In 1995/6, spending on the arts in the South East Arts Board region was £7.90 per head, compared with £39.57 per head in London.
14. In July 1990, David Mellor replaced Richard Luce as minister for the arts and was then promoted to chief secretary to the Treasury later the same year. At the Treasury, Mellor was able to help secure substantial increases in arts funding in 1991 and 1992.
15. Statistics supplied by the Theatrical Management Association.
16. Lord Gowrie, phone interview, 6 June 2003.

Part Three: Casualties and Survivors

These chapters on casualties and survivors profile the problems seven regional producing theatres struggled with as they tried to digest the changes in cultural and economic policy brought in by the Conservatives and adjust their working procedures to accommodate the demands of functioning in a market economy. All seven theatres experienced substantial difficulties during the 1980s and 1990s. Some experienced a steady decline in all areas of operations as the security of their financial base was gradually eroded. Others adjusted more effectively to the challenges they faced in the Conservatives' eighteen-year administration, but were precipitated into a sudden crisis when one anomalous factor caused the other problems enveloping regional theatres at the time to spiral out of control. Of the seven theatres profiled here, all, except the Yvonne Arnaud Theatre, Guildford, were forced to go dark at least once during this period. One never reopened.

The theatres included in this examination were chosen to illustrate a broad range of venues, taking into account geographical location, audience demographics, scale of theatre, range of activities and artistic policy. The selection of theatres was also based on the types of challenges they faced, the methods they employed to deal with them and the ultimate outcome. Thus, the moderate-sized Salisbury Playhouse caters to a primarily rural population with a very definite audience profile, and the multiple difficulties the theatre experienced leading up to its closure effectively offer a textbook example of the negative effects of Conservative cultural and economic policy on regional theatre.

The Thorndike Theatre in Leatherhead, the Redgrave Theatre, Farnham, and the Yvonne Arnaud, Guildford, are unique in their circumstances as The Surrey Cluster. They provide an interesting illustration of the difficulties regional theatres faced during this period because of the way that financial restrictions led to their individual fates being intricately intertwined. Situated on the London commuter belt, the trio was the collective responsibility of the nation's lowest funded regional arts association, South East Arts, during this period. Consequently, these theatres offer a powerful demonstration of the damaging ramifications of what William Emrys Williams disparagingly referred to as the 'horse-trading mentality', when declining audiences and funds forced them into competition. Their individual attempts to deal with the various challenges posed by the Conservative climate offer a revealing insight into the practical effects of the Arts Council's and regional arts associations' ambiguous policies. While the Yvonne Arnaud was an early victim of *The Glory of the Garden* and lost all its Arts Council/South East Arts funding because of its overly commercial policy, the Thorndike's attempts to overcome its problems through a formal association with a commercial producer were actively encouraged by the same regional funding body. Meanwhile, as the only theatre that attempted to follow the requirements of subsidy by maintaining an artistic policy in line with Arts Council directives, the Redgrave Theatre was the first to go dark.

Three theatres from the north of the country complete the series. The Harrogate Theatre illustrates the slow-drip effect of government policy on a small-scale rural theatre with a wide catchment area and white collar audience, while the combined examination of Liverpool Playhouse and Merseyside Everyman, whose management merged in 2001, shows the devastating consequences for arts organizations when the effects of urban decay were piled on Conservative cultural policy between 1979 and 1997. The problems they experienced in terms of plural funding, particularly the Arts Council's emphasis on parity funding, adopted as official policy in 1986, were further fuel for disaster.

5

SALISBURY PLAYHOUSE

Since its creation after the Second World War, the Salisbury Playhouse, formerly known as the Arts Theatre, has played a vital and successful role in the small rural community in the heart of the south west. After the Arts Council pulled out of direct management of the theatre in 1951, a plea for greater support from the local population and authorities resulted in a thriving theatre that, by the beginning of the 1980s, boasted the highest regular attendance rates of any English regional theatre and simultaneously operated a 100-seater studio theatre, a permanent TIE company and a youth theatre group alongside its main-house productions. In 1995, however, a huge accumulated deficit and falling attendances saw the theatre on the brink of ruin and forced to go dark for a period of seven months. In the Playhouse's decline, the events were propelled by problems endemic to many subsidized regional theatres during the Conservative administration.

* * *

At a public meeting in December 1994, representatives of Bonnar-Keenlyside, the consultants who had been called in to review Salisbury Playhouse's operations, revealed their findings. Hilary Keenlyside summed up the Playhouse's problems in a brief, but poignant sentence: 'Everything that could go wrong, went wrong.'[1] At the time, the Playhouse was carrying an operational deficit of almost £300,000, something the consultants noted to be a consequence of long-term under-funding and plummeting box office revenue. This figure almost doubled when examined in terms of the accumulated deficit. Taking into account the problems of the dilapidated, twenty-year-old building, which had not been refurbished since its construction in 1976 and was deemed 'unsafe' by surveyors, the consultants estimated the deficit to lie somewhere between £300,000 and £600,000.[2] Based on the consultants' recommendations, the Playhouse was closed for a period of seven months in order to make a saving of £100,000 in costs, revise existing operations and receive extensive refurbishment financed by Southern Arts and the Arts

Council. This period, during which the Playhouse went dark, involved the loss of 58 jobs and the replacement of the entire board and executive.

Seemingly, until the appointment of chief executive Deborah Paige in 1991, the Salisbury Playhouse had run a highly successful operation. It claimed the highest attendance figures of the 41 regional theatres operating in the country at the time, with houses officially averaging 84 per cent capacity. The reality of the situation was somewhat different. Long before Paige's arrival, attendance figures had begun to show signs of decline. The older end of the loyal audience who had been committed theatregoers since the 1950s was literally dying off, while others were becoming increasingly unhappy with the standards of production under Paige's predecessor, David Horlock.[3] And because of an inefficient system of administration that had been organized manually, lacked the involvement of a fully qualified accountant and employed only a part-time bookkeeper, the discrepancy between attendance figures and financial capacity was potentially huge. The disparity came mostly from the large number of complimentary tickets for loyal theatregoers and friends of the staff that were consistently given out, as well as deals that benefited large coach parties and those who bought into the subscription scheme more than they did the theatre.[4] Unfortunately, the same system meant that the extent of the problems was impossible to substantiate. The lack of a computerized box office meant that, before 1991, an audience profile could not be built up from anything more than sporadic surveys conducted once every three years. Similarly, systematic statistical records were never kept, even though these might have allowed the financial success of the subscription scheme to be properly monitored and the number of complimentary tickets given out in any one season noted.

Any attempts to improve this situation came up against the impenetrable force of the one-man-show run by artistic director Horlock – a force that applied both during his lifetime and in the legacy he left following his sudden death in a car accident in 1990. During Horlock's time as artistic director, his power was so absolute that even the board of directors were unable to get access to the books. In turn, the tragedy of his death meant that subsequent management was loathe to speak ill of his administration in any way, including making public any problems that had begun at the theatre during his time in charge.[5] Horlock's local popularity also prevented the new management from speaking out. Even when problems began to spiral under the new chief executive, Paige, it was believed that going public would only aggravate the situation.[6] This meant that the problems Horlock left his successor were not limited to the sizeable £125,000 operating deficit Paige inherited on her arrival, but included the legacy he left in people's minds of the 'good old days'. As such, when administrative or artistic changes were made to improve the Playhouse's antiquated, inefficient operation, it was hard to sell the changes locally. Thus, improvements were typically greeted with hostility and used to frame the new management in an unfavourable light when compared to the perceived golden days under Horlock. These circumstances were in certain ways unique to Salisbury. Nonetheless, they simply aggravated the problems discussed in previous chapters that had become common to many regional theatres under the Conservatives.

Like so many others, Salisbury Playhouse blamed many of the problems that led to its closure on long-term under-funding. Since the mid-1980s, annual budgets were based on attendance figures, officially given by the Playhouse as averaging 84 per cent. According to the system of deficit budgeting, such figures formed the basis on which grants were allocated by the major funding bodies – the Arts Council (the Playhouse was devolved to the Southern Arts Board in 1992), Wiltshire County Council and Salisbury District Council. Notwithstanding the fact that there was a vast discrepancy between official audience figures and the income they should have generated, it was widely believed the theatre was a victim of its own success. When debts mounted, claims that 'the Playhouse suffers financially because of its earlier success. High attendances in the past have meant lower subsidies compared with other theatres' became commonplace.[7] From 1984, total subsidies meant the Playhouse had been expected to earn in the region of 72 per cent of its income.[8] The Playhouse received a far lower level of funding than other regional theatres of similar size and operation. And it was widely acknowledged that this was a case of under-funding with regard to Salisbury, rather than generosity to other theatres.

The Playhouse, with its low levels of subsidy, was also a long-term victim of problems arising from the Arts Council's emphasis on parity funding. Financial threats had dogged the Playhouse throughout the 1980s when, on three separate occasions, the Arts Council froze its grant and on one occasion threatened to withdraw funding altogether unless local authorities brought their funding up to matching levels.[9] In 1981, Arts Council provision accounted for 84 per cent of the Playhouse's subsidy. By 1985/6, there had been little improvement on this situation, with the combined contributions from local authorities amounting to only 37 per cent of the sum given by the Arts Council. Although this figure improved from 1988/9, local authority failures to follow through on promises made to the Arts Council aggravated the Playhouse's difficulties. Numerous occasions saw local government agree to increase funding and then fail to do so. In 1992, for example, Wiltshire County Council had committed an additional £15,000 over two years, but failed to deliver. In fact, partly in response to the recession in the early 1990s, Wiltshire County Council's grant to the Playhouse was frozen for these two years and actually decreased in real terms. At the time of the theatre's closure in 1995, funding was still far from at parity levels, with local authorities collectively contributing over £120,000 less than Southern Arts.

Although the Arts Council recognized that the Playhouse was severely under-funded relative to comparable theatres, any possibility of improving the situation was complicated by the delegation of responsibility for the theatre from the Arts Council to the Southern Arts Board in 1992. This, in the view of Fanshawe, chairman of the Salisbury Playhouse Board of Directors 1993–5 'absolutely limited the budget [Southern Arts] had to spend. They had no flexibility whatsoever. At least the Arts Council had a slush fund.'[10] Compounding the situation, devolution coincided with a freeze on government spending on the arts. This inevitably meant that Arts Council grants to regional arts boards were frozen, and so, in turn, were the grants made through the regional funding bodies to the theatres. In the financial years 1993/4 and 1994/5, the Playhouse's grants suffered this fate and the theatre's already inadequate subsidy was further devalued in real terms; meanwhile, production costs were increasing at a rate faster than inflation. Unfortunately, while these factors collectively meant an increased dependence on earned income, the box office had been showing signs of a sharp decline, some of the reasons for which can be traced back to earlier changes made as a result of under-funding.

All these factors combined to create a situation whereby the theatre found it could no longer keep running its various activities at existing levels. In addition to the main theatre, the Playhouse also had a studio theatre, the Salberg Theatre, a TIE programme called Theatrescope and an affiliated youth programme, Stage '65.[11] A mounting deficit, which escalated to £125,000 during the period of confusion following Horlock's death, meant that within six months of Paige's arrival in 1991, cuts had to be made.

The first area to be affected was the TIE department. Here, the traditional practice of taking productions out to schools was abandoned in favour of a reduced, more economical in-house programme providing workshops at the Playhouse based around the current production in the main auditorium. Initially, the cuts to the TIE programme were far less severe than at many other theatres, with the Playhouse only reducing Theatrescope rather than cutting it altogether. Nevertheless, there was a huge outcry in the local community, partly because the changes put the onus of bringing children to the theatre on the schools, something the 1988 Education Reform Act had made increasingly difficult. The situation was particularly sensitive for the local community because the cuts entailed a loss of six of the eight jobs in the TIE department. Given that the TIE staff had traditionally run the affiliated youth programme, Stage '65 also had to be restructured on a more modest level.

The cuts to Theatrescope and Stage '65 were very badly received, not least because of the way they were handled by the Playhouse's management. 'Why do the children of Salisbury and district, who are tomorrow's audience, have to bear such a large part of the cuts?...The theatre is being short-sighted and shooting itself in the foot' (Stewart 1991), a disillusioned Playhouse supporter wrote to the local paper. The result was a mass boycott by those previously involved with the programme, including relations and friends of the children affected, who represented a substantial part of the regular audience in the main house. Consequently, while the reductions to the YPT and TIE programmes initially cleared £80,000 of the Playhouse's deficit, falling revenue from the box office almost immediately meant that the deficit began to mount again.

The reasons behind the fall in theatre attendances at this time, and the sectors of the audience it affected, cannot be seen exclusively in terms of these cuts. The decline was gradual, taking place over the course of two years, and it was arguably during this period that the recession caught up with Salisbury. As subsidy grants were frozen and income from commercial sponsorship fell, something blamed locally on the 'short-sighted' decision of a new marketing director from London to increase minimum levels of sponsorship, the Playhouse was hit particularly hard at the box office. Low levels of subsidy had forced the theatre to raise ticket prices at an annual rate of 10 per cent since 1982, and, during the recession in the early 1990s, this contributed to a huge drop in ticket sales. This was particularly true of the subscription scheme, where the

Playhouse's previous success with seasonal passes had in large part accounted for the theatre's high attendances over the previous decade. In particular, the theatre was heavily reliant on the associated coach parties that brought people from as far away as Cheltenham and Oxford and regularly packed the main house at matinees and weekends. During the recession, paying for individual tickets was considered less risky than paying for an entire season. With rising unemployment, a poor economy and high inflation, 'people were increasingly wary about handing over £60 at a time'.[12] Many customers were additionally concerned that were they to continue subscribing to the theatre, it might not be for the type of programme they wanted to see.

Mounting hostility to the 'sophisticated and avant-garde' (Hawkins 1993) programming supposedly introduced by Paige on her arrival penetrated deep into the traditional 'loyal' audience. Accusations of 'Kulture Vultures' were levelled at the chief executive and her management by members of a committed audience used to 'a staple diet of Ben Travers, Agatha Christie, Kenneth Horne, Alan Ayckbourn, et al.'[13] The likes of these had tended to dominate the programmes of her predecessors, Horlock, Roger Clissold and Reggie Salberg, and had earned the Playhouse a reputation for 'Strip, strip, hurray' and 'proscenium curtains and box sets' productions.[14] Criticisms of the Playhouse's new programming dominated the local media, particularly the letters page of the city paper, the *Salisbury Journal*.[15] The following comments are representative:

> Experimental theatre should be abandoned. It is a total commercial and artistic waste of time...Playhouse-goers want productions which will lift their spirits, provide enjoyment and be fun. They don't want to be forced to understand the angst and despair of kitchen sink artists who belong in the kitchen or down the plughole.
> (Strand 1994)

> We don't go to the theatre to be educated – we go to relax and be entertained.
> (Brind 1994)

Despite such protests, there had actually been no deliberate change in artistic policy. Although Paige admitted that one of the reasons for her appointment was that 'the board were aware they wanted to be more adventurous', she also emphasized that her own plan had been 'to continue more or less the same sort of programming policy, but to work on improving standards or direction, design and casting'.[16] As such, where changes were made, they were less to the Playhouse's programming than to the production values of the dramas. And even this was limited. Analysis of individual criticisms, and interviews with Paige and Allanah Lucas, the then administrative and development director, reveals that local concern was only really connected to four main-house productions: *Down and Out in Paris and London*, *The Europeans*, *Celestina* and *The Office Party*. The last three were all staged in 1991/2. The fact that four productions could cause such a furore, particularly when staged over the course of two seasons, during which time more than twenty plays were put on, raises the question of the limitations of artistic policy in regional theatres during this period. Here, the sense of ownership and parochial attitudes often endemic to the old and loyal audiences militated against the possibility of trying anything different, no matter what the Arts Council/Southern Arts might say. As Nick Bourne emphasized, '[in the provinces] people resent change'.[17]

In Salisbury, this problem was particularly acute with regard to the loyal body of theatregoers whose profile was itself generating a certain amount of anxiety at the theatre, and had been even before Horlock's death. Audience profiles gathered by the Playhouse in 1992/3 using the newly installed computerized system revealed that almost 80 per cent of 'the very definite audience' were over fifty years of age and from social class AB.[18] When compared with surveys conducted sporadically over the previous decade, it appeared that, notwithstanding the decline in attendances, there had been little change or development in the audience's profile. On her appointment, Paige was encouraged to consider the need to attract and develop a new, younger audience alongside the existing, older body of theatregoers. In response, she attempted to employ a more contemporary and varied style of repertory in an effort to attract a wider range of people.

Following the move away from weekly repertory, limited finances and facilities have traditionally worked against the staging of audience-specific productions in Britain's regional theatres. Since the 1960s, the average run of a main-house production has been three or four weeks. The increased dependence on earned income under Thatcher, combined with escalating production costs and low levels of subsidy, meant that consistent artistic success was crucial in the 1990s. Even one unpopular production could prove potentially fatal to a theatre. In the case of the Playhouse, this was particularly true with respect to its traditional audience and the baggage of feelings they brought with them regarding the theatre. As one individual put it, 'the Playhouse was built with massive donations from the public' (Johnstone 1994).

The Playhouse's staple audience was one that had been largely responsible for creating the theatre after the Arts Council pulled out of direct management in 1951. Similarly, they had been involved in supporting it in the ensuing years, raising the capital for a new building in the 1970s that allowed the theatre to move from its original home in a converted chapel to the purpose-built venue near the centre of town. Consequently, many local people held strong proprietary feelings towards the theatre, which translated into very specific ideas of how it should be run and how much say they should have in those decisions.

> The audience wanted to return to something perceived as the good old days, and looked back as a way of going forward.[19]

> I say 'our Playhouse' because it was built with subscriptions from many local theatre lovers and businesses, coupled with efforts from a number of dedicated people…The average age of theatregoers is well over 40 and they remember the excellent performances in the past from the likes of Nancy Herod, Sonia Woolley, Lionel Guyatt and many others.
>
> (Soutar 1994)

For the theatre, the challenges posed by such feelings went far beyond the fact that 'the [public] won't allow anything new into their lives and they think that everything should be done their way'.[20] The local community's history of investment translated into a belief that official decisions about the operations of the Playhouse, ranging from artistic policy to education and youth programmes, should be taken with specific, if not exclusive, reference to them. Consequently, any alterations about which they were not directly consulted gave rise to feelings of alienation and exclusion, articulated in accusations of high-handedness and tactless behaviour amongst the theatre's senior management. Comments such as 'Miss Paige has shown a total disregard for the tastes of her audience' (Pinder 1994) constantly littered the letters pages of the local paper.

In practice, Paige's efforts to attract a specifically younger audience were only realized in one main-house production. Unfortunately, 'the problems began the summer *The Office Party* was staged and *Celestina* put on', according to consultant Keenlyside.[21] *The Office Party*, a modern comedy by John Godber, who at the time of the Playhouse production in 1992 was the fourth most performed playwright in Britain, was actually a huge popular success. Such was the play's appeal that it actually broke box office records at the Playhouse and brought in the target younger audiences. But, as Paige commented in hindsight, 'it was possibly a little too contemporary' and 'not homely enough' for the conservative, older audience.[22] It contained some strong language, which gave rise to numerous complaints published in the local paper protesting that it 'was so full of four letter words, [it] was an embarrassment to those with female or young company' (Jones 1992).

Taken exclusively, the damage might have been contained. Unfortunately, what Paige conceded to be 'an error in scheduling'[23] meant that *The Office Party* was staged immediately before a received production of *Celestina*, a little-known Spanish Renaissance play that was considered to be experimental because it was performed in modern dress against a contemporary set and used non-realistic acting styles. The subject matter of the play was also highly sexual and called for some scenes of nudity. Ironically, given that many criticisms focused on the postmodern concept of a period drama presented in a modern framework, further complaints were raised by the use of Renaissance English. This was variously described by spectators writing to the *Salisbury Journal* as 'complete gibberish' and 'gobbledy gook'.

The departure from conservative styles of proscenium realism in two successive productions apparently gave credence to the suspicion that Paige was imposing an experimental, educational programme of productions that were not 'what regular theatregoers want to see, but what the producers think is good for them' (Stride 1994). The scheduling also meant that these two productions were presented mid-season, the period which Lucas emphasized could determine the success of an entire season in a regional theatre, ostensibly either by repairing any damage already incurred from unpopular productions and boosting sales for the remainder of the season, or the opposite. In this particular case, ticket sales dropped at an alarming rate as loyal theatregoers began to desert the Playhouse, despite a comparatively safe repertory scheduled for the rest of the year.

If the safe repertory was not a big enough concession to persuade the traditional theatregoers to keep coming, neither was it conducive to developing the new, younger audiences first targeted by *The Office Party*. Any chance of sustaining this new group gained by Godber's play was also undermined by the simultaneous announcement that it would be necessary to cut the Playhouse's youth theatre activities. Under the circumstances, the Playhouse 'was not as successful at developing new audiences as the board had hoped'.[24]

Many of the aggrieved public considered their protests were made in the interests of saving the theatre. While ignorant of many of the administrative challenges faced by senior management, the vocal members of the local community were perhaps equally unaware of the damage they were doing through such vociferous criticism. Of the voluble public outcry, Paige commented, 'I regret that people feel able to criticise in the way they have done, which I think has ultimately been very destructive to the Playhouse.'[25] This sentiment was echoed by the arts editor of the *Salisbury Journal*, where most such complaints were published. 'If [the Playhouse] closes, I will blame those "friends" whose strident criticism, the point of which I never could grasp, created a climate to turn off potential audiences' (Blacklock 1994), he wrote.

The devastating effects of such vocal grievances were not limited to box office sales. Under these circumstances, the increasingly unpalatable working conditions characteristic of so many regional theatres during this period became so bad at Salisbury Playhouse that in 1994 the entire executive resigned in protest.[26] Although problems with internal management, particularly between the chief executive and the board, played an important role in this, both Paige and Lucas stressed that external, often stinging personal criticism, which in the case of the artistic director ultimately resulted in calls for her resignation, 'created unbearable working conditions' where management was 'practically blackmailed into submission'.[27] But it was effectively a lose–lose situation. In an attempt to appease the community and reduce declining audience figures, Paige ultimately retreated too far into the terrain of safe, traditional repertory in the last season before the theatre's closure. She was later criticized by the consultants for being 'disproportionately affected by perceived public failures resulting in retrenchment' (Bonnar-Keenlyside 1994). Bonnar-Keenlyside argued that had Paige defined and continued with a definite new artistic style, she might have successfully developed a new audience, even if at the expense of the old one.

From the time of Paige's arrival in 1991 until the theatre's closure in 1995, criticism focused heavily on senior management. Accusations such as '[the Playhouse] has now suffered the sad decline inevitable when an arrogant management sets out to educate its customers, and by patronising them cuts off their goodwill and its own revenue stream' (McClean 1994), made the possibility of doing a good job extremely difficult. Nevertheless, a lack of diplomacy in the new management's handling of the changes did not help the situation. In their findings, the consultants deemed the Playhouse's handling of public relations 'to have been a failure' (Bonnar-Keenlyside 1994).

The need for senior management to ingratiate themselves with the local population is a vital part of the British provincial theatre's operation. One audience member at Salisbury Playhouse commented in 1994, 'theatre is not a one-way business – it needs to build on a real support between community and theatre, and the more personal the relationship comes to be, the greater the success' (Wootton 1994). Such a sentiment has become increasingly important for the country's regional theatres, as many of the older theatrical traditions with which audiences can identify have gradually disappeared. Salisbury, in particular, longed for the good old days when a resident company lived and worked in the community for an entire season:

> When we had a resident company, if the play was a doubtful draw, a lot of people would go to see what Roger Hume, Stephanie Cole, Robert Frost, Christine Edmonds, or whoever their favourite was might be doing that week/month/production. In fact, a couple of people have said to me recently 'nice to see Stephanie Cole is coming back', meaning not Stephanie Cole the famous TV star, but our Steph Cole.
> (Anderson 1994)

In the absence of such conventions, the responsibility of being an ambassador to the community falls squarely on the shoulders of senior management. Unfortunately for the Playhouse, as Paige acknowledged, she was not 'a great diplomat'.[28]

Before she even arrived at the Playhouse, Paige was at a huge disadvantage because of the popularity and circumstances of the death of her predecessor. 'It was Deborah Paige's misfortune to succeed to the post while we mourned David Horlock' (Stride 1994), and there was little hope she could ever live up to his reputation. Nevertheless, Paige did not help the situation by refusing to move up to Salisbury from London, or make any attempts to take an active part in the local community. Perhaps had she been explicitly seen to care about the feelings of local theatregoers, the traditional audience might have felt less incensed 'as traditions were trampled and changes imposed upon them rather than negotiated' (Stride 1994). The same principle could be applied to certain members of the new staff Paige brought with her, such as marketing director Danny Moar, whose 'aggressive marketing methods were alien to Salisbury' (Stride 1994). Unfortunately, with the memory of Horlock so fresh in people's minds, Paige's approach simply encouraged nostalgic memories of the past, such that many complaints in the local paper harped on the 'good old days' as a model of what the theatre should aspire to:

> How many remember, like me, the days when the auditorium was full, the director was known by everyone, and he played an active part in our community?
> (Colston 1994)

> Reggie Salberg, Roger Clissold, David Horlock promised and delivered commitment to the community…dwelling in the city they identified with local issues. Recognised, greeted in the street, they responded and respected people as individuals. Aspiring to, and achieving high fund-raising targets, they were encouraged and inspired by personal effort.
> (Stride 1994)

Partly as a result of this situation, and certainly an important factor in the failure of public relations, there was a fundamental lack of communication between senior management and the public. This was true of almost all of the theatre's operations. Artistic policy, for instance, was described by the consultants as 'unfocused, un-communicated, and misunderstood' (Bonnar-Keenlyside 1994). In other words, it was not just the productions the loyal audience disliked, but the motivations they perceived to be behind them. In retaining her London base, and through the perceived alterations to artistic policy and the new administrative positions that were created on her arrival (including the introduction of a marketing director and an administrative and development director), a suspicion grew that Paige largely saw the Playhouse in terms of personal ambition. Since Paige never explicitly corrected them on this, the traditional audience became 'predisposed to hate anything like [Celestina] because Deborah had brought it in'.[29] So strong was local resentment that even Paige's successes were turned back on her. It was generally recognized that, following her arrival, there was a 'marked improvement in the quality of productions' (Bonnar-Keenlyside 1994) at the Playhouse, an opinion reiterated in the national press, where certain of Paige's productions received critical acclaim. But what should have been a focus of local pride became one of resentment when artistic quality was perceived as providing evidence of the chief executive's personal ambition:

> The much vaunted regional and national acclaim will count for nothing without local support.
> (Docherty 1991)

> The Playhouse exists primarily for the people of Salisbury and the surrounding area.
> (Vines 1994)

As such, 'artistic successes were not commensurate with box office successes', and Paige herself finally conceded that the local population 'liked [a production] better when it was a bit more homely, even if this meant the standard of production wasn't so high'.[30] The toured-in performances, Celestina and The Europeans, fell into this category. Both were postmodern in their aesthetics and acclaimed in the national papers. But the chief executive was indicted for the productions, perceived locally as evidence of her experimental policy, largely because of the Playhouse's failure to communicate that these had been brought in from outside. Such was the hostility Paige engendered in the local community, that by the time this mistake was realized, attempts to rectify the situation simply added fuel to the fire. A public statement asserting that Paige and the Playhouse management had little control over the content of received productions simply resulted in an outcry that the productions were not home-produced, something which had been a traditional source of pride to theatregoers in the past.

Similarly, while some opposition to the changes to the youth programmes in Theatrescope and Stage '65 could be expected, the overwhelming resentment they caused came in part from a failure in the Playhouse's public relations. The lack of rapport between the theatre and public meant that the new management underestimated the popularity of the youth programmes. Consequently, cuts were made very quickly, without reference either to the teaching profession or local funding bodies. And they were only made public after they had been implemented, resulting in a widespread feeling of a fait accompli, as the writer of yet another letter to the *Salisbury Journal* observed: 'Perhaps the most worrying aspect of the whole issue is the way the cuts were made public only after they happened, too late for anything to be done about them' (Gahan 1991).

The recognition of the need to avoid speaking badly of the previous administration, which the consultants had noted, meant that there was a wholesale failure to communicate to the public the financial necessity of making cutbacks. This was particularly true with regard to Stage '65. The announcement about the reduction of the youth programme was made immediately following a sell-out production of *West Side Story* that the youth group had performed in the main house and which had generated over £6,000 at the Playhouse box office:

> With direct and indirect grants for the youth theatre and TIE, the Playhouse receives £130,000 plus £7,000 Stage '65 subscriptions – not to mention profits from productions. *West Side Story* had 99.9% occupancy.
>
> (Leversuch 1991)

Factually, this information is far from correct: separate grants were never allocated for specific departments or projects, and annual membership fees of just over £10 for each of the two hundred members of Stage '65 would have generated not £7,000, but just over £2,000 per year. This sum accounted for less than a third of even one of the seven professional TIE members' salaries and took no account of the capital costs of running the operation. But the common belief that Stage '65 traditionally generated a profit for the Playhouse, and the efficacy of the programme, meant senior management were unable to prevent 'a suspicion in many people's minds that TIE and Stage '65 are being sacrificed for Miss Paige's artistic ambition' (Sayer 1991). Exacerbating the suspicion was the evident fact that the money spent on paperwork was simultaneously escalating as the administration department increased in size.

Paige's overhaul of the administrative system, including the appointment of a marketing director in a newly created position, and a qualified full-time accountant, was an attempt by the chief executive to establish a more efficient and cost-effective operation. These changes had the full backing of the board, particularly because of the burgeoning but unknown deficit left over from the previous regime and the theatre's failure to develop a new, younger audience. Nevertheless, increased administrative costs partly contributed to the fact that the budget for production costs was reduced from £750,000 in 1989/90 to £660,000 in 1994/5, a figure that was reduced further when inflation was taken into consideration. Combined with the hostility in the community and rumours of a mounting deficit, increasingly costly administration ensured that any efforts by the Playhouse to explain the reasons behind the new system failed to make an impact. So while the board's chair told the local paper that 'comparisons [regarding the size and budget of the administration] were being made with twenty years ago', his comments were drowned out by the much louder complaints about 'the seemingly endless list of administrators'.[31]

Perhaps the public would have been more inclined to listen had the Playhouse presented a united front. Unfortunately, the board themselves never adequately communicated that the theatre's problems should by no means be entirely attributed to Paige. Worse, they allowed internal tensions to be played out in the public eye and encouraged by the vocal criticisms in the local media. Summing up the theatre's problems prior to closure, the consultants criticized the board of directors as:

1. Divided and not acting corporately
2. Openly split and unsupportive
3. [Displaying] poor financial understanding and management.

(Bonnar-Keenlyside 1994)

At the time of Paige's arrival, the existing board operated under the auspices of a system that imposed no time limit on the length of service. Annual general meetings at which new members were elected or re-elected were only open to existing and former board members, who were also the only people allowed to nominate and vote on individuals standing for election. The inevitable result was a 'self-perpetuating oligarchy' dominated by a significant number of members who had served over ten years, including former artistic director Salberg.[32] This element shared a nostalgic idea of the past, and the sympathy of the Playhouse's loyal audience, and consequently carried strong ideas about what the theatre's priorities should be and how it should be run. Many of these ran contrary to those presented by the new chief executive. But although these tensions should have, at least, been resolved in private, this was rarely the case.

One of the reasons for this is highlighted by the 'confusion from the beginning over the reasons for appointing Deborah Paige', who, according to a board member, was recommended by a select committee of only three members from a board of sixteen.[33] Furthermore, 'the board was in conflict with itself' over such issues as artistic programming and alterations to Theatrescope and Stage '65, and to the system of management.[34] Decisions were difficult to make internally because of the excessive size of the board, a factor that delayed any agreement on a coherent policy. Under normal circumstances, the board only met once a month for two hours. Complicating matters further, on top of the long-serving element heavily involved with the operations of the theatre, membership also included a number of professionals from outside the immediate community who had little knowledge of theatre in general, or the Playhouse in particular, beyond the professional interest merited by their responsibilities as board members.

The full implications of the changes proposed for Theatrescope and Stage '65, and those allegedly made to artistic policy, were therefore only appreciated by a minority of the board. Consequently, when they were voted through, those who had been unhappy with the decisions 'aired their dirty linen in public'.[35] Salberg expressed his views over Paige's artistic policy on numerous occasions. In 1994 he told a BBC interviewer, 'When she arrived she put in the wrong programme and we lost a lot of people...Her policy of exciting theatre did not work, but the programming has gone too far the other way now. I personally would be happy if she resigned.'[36]

Because of his local popularity, his sympathy with the views of the most vocal protesters and his record of long service at the Playhouse, Salberg's comments carried considerable weight.

> Modesty prevented [Reggie Salberg] from pointing out that he and his successor were not only experienced professionals who knew how to fill a theatre, but were blessed with personalities that enabled them to work in mutual confidence with the board and also made them popular and respected in the city.
>
> (Hamilton 1994)

Salberg's sentiments were echoed by other members of the board, where feelings ran so high that two of them resigned. Their resignations in the midst of such debates incensed public feeling further, with the overwhelming opinion being that they had been badly treated by the Playhouse management.

While poorly contained divisions within the board created adverse publicity, so did their handling of many of the theatre's affairs. An unsanctioned 'leak' over the Playhouse's proposed closure, for instance, caused the consultants to criticize the board as 'poor ambassadors for the theatre' and almost certainly expedited the closure through an adverse effect on ticket sales. 'The leak annoyed the theatre – already saddled with a six-figure debt as a result of funding difficulties and poor audience figures – because of the danger that audiences will start to drift away a year early' (Blacklock 1994), wrote the arts editor of the local paper. On the one hand the board members were considered to be too outspoken, yet on the other they were criticized for excessive secrecy, in part because they failed to communicate the theatre's problems and financial situation to the public. On certain occasions, such information was deliberately withheld by the board because it would have involved publicly contradicting certain of their own members. Many felt this would simply aggravate speculation over internal divisions. In hindsight, the decision not to speak out was recognized as having fuelled the rumours. For instance, feelings ran high over the fact that it took over 'two years of media pressure'[37] to extract publicly the financial position of the theatre from the board, which prevented the local community – and their official representatives, the Friends of the Playhouse – from taking the opportunity to actively help through fund-raising activities. When the consultants condemned the board for failing to retain either 'external or internal confidence' and called for their complete replacement, public response overwhelmingly concurred. 'We are told that the board is to be replaced; many think that it has been weak, secretive and largely to blame for the current situation', the Friends informed board chairman Fanshawe.[38]

Echoes of the animosity between the board of the Nottingham Playhouse and John Neville in the 1960s can be seen in the board's dealings with Paige. Their own internal divisions and failure to anticipate the extent of the animosity that changes to the theatre would generate meant that the outsider Paige was never properly briefed, but was still squarely blamed for a series of situations in which they were equally culpable. The increasingly unpleasant working conditions for practitioners in regional theatres were clearly aggravated, in this case, by the board's failure to support their chief executive, who resigned in 1994 in protest at their treatment.

> I wasn't prepared to work for a board which didn't have confidence in me but weren't forthcoming about what I had done. [The resignation] followed a meeting where members had called for my contract to be terminated. Unfair dismissal?[39]

The situation was made worse by the interference of local funding bodies, some of which had representatives sitting on the board. One of the individuals who called for Paige's resignation was the representative for Wiltshire County Council, Peter Chalke. The county council traditionally insisted on having a councillor on the board as a condition of funding. By 1994, confidence in the Playhouse had dropped so alarmingly that Wiltshire refused to hand over a loan of £58,000 despite an existing agreement with the other two funding bodies, Salisbury District Council and Southern Arts. Their condition for releasing the agreed amount was the dismissal of the current senior management and consultation/power of veto over artistic policy and all appointments of senior management in the future. Such calls for Paige's dismissal were contractually illegal; the board were legally bound to make their own decisions on such matters.

'Wiltshire must have known it was setting a condition that we could not possibly accept because it was seeking to take away the board's power and put the board in an invidious position', Fanshawe noted.[40]

The implications of allowing funding bodies to interfere with artistic policy in this way were considered potentially devastating. Southern Arts, an organization that operated under the arm's length principle and only reserved the right to have a representative present at Playhouse meetings, commented, 'It is our belief that the theatre would be in an extremely vulnerable position were it to lose at this crucial time the artistic vision and continuity for which it has rightly gained a national reputation.'[41]

In one sense it could be argued that Salisbury Playhouse had already been a victim of such a practice. According to the chair of the board at the time of the theatre's closure, the inclusion of the county council representative on the board consistently delayed and increased the difficulty of making and following through policies that might have eased the crisis. Concerning possible measures that could generate income for example, 'he stultified the debate; it was always brought back by him to questions of expenditure'.[42] Similarly, the county council representative led the way in insisting that immediate financial considerations be addressed first to reduce the deficit. But any decisions that were made to accommodate such demands had negative long-term implications. The decision to slash the marketing department's budget to under £20,000 in 1994, for instance, when, according to the administrative and development director, 'it should have been doubled' to address the problem of poor public relations, directly stemmed from the county council's demands to reduce the deficit.[43] Funding body representatives do not necessarily have any practical experience of or expertise in theatre affairs. Their traditional emphasis is on financial considerations, which typically put their concerns in diametrical opposition to the concerns of the theatre. The Redgrave Theatre in Farnham, which closed on the same day as Salisbury, suffered equally from such problems.

After a period of seventh months being dark, the Playhouse reopened in September 1995. During this time, the building was completely refurbished through funds provided by Southern Arts and Salisbury District Council, and following the recommendations of the consultants, the entire executive and board were replaced. Under the new terms of agreement recommended by the consultants, board members were limited to serving a maximum of two terms of five years. The new artistic director, Jonathan Church, meanwhile, moved down from Derby to live in Salisbury and opened with a production of *Tess of the d'Urbervilles*, an astute choice given the classic novel's specific association with the local area. In his first interview with the *Salisbury Journal*, Church commented, 'I have no desire to shock people...my aim is to illuminate' (Church 1995).

Notes

1. Comment made by Hilary Keenlyside at a public meeting held at the theatre on 15 December 1994, in which the results of consultants Bonnar-Keenlyside's investigations and recommendations about the operations of the Salisbury Playhouse were revealed.
2. Statistics and information supplied by Allanah Lucas, Salisbury Playhouse administrative and development director 1992–4, and Southern Arts.
3. David Horlock, artistic director, Salisbury Playhouse 1982–90.
4. Lucas, interview with the author, 20 December 1995.
5. Nick Bourne, chairman, Salisbury Playhouse board of directors, 1991–3, interview with the author, 10 January 1996.
6. Paige was appointed as chief executive. The role incorporated responsibility for artistic and financial policy, which was problematic since the responsibilities of one job were often in direct contradiction to the requirements of the other.
7. Bourne, interview with the author, 10 January 1996.
8. Information and statistics supplied by Salisbury Playhouse. Reggie Salberg, artistic director of Salisbury Playhouse, 1955–76. 'Our Future in Danger', audience pamphlet, Salisbury Playhouse, 1984.
9. The 1986 Cork Report included Salisbury Playhouse as one of the theatres in imminent danger of closure.
10. Antony Fanshawe, chairman, Salisbury Playhouse board of directors, 1993–4, interview with author, 7 January 1996.
11. Stage '65 was so called because it was founded in 1965.
12. Lucas, interview with the author, 20 December 1995.
13. Comments taken from various letters published in the *Salisbury Journal* in 1994.
14. Comments taken from various letters published in the *Salisbury Journal* in 1994.
15. Typically, local newspapers like *The Salisbury Journal* focus on local news for the community. While generally supportive of local amenities such as regional theatres, the concern is to provide

impartial coverage of stories of interest to the community regardless of whether overexposure could be construed as harmful.
16. Paige, chief executive, Salisbury Playhouse, 1991–4. Letter to author, 1996.
17. Bourne, interview with author, 10 January 1996.
18. Information supplied by Salisbury Playhouse and Southern Arts.
19. Dee Adcock, *Salisbury Journal* assistant arts editor, speaking on *Southern Eye*, BBC South, December 1994.
20. Lucas, interview with author, 20 December 1995.
21. Keenlyside, speaking at Salisbury Playhouse public meeting, 15 December 1994
22. Paige, letter to author, 1996.
23. Paige, letter to author, 1996.
24. Fanshawe, interview with author, 7 January 1996.
25. Paige, letter to author, 1996.
26. This included the chief executive, the administrative and development director, and the marketing director.
27. Lucas, interview with author, 20 December 1995.
28. Paige, letter to author, 1996.
29. Lucas, interview with author, 20 December 1995.
30. Paige, letter to author, 1996.
31. Fanshawe, interview with author, 7 January 1996.
32. Fanshawe, speaking at Salisbury Playhouse public meeting, 15 December 1994.
33. Playhouse board member, interview with author, September 1995.
34. Keenlyside, speaking at Salisbury Playhouse public meeting, 15 December 1994.
35. Lucas, interview with author, 20 December 1995.
36. Salberg, speaking on *Southern Eye*, BBC South, December 1994.
37. Comments taken from various letters published in the Salisbury Journal in 1994.
38. Correspondence from Friends of Salisbury Playhouse to the chair of the board of directors, November, 1994.
39. Paige, letter to author, 1996.
40. Fanshawe, interview with author, 7 January 1996.
41. Sue Robertson, executive director, Southern Arts, 'To all leaders of political parties in Wiltshire', (memorandum), 9 November 1994.
42. Fanshawe, interview with author, 7 January 1996.
43. Lucas, interview with author, 20 December 1995.

6

THORNDIKE THEATRE, LEATHERHEAD

As with many subsidized regional theatres that experienced difficulties under the Conservatives, the Thorndike Theatre in Leatherhead developed out of a smaller repertory theatre established after the Second World War. The 9,000-strong town of Leatherhead, situated in Surrey on the London commuter belt, has a history rich in theatrical tradition that officially dates back to Henry VIII. When the war ended in 1945, Leatherhead was considered a potentially lucrative place to open a repertory theatre. An old-fashioned traditional actor-manager named Ross Barrington noted that the old Ace Cinema held great potential as a theatrical venue and was granted the rights to convert it and open it as a weekly rep in 1949. The year-long venture was a failure, but more on account of some bad business practices than inadequate support. In fact, the enthusiasm from the local community that greeted the project was extensive enough to persuade others of the potential merits of maintaining a permanent repertory theatre in Leatherhead.

A year after Barrington's involvement came to an end, the theatre, by this time known as The Green Room, was spotted by Hazel Vincent Wallace and her business partner Michael Marriott, who were subsequently to become the managing director and administrator of the repertory theatre. At the time, Wallace was running a successful London company called the 'Under Thirty Theatre Group', a group established at the end of the war to give young actors a chance to gain experience and exposure on the professional stage. In 1950, the success of the company's efforts, which concentrated on mounting a series of new dramas on Sunday evenings in cooperation with West End producers, had reached such a level that the management felt further growth would involve settling in a permanent venue.[1] In terms of both its proximity to London and the enthusiasm of a discerning audience evidenced in the local response to Barrington's venture, Leatherhead seemed to offer the ideal location. The 300-seater venue that Barrington had converted from the Ace Cinema was equally attractive, particularly because of its intimate size and the fact that it offered potential premises for social amenities, such as food and drink. In 1950, Wallace and Marriott took over the lease of the theatre. With a small amount of support from the local authority, Leatherhead Urban District Council, they established the Leatherhead Theatre, run by the Leatherhead Theatre Guild, a non-profit-distributing company with charitable status.

For the next two decades, Leatherhead Theatre was a vitally successful repertory theatre. Under the firm leadership of managing director, Hazel Vincent Wallace, the company's principles – to provide an exciting setting for new and newly established plays and artists with particular emphasis on involving young people and developing their skills – saw Leatherhead become one of the most popular and highly acclaimed repertory theatres in the country. The theatre initially operated as a weekly rep, but the company was nonetheless proud of its high standards. In part, it was able to maintain these through an agreement with the Arts Council that for a number of years in the early 1950s allowed them to simultaneously use the Marlowe Theatre in Canterbury. Under this arrangement, Leatherhead divided its company into two, such that every play the company produced would run for a week in each theatre, allowing two weeks' rehearsal for each production. Although only a temporary arrangement, thanks to a small subsidy from the Arts Council and consistently high box office, the Leatherhead Theatre was able to officially adopt a two-week programme by the end of the 1950s and a three-week programme in the 1960s.

Until 1969, the theatre operated as a private club on a subscription basis. Part of the motivation to move to a larger space at the end of the decade lay in the fact that the 12,000-strong club membership, which had a waiting list of 5,000, had for years ensured that entire seasons were sold out at the theatre before they even opened. Such a demand could not be accommodated by the restrictions of the small original venue. This consideration, together with Leatherhead Theatre's proven track record and the national fervour for urban renewal in the 1960s, led to promises of long-term support from the local authorities. Moving the company into a larger, more technically advanced building seemed entirely justified.

The Thorndike Theatre, named for the actress Sybil Thorndike, was built through a combination of efforts. The Housing the Arts scheme enabled Leatherhead Urban District Council and the Arts Council to contribute to building costs, while the bulk of the money was raised through the fund-raising efforts of the Leatherhead Theatre Guild and the local community.[2]

Designed by the celebrated theatre architect Roderick Ham, the new 526-seat venue opened on 17 September 1969 in Church Street, in the centre of Leatherhead.[3] Built on the site of the Crescent, a torn-down cinema, some of whose walls the theatre retained in its architecture, the new building was widely acclaimed as a flagship for the new ideas of community theatre fashionable in the 1960s. It provided both the social emphasis advocated by the local authorities and the high art central to Arts Council thinking. As such, from the outset, the new purpose-built venue was very much set up as a community or arts centre, with the theatre at the heart of its activities.

While the main programme was intended to incorporate new and adventurous works alongside quality productions of classics, the venue also incorporated a small, purpose-built studio theatre named the Casson Room, specifically intended to maintain the original aims of the Under Thirty Theatre Group from two decades earlier. Designed to stage new, experimental works, this was also specifically designated as the site for the weekly meetings of the Young Stagers, the young people's theatre group attached to the Thorndike. Members of the Young Stagers were able to use the studio as a forum for writing, directing and performing in new works and as a place where they could get hands-on experience in the backstage areas of costume, design and stage management. Adding to the community feel was the Theatre Exchange, a TIE programme set up at this time and operating out of the Thorndike. And there was also an array of non-theatrical offerings such as film screenings, concerts and art exhibitions, which were constantly held on the premises.

In many ways, the new theatre functioned as a thriving multi-purpose arts centre and as such was extremely popular with local authorities. A spacious lobby doubled as an art gallery, and for the first decade, Sunday evenings in the main auditorium were devoted to holding concerts or showing films of local interest. Finally, the Green Room, the theatre restaurant and a café-bar saw the Thorndike at the hub of local social activity for theatregoers and non-theatregoers alike. Its popularity was such that membership of the 'Green Room Club', effectively the friends of the theatre group that had carried over from the days at the Leatherhead Theatre and which operated as a private club on the subscription basis, was consistently oversubscribed in the first decade.

Despite the Thorndike's initial popularity, the theatre had a history of financial difficulties. When it finally closed in 1997 with an accumulated deficit of nearly £1.2 million, it came on the back of twenty years of financial crisis. While the theatre experienced an assortment of difficulties that combined to propel it into a spiral of decline, primary amongst its problems was the perennial issue of low funding, something that had plagued it from the outset. With a small pool of money serving an ever-growing body of theatres, inadequate levels of funding meant that in 1974, in only its fifth year of operation, the Thorndike experienced the first of many cash crises. At this time, the theatre claimed that, in order to continue operations at the level expected by its funding bodies, it needed an extra £25,000 annually. This sum was larger than either of the local authorities' allocations. By 1978, the situation had deteriorated to the point where the theatre was carrying an operating deficit of £11,000. Despite good audiences, high inflation rates had sent maintenance costs soaring, and the theatre's labour-intensive nature meant costs were far outstripping income. Such a situation prompted the first of many threats of closure.

In common with many other theatres, subsidy was always a condition of survival for the Thorndike. And along with many of its colleagues, insufficient funding was also a constant complaint.

Along with the Redgrave Theatre, Farnham, and the Yvonne Arnaud Theatre, Guildford, the Thorndike Theatre formed part of the The Surrey Cluster. This appellation was given to the trio of producing theatres by the national press in the 1980s, when their continual and much publicized difficulties in the years following *The Glory of the Garden* effectively saw at least one of them on the brink of closure at any given time.

All situated in Surrey, the theatres' collectively low levels of subsidy historically compared badly by national standards, a fact the theatres believed was based on their geographical location. There is a national perception of Surrey as a particularly affluent area, situated near to London and with a largely middle-class population. When the three theatres were first established, it was noticeable that compared with playhouses of similar scale and operation, their grants were lacking. The theatres claimed this was a result of the Arts Council's belief that The Surrey Cluster could easily find compensation from amongst their wealthy constituents. Over the years, and despite the fact that it undermined the ideological justification of subsidy, the central funding body constantly implied that larger amounts of disposable income in the local community should translate into higher ticket prices, as well as better sponsorship and patronage of the theatre from local authorities and businesses.

The same theory was also offered to account for the Arts Council's low level of support to the local regional arts association, South East Arts, who became the Cluster's primary funding body in 1984 following devolution through *The Glory of the Garden*. Since its creation, South East Arts always received the smallest of Arts Council grants annually made to regional funding bodies. As with the theatres, the traditional belief was that this was a direct bias regarding the wealth of the area. The Arts Council perspective, according to South East Arts, was that they were likely to receive higher sums from the local authorities than other regional arts associations in poorer areas. They would therefore need less from the central disbursement agency. As the last regional arts association to be established in 1973, South East Arts also believed it was a low priority and suffered because of the strains already incumbent on the Arts Council's overstretched budget. In 1997, the year of the Thorndike's closure, South East Arts received approximately £1 million less from the Arts Council than any other regional arts board:

> This situation is a product of Arts Council history, an increasingly outdated concept of the South East as exclusively wealthy and a misguided perception that the region's arts audiences are only interested in the safe and mainstream.
> (*Surrey Advertiser* 1997b)

If this perception did account for the relative paucity of the Arts Council's grants to the Thorndike and South East Arts until 1984, it was misguided in its belief that any shortfall would be made up locally. As part of its liberal emphasis, many of the Thorndike's mandated activities, such as its TIE and Young Stagers programmes, were typically unprofitable ventures. And affluent or not, theatregoers would happily respond to inflated ticket prices by changing their allegiance to the West End.

In 1973 the theatre reluctantly succumbed to Arts Council suggestions to raise ticket prices for the first time, with a consequent drop in box office. Consistently good attendance figures continued to be recorded after this date, but the rise saw the end of a decade of regularly sold-out seasons at Leatherhead. Good houses were a condition of subsidy as well as generating vital revenue, and falling attendances were a trend the theatre was keen to avoid.

More than other regional theatres, the Thorndike was in a particularly difficult position because of its proximity to London. Located on the commuter belt and within easy access of nearby regional theatres in Farnham, Guildford and Woking, local audiences were by no means reliant on Leatherhead for theatrical entertainment. If prices were seen to rise out of proportion to the quality of the product there was a simple solution readily available elsewhere. Audience surveys conducted in the early 1970s showed that although the Thorndike retained a large, loyal following, only one-third of its regular patrons came from the immediate Mole Valley area. The rest came from the surrounding environs of Epsom, Ewell, Elmbridge and Sutton. As such, they were not only regular patrons of the Thorndike, but of Guildford and the West End too. And if the Arts Council was misguided in thinking any shortfall could be made up from this source, it was doubly so in thinking it would come from the local authorities.

Parity funding, the policy intended to protect the Thorndike from insufficient funding, was always one of the theatre's worst nemeses. From the time of the theatre's opening, the wavering support of local government was constantly cited by the Arts Council, and later South East Arts, as the reason for their refusing to increase their own contributions. In 1974, when the theatre first reported financial difficulties, the fact that local authority contributions only accounted for 3.9 per cent of the Thorndike's income, while Arts Council grants provided 38.2 per cent, simply reinforced the latter's argument that local government should be doing more. By 1984/5, the Arts Council contribution had dropped to only 23.8 per cent of income, while local authorities accounted for 7.2 per cent.[4] At this time, the theatre recorded a deficit of £62,000.

Questions of parity funding were never adequately resolved, and failure to agree on divisions of responsibility was constantly used by the various parties to justify withholding the theatre's grants. The situation particularly saw the Arts Council and South East Arts at loggerheads with Mole Valley District Council, whose low levels of funding underscored their long-held reservations about the need for a theatre in Leatherhead. This is somewhat ironic given that changes in political affiliation and a declining town centre turned Mole Valley into the Thorndike's biggest champion in the 1990s, when the theatre became key in plans for the town's regeneration. In its early years, however, the Thorndike's relationship with Mole Valley was precarious, and various Thorndike press releases, in times of strife, contained comments like, 'We have already heard from the financial director of the Arts Council that if Mole Valley's grant is cut then we can expect a comparable cut from them' (*Surrey Avertiser* 1980).

The district council established a pattern of behaviour early on. Constant threats to slash funding, or withholding of monies until the cash-starved theatre got its books in order, would typically be followed by one-off grants to help relieve mounting debts, which had invariably worsened in the meantime as a result of Mole Valley's behaviour. The district council's actions in the years following *The Glory of the Garden* demonstrate this pattern.

Following South East Arts' agreement to help pay off the Thorndike's £62,000 deficit in 1985, Mole Valley went on an economy drive and cut their grant by almost a sixth. Within the space of a year, the theatre's debts mounted. Subsequent threats of closure and pressure from its funding partners forced Mole Valley to grudgingly give the Thorndike a handout of £36,410 to make up the shortfall, a sum larger than its original grant. The situation became a convenient opportunity for the theatre's opponents at Mole Valley to point out that the Thorndike had been experiencing a cash crisis for the previous decade and publicly resurrect the argument that Leatherhead was not set up to support a theatre. The following year, Mole Valley again withheld a third of the Thorndike's annual grant, believing that the theatre was in further financial trouble when its accounts were nine months late in being submitted.

Such events are largely representative of the chequered support the Thorndike received throughout its history. Similar behaviour characterized Surrey County Council's approach. If Mole Valley regarded the Thorndike as a money pit, Surrey's support was often compromised by the fact that it was historically a Conservative-run council whose emphasis on arts funding has traditionally been low. Since the 1960s, it had also been expected to support three large producing theatres, when most local authorities might reasonably expect to support one.[5] Following a patchy history of support for the Thorndike, Surrey was the first major funding body to withdraw its entire grant of £42,000 in 1996. Together with South East Arts' alterations to its procedure for allocating funds at this time, it was Surrey's actions that ultimately sounded the death knell and ensured that at the end of that fiscal year, the Thorndike could not continue operating.

The Surrey Cluster may have been right in thinking that the Arts Council originally offered them low levels of funding in the belief that local government would help make up the shortfall. But if so, it's ironic that they later claimed London's frustration with its funding partners was behind the decision to devolve all three theatres following *The Glory of the Garden*. The Arts Council offered no clear explanation as to why certain theatres were delegated to regional arts associations at this time, but the general consensus focused on a strategy of removing the body's most troubled customers in a case of passing the buck. A consultant who looked into the three theatres' problems noted:

> [South East Arts] accepted devolution from the Arts Council of the three Surrey theatres with all their inherent issues: proximity to London, close relations with West End producers, an undue bunching of similar facilities, and above all, an aggregate subsidy that was very unlikely to be enough to sustain three theatres through hard times. In devolving these theatres to SEA in 1984, ACE was handing on its own irresolution of the seventies and early eighties.
>
> (Blackstock 1997: 8)

While instrumental in its misery, the Thorndike's problems cannot be blamed on insufficient funding alone. Numerous other factors conspired to exacerbate the problems. Amongst them was the loss of the local support that had been so vital in the theatre's early successes.

A sense of community had underlined local government's initial investment in the Thorndike and was an ideal close to Wallace's heart during her nearly three decades as managing director. From 1951 to 1980, when she occupied this role, Wallace herself was a symbol of this dedication to the community. She pioneered such groups as the Young Stagers, the Green Room Club and the Leatherhead Theatre Club – an advisory committee of local representatives whose involvement with the theatre ranged from advising on artistic policy to fund-raising. She had also worked closely with Ham on the original design of the Thorndike. It was also at Wallace's insistence that the building incorporated a studio theatre, café-bar, restaurant and lobby-cum-art-gallery. She was also subsequently responsible for introducing the weekly concerts and film screenings held on the premises. Wallace, as she describes herself, was 'from the old school of artistic directors' and would stand in the lobby of the theatre each evening and personally greet audience members before the show.[6] With no single permanent artistic director during her time of leadership, she was very much the figurehead of the Thorndike for the local community and, as such, engendered a strong loyal following.[7]

Given the strength of the loyalty she inspired and the length of her service, any successor was going to have a difficult act to follow. When Wallace retired in 1980, it was imperative that the new appointment be both aware of and careful in their handling of local community feeling.[8] Unfortunately, the stream of artistic directors that succeeded her – three in three years – were neither as dedicated to, nor as knowledgeable about, the needs of the local community. A report commissioned by South East Arts prior to the theatre's 1997 closure noted that after Wallace's departure, 'There followed several years of ineffective leadership, with audience figures dropping to an average of 56 percent and 57 percent in 1981/2 and 1982/3 respectively' (Blackstock 1997: 3).

At a time when the theatre 'seemed to lose direction' (Blackstock 1997: 3), a series of problems conspired to make the situation worse. The sharp drop in attendances was almost certainly aggravated by the fact that Wallace's departure coincided with major urban developments in the centre of Leatherhead, where new pedestrianization made the theatre less accessible.[9] It was yet another problem that faced Roger Clissold, the new director brought in from Salisbury Playhouse to take charge after two short-lived appointees had left. When he arrived, Clissold was clearly aware of Wallace's formidable legacy and the loss of loyalty engendered by her departure. Nonetheless, rather than build on her success and associate himself with the old regime, Clissold chose to distance himself from anything to do with the Wallace era. A refusal to employ actors who had regularly appeared in the previous decades saw the disappearance of familiar faces from the Thorndike stage. And criticism of his artistic policy by the Leatherhead Theatre Club caused Clissold to disband the committee in the mid-1980s.

Clissold was certainly within his rights to dissolve the club, which never officially occupied more than an advisory position, but it probably wasn't the wisest move. In addition to its role as the Thorndike's fund-raising body, the club was also its lifeline to the community, comprised as it was of representatives from the different geographical and social areas from which the theatre drew its audience.[10] As such, it was in large part responsible for sustaining the sense of ownership and involvement vital to retaining local support – something that had translated into the constant fund-raising successes over the years. It also provided the theatre with direct contact with its audience; via the Leatherhead Theatre Club, staff gained grass-roots access to local feeling about theatre policy. With its closure, these links were lost, and the bad feeling engendered lost the theatre a lot of loyal customers at a time when audiences were already flagging.

Clissold may not have endeared himself to the locals, but there is no question he was placed in a difficult position. Vocal criticisms were made by the Theatre Club just prior to its dissolution about the decline in standards and the increasingly safe and populist repertory that dominated the main programme. While this was a sentiment shared by South East Arts, who recommended Clissold's contract not be renewed on just such grounds in 1990, such complaints were likely tainted by the director's refusal to listen to the club's advice on theatre operations. But any unfavourable comparisons with the earlier regime failed to consider the restrictions placed on Clissold's artistic policy by the board of directors. At the time of his appointment, Clissold's priority was to boost falling audiences.

On his arrival, Clissold adopted a significantly safer, more popular programme than had been typical under Wallace in an attempt to offer broader appeal and bring back lost audiences. Based on the fact that audience figures started to increase a little, to a certain degree pursuing this course worked.[11] Unfortunately, the short-term solution was heavily qualified by the long-term drawbacks. The programme did little to promote Clissold in the eyes of the Arts Council/South East Arts, whose emphasis on standards and innovative work could not be answered by the middle-of-the-road repertory. And Clissold himself was often outspoken about how trapped he felt having to put on such safe, popular repertory, a policy he had initially adopted through a feeling of necessity and pressure from the board of directors, rather than personal choice. However, once the new programme had been implemented there was no going back: a more adventurous repertory risked losing any new audiences it had attracted, but made no guarantees that the old ones would return. A theatre survey conducted in 1985 revealed an increasingly conservative trend in audiences and confirmed such fears. In the survey, favourite playwrights were listed as Alan Ayckbourn and Noel Coward. Anything controversial was anathema. David Hare's *Knuckle*, a play staged in 1987 and involving some strong language and explicit material, was met with a pointed mass exodus. Most attempts at something slightly more adventurous were greeted with similar responses. On each occasion, the damage to the theatre would be countered by increasingly sedate programming.

The new policy of safe theatre didn't help the Thorndike's need to attract new customers. As with the producing houses in Salisbury, Guildford and Farnham, by the beginning of the 1980s, the theatre had noticed the growing problem of an aging audience, many of whom had been supporters since the opening of the original Leatherhead Theatre in 1951. In 1985, the average age of audience members was over 60, with less than 20 per cent under 40 years of age and only 9 per cent in their twenties. Quite aside from the limitations this very select audience placed on programming, such a situation did not bode well for the future. Unfortunately, the vicious circle of inadequate funding made it difficult for the Thorndike to actively tackle such problems.

Low levels of subvention had removed the much-vaunted 'right to fail' that ideologically lay at the heart of subsidy, and it was difficult to attract new audiences without alienating old ones. In a similar vein, the continued cash crisis meant that all possible areas of operations that could be downsized without tangible damage to the theatre were targeted in the 1980s. On stage, this meant productions of family favourites with small casts. In the theatre's administration it meant 'staffing [was] kept to a minimum and casualised where possible' (Blackstock 1997: 4), with many employees brought in exclusively for individual projects.

As a result, long-term strategies for solving problems such as aging audiences inevitably took second place. There were constant short-term efforts made to find resolutions to such problems – Surrey County Council's decision to devote an extra £30,000 to help update the theatre in 1989 and help attract new, younger audiences into the theatre, for instance. But with a lack of long-term planning, such efforts rarely fulfilled their potential. The 1985 survey noted that while 40 per cent of the Thorndike's audience heard about the artistic programme through the theatre's mailing list, there were no specific efforts taken with this or through publicity to reach a younger audience. By the time Clissold left the Thorndike in 1990, there had been little done to improve the situation.

The major innovation Clissold made to the theatre's operations in attempts to improve its fortunes was to establish a tradition of public and private partnership with a series of commercial producers. Joint productions typically meant the theatre was responsible for a maximum of half the costs and, supposedly therefore, incurred only half the risk. Equally, the potential benefits to the theatre theoretically doubled. As joint productions, the theatre should profit if the performance was successful enough to merit a transfer to the West End or be taken on tour. Prominent amongst such partnerships was that formed with Bill Kenwright, the West End impresario and founder of Bill Kenwright Limited (BKL). Clissold had a number of successes collaborating with BKL at the Thorndike, most notably staging the British premiere of Richard Harris' *Stepping Out*, which transferred to London for an extended run in 1986.

Despite a number of such commercial successes, which suited the loyal Leatherhead audience, who typically also patronized the West End, these partnerships were not enough to solve the ongoing financial crisis being experienced by the theatre. In July 1990, the Thorndike was closed indefinitely when the bank, weary of the constant funding crisis, refused to extend the existing loan any further and demanded immediate repayment of the outstanding debt of £40,000 then owed. The theatre was only able to reopen after Kenwright, whose latest collaboration with the Thorndike had been rehearsing in the theatre at the time of closure, stepped in and negotiated a deal with South East Arts to clear the theatre's deficit and allow it to continue operating. In exchange for £100,000 cash up front, to be used in conjunction with a slush-fund donation from South East Arts to clear the outstanding deficit, Kenwright agreed to underwrite all losses incurred by the theatre in the subsequent six years in exchange for complete control over the operations of the theatre, where he planned, through his company BKL, to produce, open and test many of his commercial shows.[12] Such an arrangement signalled the first such partnership between the subsidized and commercial sector in British regional theatres.

In many ways, the Thorndike's association with BKL provided the theatre with enormous benefits. Quite apart from the fact that BKL rescued the theatre from almost certain insolvency in 1990, in terms of quality, scale and volume, the productions presented under his leadership extended far beyond what would have normally been expected from a moderate-sized provincial playhouse. In 1992, after trying various combinations of programming, Kenwright decided to embark on a policy of creating more large-scale productions in-house and increase income by touring and transfers to the West End. As such, the Thorndike regularly played host to celebrated actors and directors of a stature unlikely to have been seen there otherwise. Most prominent amongst these was Peter Hall. At the time, Hall was a close friend and business associate of Kenwright, and following the success of a number of productions that opened in Leatherhead in the early 1990s, the collaboration between the two meant that the Peter Hall Company unofficially made its home at the Thorndike in 1995/6 when Kenwright became the company's largest producer.

Kenwright's policy was initially very successful. Despite sporadically low attendances for some productions, particularly when the recession hit Surrey, overall attendances at the Thorndike improved, rising from 82,000 in 1990, to 126,000 by end of 1992/3.[13] A large number of the performances produced during BKL's tenure, including all collaborations with the Peter Hall Company (such as the 1996 productions *The Master Builder*, starring Alan Bates, and *Emily Needs Attention*, with Felicity Kendal), went on to successful runs in the West End and/or on national tour.[14] Moreover, the productivity of the theatre was increased manifold, with the number of performances taking place at the Thorndike increasing from an average 240 to 400 annually. Similarly, Kenwright, who was also at the time a good friend of Wallace, reintroduced the Sunday night concerts that had been abandoned under Clissold and had film projection facilities installed to allow the theatre to double as a cinema. As such the theatre was rarely inactive.

While BKL's association with the Thorndike provided the theatre with clear benefits, it also raised questions about the efficacy of public and private partnerships. Given the extent and history of shortfalls in public funding of the arts in the 1980s and 1990s, such collaborations gained substantial support in the subsidized sector, seemingly offering one possible solution to regional theatres' ongoing problems. At the time Kenwright's association with the Thorndike was initially formalized, one of the most outspoken advocates of this system was Chris Cooper, chief executive of South East Arts until 1996. But it equally had its critics. One of the major concerns expressed about such partnerships related to the inevitable problems in reconciling the profit and civic motives that underscore the investment of the respective parties. With regard to the Thorndike, it could be argued that association with a profit-motivated impresario ultimately ensured the theatre had a shelf life and prevented it from realizing the possibility of continuing as a regional theatre after the association ended.

Between the years of 1990 and 1996, BKL ran the theatre absolutely, deciding what appeared on the Thorndike's main stage, setting the budget and keeping the books. Kenwright was officially still accountable to the board of directors, who theoretically represented the long-term interests of the theatre. However, the degree of control exercised over Kenwright's activities was questionable, given the fact that, under the terms of the association, 75 per cent of the board was replaced with employees of BKL. From 1993, the chairman of the Thorndike Theatre Limited was also Kenwright's solicitor.

This arrangement offers one possible explanation as to how the Thorndike was allowed to go into debt, a situation that the partnership should have protected the theatre against. According to the terms of Leatherhead's non-profit, charitable status, the Thorndike's share of any income generated from performances produced in association with BKL would be ploughed back into the theatre's operations. Any losses incurred by the theatre would be written off by Kenwright. As such, theoretically, the theatre was completely protected. Despite poor houses for many productions produced during the association, as Judith Hibberd, drama officer for South East Arts, noted, any losses incurred by the theatre should have been offset by the income generated from West End transfers and national tours.[15]

Despite this situation, during this period, Kenwright was extremely vocal about how much his association with the Thorndike was personally costing him.[16] In regular press conferences and interviews with the local paper, he consistently attacked South East Arts for its lack of interest in the Thorndike and low level of financial support, and expressed his frustration at the poor attendances.

> I have not had one piece of contact from SEA in four years other than round a board table. I would have thought if you care for your theatre and your region you at least go to the man who is putting in the money. They have no interest in the Thorndike. That is the answer…The Thorndike is underfunded by £350,000 a year and the response of SEA is to cut funding even further.
>
> (Gurney 1997)

Based on the agreement made with the Thorndike, whereby BKL was responsible for underwriting any debts incurred by the theatre, such complaints may have been justified if considered exclusively in terms of the running costs of the Thorndike. Regarding the number of activities it was supporting, sporadically poor houses and the large scale of the productions, in this context, Kenwright's losses were probably substantial. But the ambiguous nature of BKL's exact financial arrangement with the Thorndike means it is only possible to speculate on the actual situation. Given that Kenwright decided to end his company's association with the Thorndike in 1997, it is probable that the partnership was not generating the kind of income he had hoped for. At the same time, as Hibberd agreed, had the theatre's actual losses not been effectively compensated by profits from transfers, it is unlikely that BKL would have continued with the partnership for six years, renewing the contract after the first term of three years came to an end. Supporting this idea, there was a clause included in the contract between the Thorndike Theatre Limited and BKL that entitled the latter to terminate involvement at any time in the 'event that it determines that there is no reasonable prospect of Thorndike continuing to trade in the foreseeable future as a solvent company'.[17] What is noticeable, however, is that in arguments documented in reports, in correspondence with South East Arts and in the local and national papers, Kenwright never appeared to acknowledge the income that should have been generated for the theatre by productions that transferred out of the Thorndike to the West End or on tour.

As a consequence, although the official accounts produced by BKL on behalf of the Thorndike Theatre showed no deficit for the financial years from 1990/1 to 1995/6, the accounts produced in the final year of Kenwright's association showed that the Leatherhead theatre owed BKL almost £1.3 million. With BKL's agreement to underwrite any losses incurred at Leatherhead, it was a bolt from the blue to discover that the theatre should owe the production company anything at the end of its association. Crucially, one of the pitfalls of this arrangement was that BKL had absolute control of the books and was answerable to a board of directors made up primarily of its own employees. So, as Wallace, one of the few non-BKL employees who continued to serve on the board of directors, said, such a situation 'should not have happened'.[18] However, given the fact that 'only BKL employees seemed to understand the details of the Thorndike's financial agreement' with the production company, and the board did not question these accounts, nothing could be done.[19] Following Kenwright's decision not to renew his partnership with the Thorndike in 1997, such a debt condemned the theatre to almost certain insolvency.

It could also be argued that the interests of the Thorndike suffered further when the commercial motives of BKL undermined the civic nature of the theatre's other operations. Certain of the theatre's activities that had previously focused wholly on the community were restructured with a clear emphasis on profit. On taking over at Leatherhead, Kenwright ensured that the Green Room restaurant contracted exclusively with a catering company run by his brother, A. T. Kenwright. Similarly, the Green Room Club began to be operated on a more commercial basis, whereby subscription rates were substantially increased while member benefits were reduced. As such, membership dropped by over 50 per cent in the five years Kenwright was in charge, with many people simply failing to renew their membership.

Inevitable problems also occurred between the grass-roots initiative of the theatre's other activities, as in the case of the TIE programme, the Thorndike Exchange, and the commercial imperatives of the main house. Symptomatic of this was the evident confusion about financial control and boundaries. Although it had traditionally been understood that Surrey County Council's annual grant of £40,000 was unofficially earmarked to support the educational work of the Thorndike, and BKL was formally contracted to continue supporting the existing civic activities of the theatre, the divisions of subsidy and the loss-making nature of such activities were anathema to the commercial interests of the production company. As Arts Council finance director Blackstock reported to South East Arts in 1997, shortly before Kenwright's association with the Thorndike came to an end, 'BKL expressed disappointment that the Exchange had overrun by £50,738 on its target of £12,500 (net cost)' (Blackstock 1997: 5).

Based on this situation, it could even be argued that the poor houses, which, with the exception of those produced in collaboration with the Peter Hall Company, played to consistently declining audiences from 1993/4 onwards, can also be directly related to Kenwright's commercial imperative and lack of understanding or interest in the local community. As Wallace asserted, decisions about the programme were not made in Leatherhead, but 'from an office in Shaftesbury Avenue'.[20] Moreover, such decisions were often heavily based on the availability of a celebrity actor, something that would often not be known until a couple of months before the start of production. The traditional season in regional theatres begins in September, and decisions about programming are typically made, at the latest, by the previous April, allowing time for promotion and budgetary planning based on subscriptions and advance ticket sales. Kenwright's concerns meant that a season might only be finalized a month before it began and then could be subject to change when star actors had to alter their schedule. Replacements at this point would often be hastily scheduled, toured-in productions, whose main purpose was to fill the gap left in the programme. As such, their quality might be questionable.

Under this system, the subscription or season-ticket system, for many regional theatres the traditional mainstay of their box office, had to be dismantled. Even so, customers often found themselves holding tickets for performances that were never produced or that were replaced with toured-in, poor quality productions. Set against some of the large-scale spectaculars that Kenwright had previously produced, particularly in the early days of his tenure, and most notably when compared with the high quality of the productions directed by Hall, this was especially keenly felt by the Thorndike's audience, who had inevitably come to hold higher expectations. In the face of such inconsistencies in the programming, therefore, it is perhaps not surprising that the Thorndike lost the confidence of its audience, and attendances declined in the last few years of Kenwright's incumbency.

The Thorndike's last artistic director, Richard Redfern, who was appointed in 1996, was, according to Wallace, extremely frustrated at the constraints placed on him by BKL's control of the operations. He was also outspoken about this situation. In an interview with the *Surrey Advertiser*, he commented, 'Bill's a mixed blessing. Financially he saved the theatre, but the relationship also caused the theatre difficulties' (*Surrey Advertiser* 1996). He then went on to criticize the use of the Thorndike as a West End test venue and question its effect on the theatre. Such comments did not endear him to the BKL management. Redfern resigned as artistic director of the theatre shortly after the interview was published, only a few months after his initial appointment, citing what the paper described as a 'mysterious illness' (Surrey Advertiser 1996).

In such circumstances, it is perhaps understandable why morale within the theatre, and support for it from outside, waned. The commercial emphasis meant that the casual staffing that had started in the 1980s to keep costs down spiralled under Kenwright's leadership. As Blackstock commented in his report, 'this is an operation run on strict rations to the point where it is tatty and uninviting' (Blackstock 1997: 4). This undermined any likelihood of creating a cohesive and concerned team who were willing and able to work towards laying a solid basis for the theatre's future. In addition, the fact that the administration was controlled from BKL's headquarters in the centre of London meant the administrative team was not only divided, but there was no evident, invested leadership on the premises to inspire personal loyalty or dedication to the theatre in the way that Wallace had done as managing director. Meanwhile, Kenwright's increasingly sour relations with South East Arts only aggravated the situation.

As his earlier, revealing comment demonstrates, Kenwright was constantly frustrated about South East Arts' attitude towards the theatre. Despite such attacks, during the years of his association with the Thorndike it should be noted that South East Arts was allocating the Thorndike more than one-third of its drama budget annually.[21] Moreover, for the duration of this time, it did so on a guaranteed three-year basis, implemented to offer the theatre the best chance of building a solid future. The reasons that no such forward planning took place, and the consequences, have already been discussed.

Although cognizant of Kenwright's personal input, and fully supportive at the outset of his involvement, as Hibberd concurred, the contradictions between the ideals espoused by South East Arts and the commercial manner of BKL's operations through the Thorndike ultimately caused problems in the partnership. In an interview with the *Surrey Advertiser*, South East Arts spokesman David Leck noted, 'the question which has been asked is should we be subsidizing a West End producer?' (*Surrey Advertiser* 1997a). Certainly, the concern that taxpayers' money was being used to help fund a commercial venture that seemed to offer little in return to the local community escalated in the last years of Kenwright's involvement, particularly as attendance figures dropped and Kenwright's public criticisms of South East Arts increased. The regional arts association found his attacks particularly galling following the outcry over the closure of the nearby Redgrave Theatre, which had traditionally received less subsidy than the Thorndike, and in the face of continued criticisms from the Yvonne Arnaud, Guildford. The Guildford theatre had teetered on the brink of closure for years, not helped by the fact that South East Arts had consistently withheld funding on the basis of supporting such commercial partnerships as the one between BKL and the Thorndike.

It is debatable whether the belief that Kenwright would not be renewing his association with Leatherhead, as he publicly threatened, influenced South East Arts' decision to withdraw funding from the Thorndike, or whether this threat merely provided them with a much needed excuse. What is certain is that on the basis of the two commissioned consultants' reports, from Bonnar-Keenlyside and from Blackstock, the funding body recognized that, in the circumstances, the Thorndike could not continue to operate solvent without BKL's support. In 1996, South East Arts announced an end to revenue funding of theatres in preference of a new system of project funding, a method of allocating subsidy that would theoretically relieve the problems and criticism engendered by its own shortage of funds. Under this system, the Thorndike was placed on an equal footing with the other seventeen theatres in the South East area, whether producing or receiving houses. As such, it became eligible to bid for funds from the regional arts association's new Drama Production Fund, through which grants were allocated on a project-by-project basis. The new system also meant that the amount the theatre was likely to receive annually would probably be approximately £100,000 lower than that it had previously received. It also made planning impossible. This decision followed Surrey County Council's earlier decision in April 1996 to withdraw its grants to all theatres across the county in order to safeguard essential education and social services. This decision was made necessary after the Major government placed a cap on public expenditure to fund tax cuts.[22] As such, by the beginning of 1997, Mole Valley District Council constituted the theatre's lone public funding body.

In 1997, after hearing of South East Arts' plans, Kenwright announced his decision not to renew BKL's partnership with the Thorndike when the contract ran out at the end of March. It was following this announcement that accounts for the theatre revealed the Thorndike's debt to the production company of approximately £1.3 million. Although Mole Valley District Council was unequivocal in its support of the theatre, particularly in terms of the part it hoped the Thorndike would play in its plans to reanimate Leatherhead town centre, their grant of £132,000 fell far short of the theatre's needs. On 6 April 1997, Thorndike Theatre Limited went into liquidation.

Following its closure in 1997, various attempts were made to reopen the Thorndike as a functioning theatre, even if only as a receiving house. Unfortunately, all such attempts failed, and despite a petition with 9,000 signatures handed to Mole Valley District Council it was ultimately accepted that there was not enough money or support for a regional theatre in Leatherhead. This conclusion was confirmed in a study jointly commissioned by the Thorndike Revival Group and Mole Valley Council, assessing the demand for live theatre and performing arts in Leatherhead. The study judged that there was already adequate provision for theatre in the Leatherhead catchment area, through a mixture of local provision, West End theatres and nearby regional theatres such as the Yvonne Arnaud, the New Victoria Theatre, Woking and Epsom Playhouse. Plans to demolish the building were prevented when the Thorndike was awarded a Grade II listing on the recommendation of English Heritage in 1998, and in 2000 the theatre was taken over by a local Christian organization, Pioneer People. Now called The Theatre, it is managed as a social enterprise and a centre for local and international support projects, where activities include frequent film showings, and occasional theatre productions and concerts. On Sundays, the main auditorium is used for Christian meetings.

Notes

1. Among those who worked with the group were Claire Bloom and Diana Dors.
2. In total, the local community raised over £200,000 towards the costs of building the theatre.
3. The now-listed building was one of the first in that style, and is said to have influenced the later design for the Royal National Theatre on London's South Bank.
4. During this period, the actual increases in funding fell far beneath the proportionate increase in running costs, such that while levels of subsidy from all sources increased by 190 per cent, the amount of earned income increased by 366 per cent. Consequently, despite increasing ticket prices, the amount the theatre needed to earn through the box office to break even increased from 49.8 per cent to 54.7 per cent. By 1984/5, the total earned income, including box office, that the theatre was responsible for maintaining had risen from 57.9 per cent to 68.9 per cent. In 1984/5, grants amounted to £196,000 while earned income was £394,000.
5. South East Arts was restructured as the South East Arts Board in 1994.

6. Hazel Vincent Wallace, managing director, Thorndike Theatre, Leatherhead, 1969–80, interview with the author, July 2002.
7. During the period of Wallace's time as managing director, both actors and directors were employed on a show-by-show basis. With regard to the former, the rationale related to the fact that Leatherhead's close proximity to London allowed many celebrated actors to commute for the duration of a run without putting themselves out of the more lucrative television/West End market.
8. Following Wallace's retirement, the board of directors decided that an artistic director and administrator should be appointed to replace her, rather than another managing director.
9. In 1981, attendances dropped by 15 per cent following Wallace's retirement and the pedestrianization of Leatherhead centre. The theatre's management blamed this on problems with parking and the fact that Church Street was now blocked off to cars, which caused the Thorndike to lose its central position in the town.
10. In their early involvement with the theatre, the Leatherhead Theatre Club played a vital part in organizing the fund-raising of the £200,000 that came from the general public to go towards the building of the Thorndike and had continued to be the consistent leader in fund-raising for the theatre in subsequent years.
11. Until 1973, audiences had been running consistently at over 90 per cent; after this time, average attendances had fallen to 65–70 per cent, a drop on previous years that followed the 1973 increase in ticket prices. In the 1980s, audience figures fell to 56 per cent (1981/2); 57 per cent (1982/3); 61 per cent (1983/4); 59 per cent (1984/5). Average attendances remained between 50 per cent and 60 per cent for the rest of the 1980s.
12. BKL initially agreed to a three-year partnership that coincided with a three-year funding guarantee from South East Arts. This agreement was renewed on both sides for a further three years in 1993/4.
13. For instance, 'sure hits' such as *Travels with My Aunt* played to poor houses, averaging 40 per cent during the recession in 1992/3.
14. Amongst the most notable plays produced in collaboration with the Peter Hall Company were *Fallen Angels* (1992, starring Hayley and Juliet Mills), *An Ideal Husband* (1992), *The Master Builder* (starring Alan Bates), *Hamlet* and *Emily Needs Attention* (starring Felicity Kendal) all produced in 1996.
15. Judith Hibberd, drama officer, South East Arts Board, interview with the author, March 2001.
16. Prior to the debts that accounts, produced in 1997, showed the theatre owed to BKL, Kenwright claimed to have personally invested in excess of £1 million in the Thorndike during his partnership with the theatre.
17. Clause 7, 'Termination', *Agreement Relating to Artistic Management of Thorndike Theatre Leatherhead (Limited)*, Tuck and Mann solicitors, Leatherhead, 20 September 1990, legal document.
18. Wallace, interview with author, London, July 2002.
19. Wallace, interview with author, London, July 2002.
20. Wallace, interview with author, London, July 2002.
21. South East Arts' revenue grant to the Thorndike was frozen at £180,000 for the three years from 1993/4 to 1996/7, reflecting an equivalent freeze in the regional arts board's own funding. During this period, South East Arts' own drama budget totalled £809,510. After the Redgrave's closure, the next biggest theatrical client, The Brighton Festival, received £128,100 annually.
22. Surrey County Council had previously allocated the Thorndike a grant of £42,000 p.a. to specifically fund the TIE and young people's work.

7

Redgrave Theatre, Farnham

The Redgrave Theatre in Farnham went dark in January 1995 on the same day as the Salisbury Playhouse. At this time, the theatre had amassed an operating deficit of £200,000, following a two-year-long battle to raise funding levels and boost flagging audiences. As with Salisbury, the size of the accumulated deficit was estimated to be almost double this figure, particularly taking into consideration the state of the dilapidated building, which had not been refurbished since its opening in 1974. Originally, the intention was for the Redgrave to reopen in July 1995, six months after going dark. But this date was put back, first until December 1995 and then to April 1996 following delays in securing funding agreements and arguments over the nature of the reopened theatre. Although the new artistic director, Roland Jaquarello, who had only been appointed in October 1994, was dismissed within a year of the theatre's closure, other issues could not be settled. As time passed, and the number of postponements increased, local interest and support for the theatre diminished. The theatre's Globe Restaurant, which had been franchised out and continued serving after the Redgrave's initial closure, had been perceived as a sign of the theatre's commitment to re-open. The restaurant's closure in July 1995 undermined such a belief. Similarly, the youth and education programmes that had continued running through 1995, thanks to a grant allocated specifically for that purpose by Surrey County Council, were terminated in April 1996 when Surrey's annual arts budget was cut. The end of these programmes meant the loss of the last full-time employee at the Redgrave. Finally, plans to reopen the theatre as a producing house that doubled as a cinema were abandoned in 1997 following the total loss of the theatre's annual grant from South East Arts. Numerous other attempts to save the theatre subsequently also failed. Although a newly formed company, the New Farnham Repertory Theatre, led by the Redgrave's original artistic director, Ian Mullins, continued to fight to be allowed back into the building and to return the Redgrave to a repertory theatre with an ensemble company, at present the theatre is empty, boarded up and awaiting demolition.

The practical reasons that forced the Redgrave to go dark in 1995 were financial. However, further investigation once again reveals a combination of factors behind the deficit that extend far beyond simple questions of money. As with Salisbury Playhouse, many of these issues were endemic to numerous regional theatres during this period, contributing to what Peter Goodrham, a member of the Redgrave's board of directors at its time of closure, referred to as 'the national disease affecting all theatres' (*Farnham Herald* 1994c).

For the majority of the two decades after the Redgrave opened in 1974, attendance levels consistently ranked amongst the highest for regional theatres across the country. Based on good attendances that continued this trend during the 1990/1 season, annual budgets for the 1991/2 season were based on predictions of maintaining an average 70 per cent attendance in the main auditorium at full price.[1] Thus, the fears of a potential cash crisis threatening the Redgrave, voiced in the programme for the January 1990 production of *Blithe Spirit*, came as a shock to everyone involved in the theatre, including the funding bodies.

Given the Redgrave's popularity and high attendances at this time, the financial problems facing the theatre related directly to long-term under-funding. In 1991, the Redgrave was being subsidized at a rate of £1.40 for every seat sold. It has long been acknowledged that, compared to theatres in many European countries, even the most heavily subsidized theatres in Britain have traditionally been inadequately funded. But, as with Salisbury Playhouse, surveys conducted by the Redgrave at this time showed their subsidy to be disproportionately low even when compared with other British theatres with equivalent demographics. One analogous venue, the Haymarket Theatre in Basingstoke, was at this time subsidized at a rate of £7.00 per seat, while the figure was £9.00 for the Nuffield Theatre, Southampton.[2] While the Redgrave's subsidy was raised to £2.85 per seat by 1994, this still compared poorly when set against the national average – at that time, a rate of £5.60 per seat. And, again, the situation with regard to the Redgrave Theatre was acknowledged to be a case of under-funding, as opposed to overly generous funding in the cases of other theatres.

Over the years, such levels of funding enforced a number of changes in theatre policy, the consequences of which combined to create an irresolvable situation in the early 1990s. The fact that things came to a head at this time is perhaps understandable given that, during this period, the real value of the already low levels of subsidy was further depreciated by high inflation rates and governments cuts in public spending. For some years, the annual increase in funding for the Redgrave fell far short of inflation. From 1988 until 1993, the theatre received standstill funding from South East Arts, whose grant from the Arts Council had also been frozen for the same period. For the financial year 1993/4, the Redgrave's funding was only raised by 1.4 per cent at a time when the national rate of inflation stood at 8 per cent. Meanwhile, production costs for the labour-intensive operation were spiralling, such that a comparison made by the Redgrave based on the theatre's January 1994 production of *Revenge* revealed that costs had increased so much in the course of a year that the theatre would have to take £65,000 at the box office to break even. A comparable production staged exactly one year earlier had only had to make £40,000.³ As Jaquarello asserted, 'The theatre must get away from funding that is still at the equivalent of 1970s levels' (*Farnham Herald* 1994b).

'Getting away' from such levels of funding had historically proven difficult for the Redgrave. In its bid to retain its subsidy, from the early 1980s the theatre had consistently marketed itself on the repertory ideal that restricted its programme to the safe identikit seasons outlined by critic Gooch in his book *All Together Now* (1984). Typically, its 'safe' programme offered 'something for everyone', kept seat prices artificially depressed and attendance figures artificially high. While such attendance figures were themselves a requisite of subsidy by the major funding bodies, over the years, pleas for an increase in revenue funding had consistently been rejected on the grounds that box office takings averaging between 66 and 70 per cent would cover any shortfalls. Effectively, as with the Salisbury Playhouse and the Yvonne Arnaud Theatre, the Redgrave believed it was penalized for its own success. But as Graham Watkins, artistic director 1989–94, commented in light of the early predictions of a cash crisis facing the theatre,

> You can't go on with an increasing decline in unearned income without being able to make that up in earned income, or by making cuts in some way...If we sold every one of our 362 seats every night and continued to produce plays all the year on present subsidy levels, we would still end up insolvent.
>
> (*Farnham Herald* 1991)

With budgets being prepared on the forecast of 70 per cent houses, the potential damage incurred by falling attendances would be devastating. In 1991, when the Redgrave first went public with its financial difficulties, there was no evidence that audience figures would ever pose a problem for the theatre. But in spring 1993, a sharp decline in attendances was recorded. This decline continued up until the time of the Redgrave's closure, when the theatre found itself playing to houses often only a quarter full. The reasons behind such declining figures are once again typical of those affecting the majority of regional theatres during this period.

It was at this time that, according to the Redgrave's finance officer, Briar Stevens, 'the recession finally hit Surrey'.⁴ Farnham is an affluent white-collar area, situated twenty miles south of London in the commuter belt, with a large proportion of the 38,000-strong town working in the city. The majority of the population fall into social class AB and traditionally have sizeable disposable incomes. Because this sector of Britain's population, which constituted the vast majority of the Redgrave's loyal audience, was typically hit last by the national recession, the effects of the early 1990s economic depression were equally delayed in reaching the theatre's box office and the town's other major businesses. It was not until two years after the recession reached most other parts of the country that individuals working in the Farnham area were therefore faced with the possibility of redundancy or pay-cuts, or felt the need to make small savings on non-essentials such as leisure pursuits. But when they did, and the Redgrave recorded a concomitant decline in audience figures, the same circumstances prevented local businesses from helping out with sponsorship. Combined with the problems incurred by long-term low levels of funding, the effects of declining audiences and the loss of sponsorship were devastating for the Redgrave. Just before the theatre's closure, board member Goodrham stated, 'We feel that we are still not out of the recession and that it obviously is at the bottom of the situation' (*Farnham Herald* 1994c).

Unhappily, because of the financial problems accrued from long-term under-funding and falling attendances, the Redgrave was forced to raise ticket prices from an average of £7.95 to £9.25 between 1991 and 1993. Such sizeable inflation in box office prices over a short period of time would have been a deterrent to audiences ignorant of the reasons behind the rise, even in a stable economic climate, particularly given the tradition of keeping prices artificially depressed courtesy of government subsidy. Local economic conditions, however, aggravated the situation enormously, prompting Watkins to comment:

> If we are forced to push [ticket prices] up too much, we will exclude whole chunks of the community – the young who we are trying to woo into the theatre, and at the other end of the spectrum, older people on a fixed low income.
> (*Farnham Herald* 1991)

As with Salisbury, the Redgrave had long had a problem with aging audiences. Although a computer system was not installed until 1994, manual audience surveys conducted sporadically over the decades recorded an audience whose average age was well over sixty. And as Stevens noted, a substantial part of the loyal body of theatregoers were already sixty when the building first opened in 1974. By the 1990s, these audience members were dying off. And, again, in spite of a long-voiced concern for the need to change the situation, the dwindling older audience was not being replaced by a new, younger one.

Despite successful youth and education programmes run through the theatre, the Redgrave itself was not structured as a fashionable and thriving arts centre, or as a welcoming venue that invited the younger members of the local community to spend time there regardless of the current production running in the main house – something that had been encouraged by many local councils and corporations when they started investing in regional repertories in the 1960s and 1970s. The theatre was not centrally located in Farnham, and its dated 1970s building had become so dilapidated that it caused a London *Times* journalist, Michael Wright, visiting in 1994, to comment that 'entering this building is like wandering into the lobby of a rundown hospital. All that are missing are the back numbers of *Country Life* and *Caravan Weekly*' (Wright 1994).

This comment included the theatre bar and restaurant, and certainly neither of these were as successful as intended in bringing in a cosmopolitan crowd. Farnham did not have a youth centre or a cinema. As such, the theatre could have easily offered an attractive retreat for a substantial section of the population without many alternative resources to fall back on. But, with the exception of its youth and education programmes, the Redgrave provided little more for Farnham's young people than its basic repertory. Despite constant assertions over the years from the board of directors, successive artistic directors and members of the public concerning the need for the Redgrave to reach more young people, youth interest rarely informed artistic policy. Caught in the subsidy trap, so long as the Redgrave attracted the high attendance figures needed to satisfy its major funding bodies, and allow the theatre to break even, the artistic policy remained unchanged. As such, after the theatre's opening, few productions provided anything that would specifically concern or involve young people. At a public meeting held in November 1994, at which the audience was invited to air their views, the theatre's lack of concern with engaging the young was consistently brought up. A teacher from a local school said that she constantly scoured the Redgrave's programme in vain for something to take her drama class to. Others in the audience spoke of the need to enthuse 'the generation that has been brought up with that stupid little box in the corner' and emphasized that 'if [the Redgrave] wants the youth involved, you must put on something the youth want to see'.[5]

The youth of Farnham and the surrounding areas were not the only ones who felt excluded from the theatre. During this same meeting, strong feeling was expressed that the local community had been excluded from the theatre's concerns. One individual commented, 'We are not included now; the atmosphere has gone.' The reasons behind this loss of community feeling have much in common with those that distanced the Salisbury Playhouse from its local, loyal theatregoers. The Redgrave was built in 1974 to replace the smaller local repertory theatre, the Castle Theatre, which had grown up organically from a small community theatre over the course of 35 years. The popularity of the Castle was undermined somewhat by the restrictions placed on it by the size and inadequate facilities of the small building in which it was originally housed. Consequently, during the theatre-building boom of the 1960s and 1970s, the local community took the decision to build a new theatre with twice as many seats, a larger stage and amenities such as a bar and restaurant. Under the Housing the Arts scheme, the local authority, Waverley Borough Council, was persuaded to give a small sum towards building costs and lease a piece of land on which the new Redgrave Theatre could be built. But the majority of money was raised through a subscription scheme financed by the local community. As such, a strong sense of ownership grew up around the theatre. Mullins, the Redgrave's first artistic director, noted:

> The Farnham company was rooted in the community that it served and there grew up that special sense that the town and audience actually owned their company of much loved, talented, and familiar repertory players. And if they belonged to each other, that great shared experience was fostered between them.[6]

Although the Redgrave never provided the arts centre ambience desired by many local councils, for years it had nevertheless been an important source of community involvement and pride. This sense of ownership and inclusion largely disappeared in response to perceived changes made during Watkins' residence as artistic director.

As explained in chapters two and four, the move away from the practice of maintaining a resident ensemble company at many regional theatres had been exacerbated by changes in the acting profession, which, following the technological revolution and the huge expansion of television, increasingly centred on the London market. The necessity of making financial cuts also aided the decline of the resident company. However, its loss invariably resulted in some estrangement of provincial theatres from the local community. Unlike many of its colleagues, the Redgrave had continued to maintain an ensemble company until 1989. On his arrival at the theatre, and partly out of financial necessity, Watkins had ended this tradition. In doing so, he precipitated the severance of the theatre from its local community. One local mourned the days 'when we could follow actors in a variety of roles and when the audience would give the actors a lift to Farnham station afterwards'.[7]

The most vociferous complaints though, were reserved for the perceived changes in the Redgrave's repertoire – and these complaints were not confined to the concerns aired at the public meeting. Comments from various letters sent to *The Farnham Herald*, over the course of 1994, underline the extent of the concern amongst locals that their tastes weren't being addressed:

> The plays are for an arty minority.
>
> We should have plays that we want to have, rather than plays that artistic directors think we should have.
>
> By all means have an interesting artistic programme, but for heaven's sake, commercial considerations have to come first.
>
> Four weeks of Molière is too much. The maximum number of people in the Farnham area who would want to see it is enough for two weeks or perhaps one.

With hindsight it appears that the changes made to the programme were seen as much larger than they actually were. In practice, as finance officer Stevens testified, very little changed, and the Redgrave continued to offer traditional repertory.

The Redgrave's artistic programme for the seasons following Watkins' arrival in 1989 did not indicate a significant move to a more risky, adventurous policy: it conformed largely to the identikit programme described earlier. Most seasons included a staple of populist British playwrights such as Ayckbourn and Godber, numerous British classics and frequent adaptations of popular novels. Riskier experimental, new or 'foreign' works were infrequent. Given that this was the case, the perceived change and related drop in box office figures can be attributed primarily to two things. The first was the introduction, under Watkins, of the occasional co-production, produced in conjunction with a commercial sponsor.

As already seen with the Thorndike, one way of cutting costs embraced by many regional theatres was in the mounting of co-productions. Production costs and, theoretically, the risks of failure could be halved when part of the money was put up by another theatre or commercial producer. Because of its proximity to the capital, the Redgrave was in a particularly good position to attract commercial producers from London looking for a place to test potential West

End productions. In 1993, Watkins took the Redgrave down this route on a couple of occasions. Working in association with West End impresarios to reduce costs and address the issue of declining audiences, the Redgrave produced two shows that offered star names and West End try-outs that would theoretically cater to a more eclectic audience than the theatre's traditional repertory. While such a move, in theory, should have relieved the financial situation, in the long term such productions arguably did a lot more damage than good.

One such production was the new musical *A Step in Time*. Starring Bonnie Langford, it was co-produced by the commercial production company Apollo Leisure Group, with a view to transferring the production to the West End. As is typical in such situations (see the profile of the Thorndike Theatre), the fact that the commercial producer was putting up the major share of the capital automatically gave them jurisdiction over the choice of show. Apollo Leisure Group was exclusively interested in the money-making potential of the production and had no concern for the Redgrave's traditional repertory or audience tastes. Consequently, while the production received average audiences, in hindsight, its long-term effects were devastating for the theatre. The production was presented during the pre-Christmas time slot with which the theatre hoped to attract large groups on their annual office-party outings and encourage loyal theatregoers to renew their subscriptions for the spring half of the season. But, as Stevens noted, the show itself was 'wholly inappropriate' for both the office parties and the traditional audience, who felt their tastes were being ignored in favour of commercial gain. Consequently, this production was blamed for losing the Redgrave a large number of individuals who until this time had remained loyal. Aggravating the situation was the fact that *A Step in Time* was scheduled only a month after another new drama, *The Secret of Beatrix Potter*, also produced in association with a commercial producer, had been a notable flop.[8]

Such commercial productions were not the norm, not entirely new and not intended to signal any major change in artistic policy. But there was a failure to communicate either this fact or the reasons for the inclusion of such productions to the public. Such a breakdown in communication had been typical of the Redgrave's relations with the public since Watkins' arrival.

Watkins' failure to work with the public caused a certain amount of local resentment. While people remained ignorant of the true reasons for ending the tradition of a resident company, and the inclusion of occasional co-productions, Mullins noted that it was also widely believed in Farnham that certain productions, such as the January 1990 musical version of Roald Dahl's *Matilda*, were primarily vehicles to further the director's aspirations as a theatre impresario. A number were produced in association with Watkins' own company, Castle Productions. Under the terms of this association, the Redgrave absorbed all the risk, while in the case of success, Castle Productions took a large part of any profits. In his petition to Waverley Borough Council to reopen the Redgrave as a repertory theatre with the New Farnham Repertory Theatre as resident company, Mullins wrote of the theatre's decline in terms of Watkins' appointment:

> A personally motivated artistic director who very quickly dismantled the whole precious repertory system and replaced it with a policy that was speculative and commercial in

its programming, and wholly at odds with the theatre's tradition, building, audience and community.⁹

Whether true or not, Watkins did nothing to diffuse such beliefs and these, in turn, did nothing to increase his popularity amongst the local people.

Such a breakdown in communication was not remedied with the appointment of Watkins' successor, Jaquarello, in 1994. If the local community already felt indignant towards and alienated by the theatre, Jaquarello's attitude on his arrival did little to reassure them. Discussing his artistic policy, Jaquarello commented that he wanted a

> wide ranging repertory of international classical writing, intended to reposition theatre with a distinct identity which will entertain and stimulate our audience...Theatre must continue to lead people. This is what all writers are about. Ibsen did not conduct market research, discover VD was a popular topic and so write *Ghosts*.
> (*Farnham Herald* 1994b)

The deliberate intention not to consult the audience implied by such remarks further incurred the wrath of many locals, who regarded the theatre as the town's property. While Watkins had appeared to be using the Redgrave to line the pockets of London producers, Jaquarello's insistence that art take priority and that there would be no swing to populist theatre for the sake of 'bums on seats' made him sound despotic and his audience inconsequential.

> Our theatre was not built with the name of a major actor to lose sight of our theatrical heritage, and we will not simplify the theatrical experience by going purely for star names. You will never see The Chippendales on the Redgrave stage.
> (*Farnham Herald* 1994b)

Although the season planned by Jaquarello was not as highbrow as some might have feared, he further alienated the dedicated audience by employing postmodern marketing techniques modelled on the more glossy, cutting-edge advertising of the larger national companies. The new style of advertising was very much at odds with the provincial sentiments of local townspeople, and the change from the traditional style of advertising consistently employed over the previous decade seemed to confirm people's fears about a change in artistic policy. This was somewhat unfortunate, given that the images were actually misleading. For instance, a straightforwardly naturalistic production of *Mrs. Warren's Profession,* scheduled to be performed at the Redgrave in October/November 1994 in turn-of-the-century period dress, was advertised with a poster depicting a modern-day prostitute wearing a 1990s miniskirt and fishnet stockings. Numerous comments made both at the public meeting and in letters to the local paper testified to the offence and misinterpretation such images caused.

Such problems, following so directly on from Watkins, ensured that Jaquarello's programme was effectively condemned even before he took up the role of artistic director in October

1994. Consequently Jaquarello only managed to direct one production before the Redgrave was forced to go dark in January 1995. *The Playboy of the Western World* was a commercial failure, criticized as 'incomprehensible' and in need of subtitles on account of the characters' strong regional Irish accents. Poor attendances for this production and meagre bookings for the coming season forced the theatre to abandon its programme and go dark directly at the end of the run.

Contributing to the declining box office, the Redgrave's apparent disregard for its committed audience also resulted in strident criticism of the theatre conducted through the local media, particularly the letters page of the *Farnham Herald*, in a campaign reminiscent of that launched against Paige at the Salisbury Playhouse. Such criticism not only targeted the successive artistic directors of the Redgrave Theatre, but the board of directors who appointed them. The case of Farnham differed to that of Salisbury, however, in that the board were united in their support of Watkins, and particularly Jaquarello, whom they had appointed with the specific intention of instituting a new, more highbrow artistic policy. Given the feelings of exclusion already running high in the community, such a decision only increased local hostility and raised questions of the board's general competence, particularly when it was discovered that not even one member of the board had any practical experience of professional theatre.

In this situation, such criticism was not limited to the local community, and the board's decision to appoint and support Jaquarello ignited long-felt tensions between the theatre and its major funding bodies. The local authorities, Waverley Borough Council and Surrey County Council, were very outspoken about the fact that they felt the board had made a serious mistake in the appointment.[10] Even South East Arts, whose arm's length principle and advisory role historically translated into public reticence with regard to clients' policies, were openly critical of the Redgrave's board of directors. 'We want to ensure that the board are experienced and committed individuals with a working knowledge of the theatre' (*Farnham Herald* 1995b), declared Chris Cooper, executive director of South East Arts, in the summer of 1995, implying that the board had not fulfilled these criteria. Jaquarello, meanwhile, saw himself as a victim of the board's unpopularity. 'I was appointed by the Board and am being made redundant as part of a process of actually running that Board down' (*Farnham Herald* 1995a), he commented after being dismissed from his post.

The feud between the board of directors and the theatre's collective funding bodies stretched back decades and had become increasingly tense in the years following Watkins' outspoken remarks about the theatre's inadequate funding. And it could be argued that the demise of the Redgrave Theatre is an example of the dangers of plural funding and an illustration of the insidious effects of funding bodies becoming directly involved in the creation of artistic policy. Typical of local authorities, both Waverley Borough Council and Surrey County Council primarily supported the Redgrave as a public amenity for the local population. As such, their primary concern was that the theatre deliver an artistic programme designed above all to be attractive and accessible to as large a section of the local population as possible. As long-term Conservative strongholds from the early 1980s, the politics of these councils also typically relegated funding of the arts to a secondary consideration. Under the terms of Thatcher's monetarism, this translated into the belief that the theatre should pay its own way, rather than become an albatross around the authorities' necks and a never-ending drain on their scarce resources. During Watkins' incumbency, the local authorities put increasing pressure on the Redgrave Theatre to pay its way by putting on a more populist programme. This encouraged Watkins to start working with outside producers on the commercial ventures the same authorities later came to attack the theatre for mounting. The local authorities' emphasis on such a commercial programme also put them at odds with the Redgrave's other major funding body, South East Arts. The fact that these disputes became public knowledge did little to stem declining audience figures.

Unlike Salisbury Playhouse, the Redgrave was in a particularly unfortunate position because of its location, and one response to an unappealing repertory and inflated ticket prices for locals was to travel elsewhere to see theatre. The town's proximity to London, and the competition that came from the capital, were finally acknowledged when consultants Bonnar-Keenlyside, brought in by South East Arts Board to examine the collective problems of The Surrey Cluster, concluded that 'people in the 25–40 age group now tend to go to London' (Bonnar-Keenlyside 1993). Stevens suggested that rather than returning to Farnham for a night out at the theatre, people would instead travel up to London to meet partners who worked there, with the now negligible difference in price easily outweighed by higher standards and wider choice, particularly via commercial West End productions that catered to all tastes.

In terms of location, the Redgrave was placed in a particularly challenging position with regard to competition for audiences. In addition to the threat from London and the three other commercial theatres mentioned earlier, the Haymarket Theatre, located nearby in Basingstoke, also operated a traditional regional repertory. And with regard to The Surrey Cluster, competition was not just for audiences but for funding from Surrey County Council and South East Arts.

With the constant reductions made to public spending by the Thatcher government, the problems of collecting local rates in the aftermath of the poll tax disaster, and the national recession in the early 1990s, neither funding body had the resources to support all three theatres within their jurisdiction at adequate levels. The appellation, The Surrey Cluster, was applied by local media in response to the seemingly endless collective financial troubles of the respective theatres. Thus, for instance, the cut in Surrey County Council's arts budget in 1996 meant the loss of their entire grant to all three theatres. In the Redgrave's case, this was the grant earmarked specifically for the theatre's education programme, which had continued after the main house went dark. The loss of this programme ensured that the theatre lost further support in its bid to reopen.

The issue of parity funding caused further problems. The loopholes in the idealistic system of plural funding were clearly evident when Surrey County Council immediately withdrew their annual revenue grant of £36,000 to the Redgrave on the theatre's going dark. This left the other two funding bodies, Waverley Borough Council and South East Arts, to make up the shortfall on a theatre they could ill afford to maintain in the first place, while withdrawing funding effectively meant endorsing permanent closure.

Relations between the three funding bodies had long been strained over the huge disparities in the levels of funding they respectively supplied. In the financial year 1995/6, for instance, South East Arts provided £180,000, a disproportionately larger sum than that supplied by Waverley Borough Council and Surrey County Council, who offered £100,000 and £36,000 respectively. South East Arts had long threatened to withdraw all funding if this situation was not remedied, becoming most vocal in their threat when the local authorities directly interfered in the Redgrave's artistic policy and pressured Watkins to introduce the disastrous pre-West End try-outs that went entirely contrary to their own ideals regarding artistic policy. But as Cooper noted, while the Redgrave remained in operation, the regional arts association could never follow through on its threat because to do so would ensure the permanent closure of the only traditional 'regional repertory' theatre left in Surrey. At one point, Watkins became so exasperated with the situation that he vented his frustration to the *Farnham Herald*:

> One of the impossible things about this job is serving many masters. Mr. Kinsella, representing one of our major funding bodies, backs the view that we are 'arty farty'. Our other major funder, South East Arts regards us as too middle of the road and wants us to become more cutting edge with more new work and so on. There is an immediate contradiction here.
>
> (*Farnham Herald* 1994a)

The unresolved differences between South East Arts and Waverley Borough Council continued after the Redgrave went dark. Rather than coming to an amicable agreement over the operating policy of the theatre, in the immediate months after its closure, consistent refusals to compromise on both sides left the Redgrave in the impossible position of attempting to satisfy diametrically opposing demands, and guarantees of funding were constantly withheld as plans for the new theatre were disputed. While problematic in terms of clearing the theatre's debts and planning its new season, such disputes also generated more bad publicity and further undermined the local community's faith in the prospect of reopening.

Again, this was far from being a new situation. In the months leading up to the Redgrave's closure, at a time when it was particularly important to present a united front and ensure the continued support of the public, encourage bookings and renew subscriptions, the disagreement between the funding bodies was carried on publicly through the local media. Headlines in the *Farnham Herald* typically read along the lines of 'Theatre funding row takes centre stage', a headline taken from an article in April 1994. Such articles constantly included direct quotations from various funding body representatives and did little to calm the situation. This comment by Denys Kinsella, Waverley Borough Council's representative, is characteristic and gives some insight into the problems Watkins faced:

> [The Redgrave] sets itself up as a culture leader, which as a result gets about thirty people in a six hundred seat theatre because it isn't putting on what the public wants.
>
> (*Farnham Herald* 1994a)

Such arguments undermined public confidence and fuelled public anger over the already volatile issue of programming, ensuring audiences stayed away at a time when the theatre desperately needed good houses if it were to have any chance of staying open. The invective levelled at the board following the appointment of Jaquarello – a man with an even more 'arty farty' vision than Watkins – meant his programme was effectively condemned before he even began.

Following the total withdrawal of all grants from Surrey County Council and South East Arts, by default, the Redgrave and all its contents became the property of Waverley Borough Council because it was built on land the council leased. After its closure, only one significant attempt made to revive the theatre was given the council's approval. Waverley leased it out to a newly formed company, Farnham Theatre Productions, which proposed to operate the Redgrave as a receiving house offering a mixed programme of touring productions. Unfortunately, the venture was badly mismanaged, and Farnham Theatre Productions went into liquidation after eighteen months. To pay off the debts incurred during this period, the Redgrave's basic infrastructure and all its equipment were ripped out, and all its costumes and props were sold off. Many of these had been given through private donation, and there was an outcry at the council's assumption of ownership of these items, a furore exacerbated by the 'disappearance' of the £21,000 raised by the local community as part of a 'save our theatre' campaign, which was generally assumed to have been absorbed into the council's budget. The theatre is now boarded up and, if plans drawn up in consultation with Waverley Borough Council to redevelop the area surrounding and including the Redgrave are passed, the building will be demolished. There is no provision in the redevelopment plans for a new theatre.

The plans, and Waverley's part in them, have been denounced by the campaigners who fought to save the theatre. In the words of one campaigner, actor Malcolm Rennie, 'If Waverley succeeds in demolishing the Redgrave, it will be the first council in the country to destroy a modern purpose-built theatre without providing an equivalent replacement, and will have committed the biggest act of cultural vandalism ever perpetrated on Farnham.'[11]

Notes

1. Figures produced by the Redgrave Theatre, Farnham.
2. Figures produced by the Redgrave Theatre, Farnham.
3. Figures produced by the Redgrave Theatre, Farnham.
4. Briar Stevens, interview with author, Farnham, September 1995.
5. Comments made at a public meeting held at the Redgrave Theatre, Farnham, November 1994.
6. Ian Mullins, artistic director, Redgrave Theatre 1974–7, interview with author, 30 August 2003.
7. Comment made at a public meeting held at the Redgrave Theatre, Farnham, November 1994.
8. *The Secret of Beatrix Potter*, starring Val Lehman, an actress from the then popular television soap opera, *Cell Block H*.
9. Public letter to Waverley Borough Council, 2002. Supplied by Mullins.
10. Stevens, interview, Farnham, September 1995.
11. Malcolm Rennie was a founder member of New Farnham Repertory Company, whose Redgrave Action Group campaigned to save the theatre and reopen it.

8

YVONNE ARNAUD THEATRE, GUILDFORD

Since 1985, Guildford's Theatre has been without Arts Council funding. Despite massive economies, reduced overheads, a flourishing mailing list with 40,000 members, record attendance figures and great artistic success, Guildford's theatre is in severe crisis.[1]

In 1995, it was announced by the Yvonne Arnaud Theatre, Guildford, that barring a miracle the theatre would close the following April. After a decade of financial crises, the theatre was running an accumulated deficit of £250,000 and claimed it could not continue to operate solvent beyond the spring unless the debt was made good in the meantime. While numerous of the circumstances leading to this announcement were common to many of the regional theatres discussed, what distinguishes the Yvonne Arnaud is that throughout this period, and to date, it has consistently run an extremely successful operation. There have been no internal difficulties in the theatre administration and no significant decline in attendance figures, which, excepting the recession years in the early 1990s, have continued to remain amongst the highest in the country. Notwithstanding, under the monetarist economy of the Conservatives, and following increased reliance on subsidy, the Yvonne Arnaud discovered that while 'highly successful, [the theatre was] still losing money'.[2]

The Yvonne Arnaud Theatre is the third theatre in The Surrey Cluster and currently the only one still operating as a producing house. Built in 1965, following the destruction of the old North Street Rep by fire two years earlier, it was paid for with money provided mainly by local fund-raising efforts, while a small contribution from the Arts Council and Guildford Borough Council were donated through the Housing the Arts.[3] In contrast to the Thorndike and Redgrave, from the time of its opening the Yvonne Arnaud adopted a fairly mainstream artistic policy. The emphasis of its programme combined typical repertory with predominantly popular productions, the latter cast separately, often with well-known actors. Occasional successes were 'sold on' to West End producers. While this practice was initially adopted with a view to ensuring the security of the theatre, and has allowed the Yvonne Arnaud to compete with the West End and retain a consistently high box office, the policy has equally meant a volatile history in the theatre's relationship with the Arts Council and, from 1986, South East Arts. Most notably, the Arts Council's 1984 decision to withdraw Guildford's subsidy heralded the beginning of two troubled decades that have seen the theatre constantly at loggerheads with the funding body, and often on the brink of closure.[4]

Even before it was devolved to South East Arts in 1984 and lost its major source of funding, cash crises were nothing new to the Yvonne Arnaud. As with many of its contemporaries, Guildford's producing theatre has primarily credited its constant difficulties to a case of inadequate funding. Like the Redgrave and the Thorndike, the Yvonne Arnaud was a victim of the Arts Council's perception that local authority funding and community patronage in the affluent south east would make up any shortfall in subsidy. That this was not the case is testified to by the Arts Council itself: in the twenty years under its patronage prior to The Glory of the Garden, the central funding body constantly complained about the unduly low levels of funding provided by Surrey County Council and Guildford Borough Council. In 1983/4 they were giving the theatre an annual grant of £12,000 and £35,000 respectively, compared with £108,000 from the Arts Council. A press release issued following the theatre's discovery that its Arts Council grant was to be withdrawn in 1984 commented:

> There has been tension for some years between the Arts Council and Guildford over the disproportion between the Arts Council's subsidy and those of the County Council and Borough Council. The rise in the Borough grant in the last three years (still little more than half of what the Mole Valley gave to the Thorndike) was too late to offset the effect of the very small annual subventions over previous years. Arts Council senior officers had more than once visited Guildford to press this point, while representatives of the council and the board had been informed that any raising of Arts Council grant level was dependent on improved local authority grants.
>
> (Penycate 1985)

On top of this, the Yvonne Arnaud believed it was targeted in The Glory of the Garden because of its mainstream programming. Although obliged to balance particularly commercial seasons with occasional seasons of more traditional rep in a manner that the first chairman of the board, Jack Penycate, described as a 'schizophrenic existence' (Surrey Advertiser 1985), the theatre had always received low levels of funding compared to other regional theatres. Prior to 1984, the Yvonne Arnaud had always had to earn at least 80 per cent of its income. The fact that it had managed to survive for two decades with such a low proportion of its income comprised from subsidy made it an obvious target for funding cuts, particularly given its geographical and financial relationship to the other theatres in The Surrey Cluster. As the theatre noted, when the news of the 1984 cuts were announced, the Arts Council's decision was hardly unexpected:

> The withdrawal of the Arts Council grant did not take the board of Yvonne Arnaud Theatre Management Limited completely by surprise. It was, in fact, an obvious victim of the policies of the new regime at 105 Piccadilly. At least one of the three theatres in

Surrey within 17 miles of each other, all subsidised and all in towns with quick and easy access to London, was bound to be on the 'hit list', and it was clear that the Yvonne Arnaud, with total subsidies only 18 per cent of its annual income, would struggle to survive without the grant, while the other two, with some 60 per cent of income in subsidy, would close without it.

(Penycate 1985)

Despite consistently selling out its shows, the expense incurred by the 590-seat venue of mounting such spectacular, named productions, on top of basic running costs that escalated over years of high inflation, meant that in 1982, two years before the decision to withdraw its funding was made, the theatre was recording an operating deficit in excess of £82,000. The situation led the theatre to make a quarter of its staff redundant and plan cuts in production costs in an attempt to get out of the red. Meanwhile, it threw itself on the mercy of the Arts Council for an increase in subsidy.

In 1985, the Yvonne Arnaud lost its total Arts Council grant following the approval of the funding body's 'strategy for a decade'. Although the central organization had been supporting the theatre with full knowledge of its mainstream programme since it opened, and had never publicly voiced any concern over the artistic policy, at this time the findings of a report declared that its programme was 'too overtly commercial' to make the Yvonne Arnaud eligible for state funding. Ironically, in preparation for some anticipated cuts, in 1983 the theatre had officially adopted a more intensely commercial programme to maximize opportunities to sell on productions to the West End or facilitate occasions to work in collaboration with commercial producers. As the theatre commented at the time, 'Recognizing that the theatre's grant-aided status was at risk, the theatre's board of directors discussed last year methods of finding a firmer basis for cooperation of this kind, and finally reached agreement with a commercial management of the highest standard, Triumph Apollo' (Penycate 1985).

The 1983/4 year-long arrangement with Triumph Apollo was the Yvonne Arnaud's first official collaboration with a commercial production company and signalled the beginning of the theatre's efforts to capitalize more on mainstream collaborations. Unhappily for the theatre, employing such a strategy effectively legitimized the Arts Council's decision to remove its funding. Any chances of fighting the decision were made increasingly difficult by the central funding body's concomitant decision to devolve responsibility to South East Arts, the nation's lowest funded regional arts association. Coupled with the low levels of local authority support then received, these decisions left the Yvonne Arnaud responsible for earning 96 per cent of its income. As such, the theatre's then artistic director, Val May, emphasized that there was no choice but to increase the commercial programming with an increased emphasis on West End transfers.[5] From this time, the theatre tailored its policy almost exclusively around a programme that would actively work to entice commercial West End producers to collaborate on productions, and the programme began to regularly include spectacular productions of musicals and ballets as well as popular plays. From 1985, attendances at the theatre were consistently 'the highest in Surrey, and amongst the highest in England' (*Guildford Herald* 1994). Over the next decade, barring the recession years from 1992/3 to 1993/4, the theatre claimed to have maintained houses averaging 83 per cent capacity, a result not only of consistently popular productions, but also of a high-powered marketing drive that built up a mailing list of 40,000 people, 11,000 of whom subscribed to the season-ticket scheme.

Despite all such attempts to maximize the box office, an economy marked by recession and high inflation meant that even good attendances did not guarantee the theatre would break even. As discussed earlier, the labour-intensive nature of theatre meant that costs spiralled during the years of high inflation in the 1980s. This was particularly true at the Yvonne Arnaud, where the extensive requirements of the commercial productions increased such costs exponentially and where, given the crisis-ridden state of theatre nationwide, the chances of selling on such productions became increasingly difficult. In talks with South East Arts in 1994, the theatre identified one of its major problems as being

> the rapid decline in the amount of high quality productions being made available to regional theatres. Partly because of spiralling costs, also because the bankable star names that the Yvonne Arnaud's audience demands are increasingly less inclined to tour outside London. The few producers able to attract these stars increasingly wish to take their productions to much larger theatres in order to capitalize on their much greater income potential.[6]

The situation was compromised further by the theatre's location, in much the same way as the two others of The Surrey Cluster. But adding to the problem, in 1990 the Yvonne Arnaud began to face new competition from Leatherhead, following the Thorndike's association with Kenwright, and, from 1992, from Woking with the opening of the 1200-seat New Victoria theatre. The comparable commercial programming that was now a staple of both these theatres made it imperative for the Yvonne Arnaud to maintain standards to retain its audience who had, by this point, come to expect spectacles comparable to those in the West End. As such, production standards couldn't be cut to save costs. The opening of the New Victoria seven miles away proved particularly ominous for Guildford because its size made it that much more attractive a proposition for West End producers looking for regional theatres they could use as try-out venues. With more than double the number of seats in its main auditorium, the potential returns on producing a piece at the New Victoria were a lot more lucrative than at the Yvonne Arnaud.

By the mid-1990s, production costs at the Yvonne Arnaud were averaging a hefty £190,000 per play. In the absence of subsidy, this meant the theatre found itself faced with a rising debt. And efforts to get around this problem constantly hit a dead end. Any attempts to appease South East Arts and persuade them to reinstate the theatre's subsidy by adopting a less populist programme were undermined by the Yvonne Arnaud's absolute reliance on box office, which loss of funding had ensured was a condition of its existence. Further, the theatre could not afford to risk alienating its very loyal and 'proper' audience, either in terms of a change of programming or in cutting standards. As Douglas May, then chair of the board of directors, noted, 'Whenever the Yvonne Arnaud has experimented 'down market', its audience has stayed away' (*Surrey Advertiser* 1992b).

In the early 1990s, the reliance on the core component of this loyal audience was intensified by the national recession, and any possibility of exploring alternative avenues of increasing income were further compromised. Financially troubled commercial producers were able to offer less capital for collaborations and became more hesitant about buying on pieces produced exclusively by the theatre, while levels of sponsorship dropped by more than half. This was one of the few occasions during the theatre's troubled period under the Tories when the Yvonne Arnaud experimented 'down-market'; the inevitable result was a disastrous box office. In the summer of 1992, for almost the first time in its existence, the Yvonne Arnaud found itself regularly playing to half-full houses, with the effect being that by the beginning of the following season the theatre had already used up any outstanding assets. A continued slump in ticket sales going into 1993, carried over from the delayed effects of the recession in the south, saw the theatre forced to close for six weeks in 1993 and eleven weeks in 1994 to save on costs. During the second closure, eleven staff were made redundant, and as a cost-saving measure only two of those were hired back on reopening. Declaring at this time that the theatre had an operating deficit of £250,000, the Yvonne Arnaud started increasingly relying on cheaper casual staff to carry out administrative duties.

Despite the problems of varying their repertory, during this period the Yvonne Arnaud found itself increasingly concerned about the need to develop a new and younger audience. A survey conducted in the mid-1980s placed the average age of the audience as between 50 and 70 years of age, of conservative taste and from income bracket AB. Actor Timothy West's experience of performing at the theatre at this time testifies to this demographic. Following an appearance in which his character uttered a couple of mild expletives, West received a £5 note and a letter from a local Guildford solicitor noting that since the actor had apparently sunk so low as to be forced to appear in such 'garbage', he must be in dire need of funds. To ensure the theatre had a future, both in light of the audience's age and South East Arts' demands for a more varied and exciting programme, the Yvonne Arnaud recognized that it was imperative to try to rectify this situation.

Unfortunately, the same difficulties that compromised any potential changes in programming equally undermined the theatre's attempts to develop other activities that could have reached new audiences. The theatre had attempted to maintain a programme of school workshops, started prior to *The Glory of the Garden*, and continued to operate an outreach programme even after being dropped as a client by the Arts Council.[7] It also had a small 50-seat studio, the Mill Studio, originally earmarked for more experimental work and new writing. Before Arts Council funds were withdrawn, this had initially been scheduled to open in 1985. In the event, it only finally opened in 1993 when South East Arts awarded the theatre a small grant of £19,000 specifically for development in its educational and experimental work. But with an increasing deficit, combined with the temporary fall in box office in 1992/3 and 1993/4, none of these activities could be operated or developed on the desired scale.

Other incentives the theatre attempted to implement to entice new audiences into the main house were also plagued by financial difficulties. Efforts to develop and expand the 'static and ageing mailing list', particularly with a view to targeting a new, younger audience were inevitably hampered by the administrative cuts and increased reliance on casual staffing.[8] And throughout the decade following *The Glory of the Garden*, increasing production costs forced the theatre to raise ticket prices annually. The slump in attendances during the recession years aggravated the situation, and the theatre admitted that ticket prices mushroomed between 1991 and 1993.

> Ticket prices generally range from £11 to £16.50. If the Yvonne Arnaud enjoyed the same grant as the Thorndike, which they dismiss as small, we could extend the normal price range so that seats cost between £9 and £15.
> (*Surrey Advertiser* 1992a)

While the Yvonne Arnaud did offer stand-by reductions on tickets unsold just prior to any performance, the theatre's previous history of sell-out successes meant that even this scheme largely failed.

Excepting the grant of £19,000 earmarked for its youth and studio work from 1993, in the decade after *The Glory of the Garden*, the Yvonne Arnaud received no funding whatsoever from South East Arts. Adding insult to injury, levels of local authority funding also compared poorly with other regional theatres, a fact that added fuel to the theatre's case against the regional arts board:

> A further hypocrisy of South East Arts is that they have been urging parity funding by local authorities, but for the Yvonne Arnaud we are urging parity funding and they won't.
> (*Surrey Advertiser* 1994b)

To receive parity funding, however, the Yvonne Arnaud was consistently told by South East Arts that it had to revise its repertoire and produce a more 'adventurous programme', a demand that the theatre felt was impossible without the security provided by subsidy.

While the lack of subsidy effectively prevented the theatre from taking measures to answer South East Arts' requirements, the Yvonne Arnaud continued to be publicly vocal about the fact that its continuance of a safe programme and concomitant good tickets sales allowed the funding body to effectively continue penalizing it for its success. Yet, in something of a lose–lose situation, the fact that it had not gone dark actually undermined the theatre's own case for subsidy.

> The fact that we play to bigger capacity audiences than the Redgrave militates against us. The Yvonne Arnaud is capable of generating £2 million at the box office, whereas the Redgrave generates about £500,000.
> (*Surrey Advertiser* 1994a)

As a part of The Surrey Cluster, the Yvonne Arnaud relied on the lowest funded regional arts association nationally to supply its subsidy while at the same time maintaining adequate levels to the Redgrave and Thorndike. But, as discussed, it was unlikely that South East Arts was ever going to have the capacity to do this. The situation thus inevitably placed the three theatres as odds with each other and created an unfortunate rivalry, as artistic director James Barber pointed out: 'My sense of fair play tells me that if there are three theatres all doing similar work they should all receive the same funding...I know if we were getting the same as the other chaps we'd be okay.'[9]

Rather than productively pooling resources, a crisis at one theatre was immediately seized on by the others; in the fight for subsidy, and ultimately survival, the easiest way of attacking funding policy was to reference one of the other theatres and sound the cry of 'not fair'. There is certainly a case to be made that the Yvonne Arnaud's constant citations of allocations to the Redgrave and the Thorndike had a direct influence on South East Arts' funding decisions and played a part in the demise of the other two theatres. While high profile supporters and patrons of the Yvonne Arnaud, including local politicians and actors, may not have understood the full extent of the situation, comments such as those made by the likes of Penelope Keith and Thelma Holt generated substantial attention from local and national media and unquestionably put a lot of pressure on the regional arts association. 'There exists a serious imbalance in the funding of Surrey's theatres. Surely there is a cast-iron case for, at the very least, "sharing the cake" equally between the Thorndike, Redgrave and Yvonne Arnaud' (*Surrey Advertiser* 1992c), Keith told the local paper.

The constant efforts by representatives from South East Arts to emphasize their own difficulties during years of standstill funding and the fact that they themselves had had no part in originally removing the Yvonne Arnaud's grant – often stressed to the local papers – bears witness to how acutely the funding body felt the brunt of such attacks. Ultimately, when the Yvonne Arnaud was finally given a subsidy at levels comparable to other theatres in the region in 1996, South East Arts noted that the theatre was being given the funds previously allocated to the now-dark Redgrave on the understanding that Guildford had a better chance of continuing to operate. Similarly, the constant pleas from the Yvonne Arnaud's quarter to 'share the cake' more evenly no doubt played some part in South East Arts' ultimate decision to change its method of grant allocation from revenue to project funding in 1997 – a decision the funding body understood would result in the closure of the Thorndike.

Such attacks were never explicitly directed at undermining the competition, but funding decisions made with regard to the other Surrey theatres' programming and policy were constantly used as a means of attacking South East Arts. Hence the Yvonne Arnaud was careful never to criticize South East Arts' decision to fund the commercial alliance between Kenwright and the Thorndike lest it reflect negatively on its own commercial programming. Nonetheless, the fact that their own commercial programme constituted South East Arts' official line of reasoning for withholding subsidy from 1985 gave validity to the theatre's accusations of hypocrisy and illogical behaviour on the part of the regional arts association. Given that South East Arts, on standstill funding itself for the majority of the early 1990s, simply did not have the funds to finance three producing houses at subsistence levels, any changes to funding allocations would inevitably be at the expense of another theatre. Had such a situation not arisen, it is possible the theatres might have been able to pursue a more mutually beneficial policy of cooperation and collaboration, something it was constantly suggested might help to cut costs and raise the theatres' collective profiles if considered in terms of marketing, programming and ticket sales. Prior to *The Glory of the Garden*, the theatres had operated just such a joint marketing system, 'The Surrey Theatre Link', which involved sharing, exchanging and touring studio programmes. But after the Arts Council's 'strategy for a decade' removed funding from one theatre and devolved responsibility for all three to the less wealthy regional arts association, competition for the inadequate funds engendered such tense feelings that The Surrey Cluster was never again able to pursue this course.

While the closure of the other two Surrey theatres heralded something of a brighter prospect for the Yvonne Arnaud, recurrent (revenue) funding was not forthcoming; instead, the theatre had to comply with the regional arts association's new policy of project funding. In other words, from 1998, grants from South East Arts had to be applied for on an annual basis with no guarantees from one year to the next. Apart from the excessive and costly administrative strain this placed on the theatre, it continued to compromise the possibility of forward planning. And the theatre's turbulent relationship with the regional arts association reached boiling point in 1999, when the financially stricken Chichester Festival Theatre was devolved to South East Arts and immediately awarded recurrent funding to the tune of £300,000 for the following three years. Given that its artistic programming was equally commercial, the decision caused an unmitigated outcry of fury from the Yvonne Arnaud.

In 2001, the theatre's ongoing financial problems seemed finally to have been resolved following the announcement that it would be given recurrent funding on a three-year basis totalling £320,000 annually, on the recommendations of the Boyden Report. While largely continuing its popular programme, this allowed the theatre to simultaneously work with the Arts Council to answer the central funding body's own priorities in areas of education, access and diversity. Unfortunately, the theatre's period of security was short-lived. In December 2007, without prior warning, it received the news that its entire Arts Council grant was to be withdrawn from the beginning of the next financial year. Plunged once again into a battle for survival, theatre director Barber commented:

> This has come as an absolute shock to everyone. Over the past few years, partly with the advice and guidance of our drama officer from ACE, we have, as an organisation, worked incredibly hard to develop all aspects of the theatre's work following the guidelines and in accordance with the priorities of the arts council. In the first five months of this year alone, 20% of our audiences were new attendees and the programme, both on the main stage and in the Mill Studio, is busier and more diverse than ever – something the arts council has readily acknowledged. Despite all our efforts, the future of the Yvonne Arnaud is now severely threatened.
>
> (*Surrey Advertiser* 2007)

Despite strong representations from the theatre, the Arts Council confirmed its decision in January 2008, with the acid-drop sweetener that it would extend its funding until March 2009, with a final year grant of £447,799, to help the theatre explore plans for its future.

Notes
1. Letter from the Yvonne Arnaud Appeal Committee, sent out to patrons in 1995. Information supplied by Yvonne Arnaud Theatre.
2. Michael Elliot, consultant, presentation to Guildford Borough Council, 6 February 1995.
3. The amount contributed by the Arts Council and Guildford Borough Council amounted to 6 per cent of the total costs.
4. *The Glory of the Garden* was released on Christmas Eve 1984; theatres on the document's 'hit list' had their funding withdrawn at the end of that fiscal year 1984/5 and responsibility for theatres that were devolved to their relevant regional arts associations was officially taken up in 1986.
5. Val May, artistic director, Yvonne Arnaud Theatre, Guildford, 1975–92.
6. Record of discussions between South East Arts and Yvonne Arnaud Theatre dealing with the theatre's financial crisis, 13 December 1994. Information supplied by Yvonne Arnaud Theatre.
7. At this time, the Yvonne Arnaud Theatre employed three youth and education officers.
8. Record of discussions between South East Arts and Yvonne Arnaud Theatre dealing with the theatre's financial crisis, 13 December 1994. Information supplied by Yvonne Arnaud Theatre.
9. James Barber, artistic director, Yvonne Arnaud Theatre, Guildford, 1992–present. Comment made during interview, 'Curtains for Yvonne', television documentary, *The Pier Series*, Meridian Television, April 1996.

9

MERSEYSIDE EVERYMAN THEATRE AND LIVERPOOL PLAYHOUSE

In the 1960s, the widespread conversion of local authorities to the idea that supporting a civic theatre could be socially beneficial to local communities bolstered the Arts Council's belief that there should be one regional producing theatre for each municipality with a population of 200,000. At this time, the industrial city of Liverpool was experiencing a period of economic prosperity and a population boom, with the large plant manufacture in engineering, cement, sugar refining and flour milling thriving around the city's docks, which then constituted the nation's northern base for transatlantic trade and ship building. The region's economic prosperity in the 1960s was accompanied by a cultural energy, particularly after the success of the Beatles raised Liverpool's international profile and made it the focus for many young musicians, poets and artists. With a population in excess of 800,000, proposals for a new, second, producing theatre in the city were greeted with enormous enthusiasm by the local community and authorities.

In terms of regional theatre, Liverpool had long been distinguished as the home of the oldest repertory theatre in the country. The Liverpool Playhouse had been operating as a producing theatre since it was first founded by Basil Dean as the Liverpool Repertory Theatre in 1911. Starting life as the Star Music Hall in 1866, the theatre in Williamson Square had originally held more than 2,000 people, half of them accommodated in the huge gallery. It was redesigned by Stanley Adshead in 1911, the year Dean established the Repertory Theatre, and was subsequently run on a successful repertory basis for the next 80 years, only closing temporarily during the Second World War. In the late 1960s, major renovations to the Playhouse saw the size of the auditorium restructured to seat 800, a capacity thought more suitable for a larger regional producing house. At the same time, a new foyer, rehearsal room, workshop space and restaurant were also added. Such additions allowed the theatre to become more socially accessible and operate more closely along the lines of civic amenity advocated by the theatre's new proprietor, Liverpool City Corporation. The local authority contributed a large portion of the money needed for the renovations carried out to the Playhouse building in 1968 and subsequently bought the theatre and began to provide a base annual grant to the resident company. Further expansion of the Playhouse's activities followed the civic model in the 1970s, with the addition of a new studio theatre, the Theatre Upstairs, and the development of a children's theatre company that was operated by the Playhouse, but had its base on separate premises.

With such extensive expansion at this time, the development of the Playhouse clearly coincided with the trends typical in the majority of Britain's regional producing theatres in the post-war years, and the theatre's artistic programming offered no exception to this rule. Despite the concern to make the programme more socially accessible in the 1960s, the theatre's artistic policy remained very much one of conventional, 'middle-class' repertory that attempted to reconcile the Arts Council's demands for high art and innovation with the local corporation's concern for broadly appealing work. As Rowell and Jackson noted in *The Repertory Movement*, from the 1960s, the 'well-established Liverpool Playhouse was providing worthy but only occasionally exciting productions of the conventional repertory fare (Shaw, Sheridan, Wilde, Priestley, Shakespeare), together with occasional forays into more recent and abrasive drama (*The Fire-Raisers* and *Luther* in 1962/3, *The Hostage* and *The Entertainer* in 1963/4)' (Rowell and Jackson 1984: 158). As such, 'there was clearly room [in Liverpool] for a theatre of a different kind appealing more directly to newer and younger audiences' (Rowell and Jackson 1984: 158).

In 1964, the Merseyside Everyman Theatre, Liverpool, was founded by a group of young men who had been students together at Birmingham University. Martin Jenkins, Terry Hands and Peter James' shared experience of student drama provided them with an idea for and the motivation to establish a new kind of theatre that would focus on innovative and developmental work, particularly for young people. Emphasis was laid on the social utility aspects of theatre education and participation, and a programme was proposed that could be tied in with local schools' curricula and timetables. In addition, Jenkins, Hands and James proposed creating a theatre with an artistic approach that stressed the ensemble and developmental areas of stage work, such that the new theatre could function as a forum for practical experimentation. In the liberal, socially minded 1960s, such an idea was immensely appealing to Liverpool City Corporation, and they greeted the trio's approach with substantial grants to set up the project.

Following the lease of a converted chapel adjacent to the city's university area on Hope Street, the characteristic house style of the Everyman slowly began to emerge. Doreen Tanner, a Liverpool theatre critic who wrote a chronicle of the Everyman's first ten years, described this style as 'a unique collective personality...moulded by coherent direction and able to shape plays to its own purposes' (Tanner 1974: 11). Initially, the theatre's early programming did not notably differ from that of the Playhouse, with the first season including productions of *Henry IV Part 1*, *The Servant of Two Masters*, *The Caretaker* and *An Enemy of the People*. But the energy of the ensemble work, which typically played at breakneck speed, and the company's concern to bring immediacy and contemporary relevance to all the plays performed, soon began to garner the Everyman national recognition as a pioneering venue for controversial work.

Over the years, the Everyman's type of programming changed. While the company sustained a concern with exploring new ideas through the text in a way that would allow them to comment on contemporary political and social trends, gradually the choice of plays moved away from the traditional repertoire to encompass a much broader range of work, with a specific emphasis on pieces topical to the local community. So early productions such as the Everyman's celebrated version of *Agamemnon*, which provided an irreverent comment on the Vietnam War, or its look at the swinging sixties in a miniskirted version of *As You Like It*, gradually gave way to topical pieces devised or written specifically for the theatre. The arrival of Alan Dossor in 1970, an artistic director 'not interested in plays that did not relate to the community outside' (Tanner 1974: 43), for example, saw the development of the musical documentaries and historical plays that became the Everyman's forte. *The Braddocks' Time*, produced in his first season, for instance, was a musical docudrama about a Liverpool Labour MP, Bessie Braddock, who had been active in the 1940s and 1950s. Similarly, *Soft, or a Girl?*, written for the theatre by John McGrath in 1971, was a rock musical about Liverpool that focused on problems in the local community caused by the generation gap. The success of these ventures later inspired Bob Eaton to write his hit musical biography *Lennon*, first produced at the theatre in 1981, and Willy Russell to try his hand at playwriting. His first effort, *John, Paul, George, Ringo...and Bert*, produced in 1974, marked one of the high points in the Everyman's early fortunes.

Despite the popular success of certain productions such as these, issues of commercial appeal and quality were never foremost on the theatre's list of priorities. Moreover, experimentation with acting styles, improvisation and interpretations of the texts often made the theatre's policy of 'casual accessibility' somewhat questionable. But as part of its ideology as an experimental theatre, the Everyman was adamant about the importance of maintaining the 'right to fail'. Consequently, with occasional exceptions, attendances at the Everyman were historically low, with houses consistently averaging between 40 and 50 per cent in the years before 1979. From the time of its foundation, therefore, the theatre relied heavily on subsidy for its survival.

Public support was also particularly vital to the Everyman in regard to its extensive outreach work. The Everyman's early policy of scheduling regular matinee performances to coincide with school hours developed into substantial TIE and YPT programmes operated through a branch of the theatre called the Hope Street Project. At the height of its work in 1973, the project established the Everyman Priority team and, with a grant awarded by the Gulbenkian Foundation, was able to base itself at one of Liverpool's Educational Priority Area schools and work extensively with children in underprivileged areas. Although this was only continued for a three-year period, it provided vital support for the Everyman's youth work, generating increased interest in the Hope Street Project. From this time, the project functioned as a quasi-autonomous operation within the theatre, providing training and development opportunities in all areas of theatre for approximately 1,000 young people each year.

With such emphases, the very nature of the theatre's policy meant it was historically enmeshed in typically loss-making activities. As such, from the outset, the Everyman was dependent on sufficient levels of subsidy to carry out its objectives. Despite a few financially difficult periods, up until the 1980s, and the arrival of the Thatcher administration, the Everyman received full support for this work from the Arts Council and local authorities and was able to function successfully as a pioneering regional theatre. This was despite the fact that, economically, the Liverpool area declined steeply after the 1960s.

* * *

In the early 1980s, the Arts Council became increasingly sensitive to the fact that the measures it took to maintain and support as wide a spectrum of artistic endeavour as possible in Britain's theatres were meeting with regular opprobrium. As central government put increasingly tight restrictions on public spending and offered below-inflation increases in its annual subvention for the arts, criticism about the national funding body's policy of 'equal misery for all' became more vociferous. In particular, criticism focused on the Arts Council's failure to move on from its traditional reactive policy of responding to circumstances as they arose, which, it was widely felt, had translated into their concomitant failure to make proper judgements of need based on individual cases. By failing to do so, it was argued that the Arts Council's methods of funding were causing anomalous differences between companies to increase.

In 1986, following the recommendations made in the Arts Council-commissioned independent enquiry, the Cork Report, the council's drama department, led by Ian Brown, decided to rethink the organization's traditional funding principles. Faced with escalating costs on one side and falling levels of state subvention on the other, the national funding body recognized that providing the desired broad network of companies with funds that would allow them to continue operating at acceptable levels could not be sustained under the prevailing system. Under financially restricted circumstances, it was clear that attempts to continue supporting the same number of companies without a redistribution of funds would have resulted in numerous insolvencies in the subsequent eighteen months. Following the outcries over the 1981 Christmas Cuts and 1984 *The Glory of the Garden*, both of which involved the withdrawal of funds from certain clients, adopting an increasingly hard line on parity funding provided an alternative, more up-to-date and pragmatic approach to dealing with local conditions and authorities, and was seen by the Arts Council as infinitely preferable to cutting clients.

The system of parity deals had existed as an unofficial policy from the 1960s when local authorities became increasingly involved in arts funding. Sir Brian Rix, chairman of the Arts Council drama panel in 1986 at the time parity funding became officially adopted, explained the idea in terms of the national funding body's concern to make the local authorities live up to their responsibilities to local arts organizations:

> A parity agreement is not simply a matter of asking a local authority to match the Arts Council grant for a theatre, or vice versa. Rather, it is a process of agreeing the

appropriate level of funding jointly between the Arts Council and local funders, and then sharing that sum equally. In some cases this may mean the Arts Council reducing its contribution, while local authorities increase theirs. In other cases it may result in local authorities or the Arts Council raising their level of funding to match that of their partner or partners. It may even mean increased support from local authorities for theatre companies. The days of the Council for the Encouragement of Music and the Arts acting as a central patron are long past. The Arts Council cannot afford in these stringent times to impose a theatre on a reluctant local authority.

(Rix 1991)

The concern to adopt a more robust approach to parity funding at this time was in large part related to the abolition of the GLC and five metropolitan county councils. At the time of their dissolution, which took effect at midnight, 31 March 1986, these authorities were collectively contributing an estimated £46 million to the arts across Britain. Consequently, from the time the proposal for their abolition was put forward in the 1983 White Paper, *Streamlining the Cities*, their loss was widely heralded as posing the greatest financial threat to the arts in Britain so far seen under Thatcher. The Conservatives were seemingly aware of the potential devastation abolition posed in this sector, and a consultation paper published at the same time as *Streamlining the Cities* suggested that a few select prestigious companies should be designated of national importance and would be protected through special grants provided by central government. This was effectively realized in the form of the £25 million abolition funding channelled through the Arts Council. In Liverpool, those organizations prioritized to receive money from the government's abolition funding included the region's seven museums and galleries, all of which had to be 'nationalized'. Unlike the other organizations included on the government's list, however, amongst which were the National Theatre, the English National Opera, the London Festival Ballet, the Royal Exchange, Manchester, and the Royal Liverpool Philharmonic Orchestra, not all of these Merseyside companies had initially been considered priorities. But given the extreme poverty into which the greater Liverpool area had descended by the 1980s, and the extent of the financial problems already being experienced by the successor authorities, failure to 'nationalize' these institutions would almost certainly have condemned them to a rapid demise. In recognition of this fact, the number of organizations included from Merseyside was extended. Meanwhile, those companies not designated as being of national importance had to do the best they could by appealing to the successor local authorities for replacement funding, through increasing income from business sponsorship and by capitalizing on the box office. The two producing theatres, Liverpool Playhouse and Everyman, fell into this category and were designated the responsibility of Merseyside's five successor authorities: Liverpool City Council, Sefton Borough Council, the Metropolitan Borough Council of Wirral, Knowsley Borough Council and St Helen's Metropolitan Borough Council.

Unfortunately for the Liverpool Playhouse and Merseyside Everyman, securing replacement funding was not as straightforward as they might have hoped. In the first place, the theatres were considered a low priority issue by the five successor authorities, given the pressing social problems the councils were dealing with in what, at this time, was one of the country's most economically and socially deprived areas.

In 1880, Liverpool had more millionaires than any provincial city in Britain. By 1984, the European Commission calculated it was one of the poorest cities in Europe in terms of population decline, job losses and unemployment levels.[1] In the early 1980s, following the collapse of the city's industry, Merseyside witnessed some of the most desperate social, economic and political problems in the country. Until Thatcher became prime minister, many large-scale industries had been supported by government subsidies. In line with Keynesian economics, during the 1970s, state funding had been used to sustain increasingly unprofitable manufacture out of fear of the consequences of high unemployment resulting from plant closures. But industrial losses supported by public monies were contrary to Conservative monetarist policy, and the declining situation in Merseyside was considerably exacerbated when such government subsidies were withdrawn at the beginning of the 1980s. During Thatcher's first term in office, Liverpool was characterized by a spate of well publicized plant closures and redundancies, leaving the Merseyside area with problems of poverty and unemployment disproportionate to the rest of the country. At the time of the metropolitan county abolition, 47 per cent of the city was living in official poverty, with 72 per cent of the local population counted as living in the most deprived 10 per cent of national conditions. Moreover, the five local authority districts in the area of the Merseyside County Council had an overall unemployment rate of 20.8 per cent, or 140,472 jobless individuals. In certain parts of the area, 90 per cent of the population's youth were unemployed. The region also had a disproportionately high number of unskilled workers, who bore the brunt of the unemployment problem. Consequently, Merseyside had to contend with a far larger number of long-term unemployed than the rest of the country.

Even prior to the abolition of the metropolitan counties, such social and economic decline had caused substantial problems for the Everyman and Playhouse. The widespread depression and concomitant loss of disposable income amongst the local population, combined with a suspicion over such 'middle-class' activities as theatre-going, had translated into declining box offices at both theatres from the early 1980s. This was particularly true of the Playhouse, which had attempted to improve the situation by changing artistic direction. In 1981, it became a 'writers' theatre', under the four-man directorship of Chris Bond, Willy Russell, Bill Morrison and Alan Bleasdale, all of whom were graduates of the Everyman. When this venture failed to breathe new life back into the theatre and create better houses, the Playhouse had adopted an increasingly safe programme, which saw attendances drop to an average of 30 per cent capacity by 1985. Comparatively, the Everyman had never had a large box office because of the nature of its pioneering, controversial and experimental work. But, as mentioned earlier, this made it heavily dependent on subsidy to give it 'the right to fail'. In such circumstances, both theatres were particularly vulnerable to low levels of support from local authorities.

Although Merseyside County Council had previously recognized their responsibility to the theatres, because of the substantial social and economic problems it had to deal with from its creation in 1972, levels of subsidy never reached anything near parity levels with those of the

Arts Council. To offer one arbitrary example, in 1984, Merseyside's support to the Playhouse was £91,000, compared with £283,000 from the Arts Council. Moreover, combined public funding had historically been criticized by the theatre as being substantially lower than needed to sustain the expected level of operation. In 1984, the combination of inadequate subsidies and declining audiences resulted in an operating deficit of £44,000 at the Playhouse. This figure dramatically increased when essential repairs were needed on the 122-year-old building and following problems relating to the resignation of the theatre's three executives. Artistic director Bill Morrison, administrator Josephine Beddoe and principal director Chris Bond offered their collective notices at the end of the financial year, citing their reasons for leaving as 'the long-term effects of struggling to support the arts on a broad front as well as see the theatre through a period of one crisis to another'. As Morrison told The *Stage*:

> We feel that most of our time and the artistic directors in particular is spent compiling huge documents. I know the others feel there is a real danger they will burn themselves out. Everybody in the arts feels this, they can't avoid it now, but there comes a time when enough is enough.
>
> (*The Stage* 1984c)

Without the unifying factor of Merseyside County Council, the disparate political affiliations of the successor authorities ensured that such problems would get worse following abolition. This was particularly true of the authority considered to hold the major responsibility for the two theatres, Liverpool City Council, within whose geographical jurisdiction the Everyman and Playhouse were located. In the years leading up to 1986, economic decline had contributed to a situation of extreme political instability in Liverpool. The far left Militant group, led by Derek Hatton, dominated Liverpool City Council between 1983 and 1987 and, in their attempts to defy the Thatcher government, deliberately overspent the city's budget on things like housing repairs and employment incentives. Rather than forcing central government to make good the deficit, the group effectively bankrupted the city and, in the process, obstructed any attempts at urban regeneration by frightening off potential business investment in the area. The situation was further exacerbated when the city council was penalized by central government for overspending with the introduction in 1984 of rate-capping. In its attempts to make up the government shortfall in its grants, the Militant group had raised the rates out of all proportion to other parts of the country, such that in certain areas of the city the domestic taxes levied on property values were three times the national average. Following abolition, Liverpool City Council claimed that it had only been allocated £20 million for £27 million worth of service and could not afford to give arts organizations what they needed. Furthermore, as a 'workerist' administration preoccupied with working-class issues such as employment and housing, the Militant group was equally hostile to any perceived middle-class pastimes, including 'middle-class arts'. Under these circumstances, theatre subsidy was not only considered a low priority issue, but a potential weapon. A war of funding attrition over the arts organizations delegated to its responsibility following abolition could theoretically score the far-left party points in its political battle against the state.

The situation was aggravated further by the fact that the other four successor authorities appointed to share responsibility for the theatres were run by different political parties. At this time, Sefton and Wirral both had 'hung' councils and were ruled by an unstable Liberal-SDP/Conservative alliance, while the authorities of Knowsley and St Helens were Labour.[2] As the Arts Council's deputy chairman, Rittner, noted at the time, this set-up led to a situation in which none of the successor authorities felt it was their responsibility to make up the deficit caused by the abolition of Merseyside Council. They uniformly rejected the Arts Council's suggestion that they form 'jointly constituted local authority boards, or committees with a power to precept on constituent authorities', and instead became embroiled in a series of heated debates over the theatres, with each alleging that financial responsibility for the Everyman and Playhouse lay at the doors of their sister councils.[3]

The Arts Council's estimate for the drama needs of the Merseyside region following abolition was placed at £1.6 million. Because of the deprived circumstances of the area, the national funding body offered to provide £1 million of this on the condition that the local authorities made up the rest. Unfortunately, due to the problems described, during negotiations conducted in the months approaching abolition, they were unable to improve on a situation in which the Arts Council's subsidy to the Everyman and Playhouse outweighed the combined contributions offered by the local authorities by a ratio of nine to one. In February 1986, only one council had agreed to make any contribution at all to the theatres. But the proffered sum of £100,000 compared poorly with the subsidy then being provided to the Playhouse and Everyman by the Arts Council, which amounted to grants of £570,000 and £315,000 respectively.

The impossibility of sustaining this situation, and a determination to prevent it from deteriorating further, translated into the Arts Council pursuing an increasingly tough line on parity funding. Although the underlying principle of parity funding was to provide a more secure support base for clients, in the cases of the Liverpool Playhouse and Everyman it made life increasingly difficult. In 1986, the combined funding from the local authorities and national funding body was already far below the amount required by the two theatres to sustain their operations at desired levels. And the situation was made worse by continuing negotiations between the funding partners that never progressed beyond a stalemate. Under these circumstances, the Everyman and Playhouse found their respective operations being slowly crippled as the theatres were used as pawns in political battles to which their own situations were peripheral at most. Clare Venables, who had a comparable experience as artistic director of the Sheffield Crucible following the abolition of West Yorkshire County Council, commented: 'In the end, you just sit there in the middle, powerless, while they fight it out' (The Times 1986).

The first year post-abolition saw increasingly difficult situations developing at the Everyman and Playhouse. In its attempts to pressure the local authorities into collectively providing more funding, the Arts Council variously threatened to cut its own support to the companies, or withheld portions of its promised grant past the dates the money should have been released. Such actions created increasingly difficult working conditions at the two theatres, which, at the beginning of the financial year 1986/7, were both already carrying sizeable deficits. In particular, the situation made forward planning impossible. At the Playhouse, for instance, the deadlock with the local authorities and Arts Council caused the situation to degenerate to such an extent that by 1987, despite frozen salaries and reduced production costs on an increasingly 'safe' artistic programme, wherein the theatre also produced fewer shows each season, financial difficulties were still crippling its activities. In February 1987, it announced that it was being forced to close its studio, the Theatre Upstairs, and was unable to plan an artistic programme beyond July. The spate of bad publicity caused by the situation was also blamed for a further decline in attendance figures, which fell to an average of below 30 per cent. The situation proved too much for Jules Wright, Morrison's successor and artistic director of the Playhouse for only fifteen months. She simultaneously announced her resignation, citing unbearable working conditions, and her despair over the future of the theatre following the abolition of Merseyside County Council. As she told *The Stage*, 'The position is intolerable; I see no indication of either will or commitment to improve the present situation on Merseyside, and have therefore decided to resign' (*The Stage* 1986a).

Negotiations between the Arts Council and the five local authorities continued into the following financial year but only managed to improve slightly, despite the 1987 suspension of the hostile Militant group from Liverpool City Council and its replacement with a far more liberal Labour consortium. However, the extra £100,000 that the national funding body was subsequently able to secure from the collective councils still left the ratio of Arts Council to local authority spending at five to one, far below ideal parity levels. At the beginning of 1988, the escalating crisis in theatres nationwide, combined with widespread criticism of the Arts Council's policies, caused the national funding body to become even more strident in enforcing its policy of parity deals. At this time, the quango announced that, in the face of the local authorities' failure to provide the required £600,000 support for the Liverpool theatres, the national funding body could no longer shoulder the burden alone. In consequence, it stated, it would be slashing grants to the Everyman and Playhouse for the coming fiscal year, 1988/9, by 5 per cent, a cut which would amount to a loss of approximately £90,000 for the theatres. In deference to the socio-economic problems of the region, these cuts were to be spread over the course of two years, such that in the first year the Everyman's grant was cut by £16,000 and the Playhouse's grant by £29,000. A statement released by the Arts Council read:

> After four years of negotiations with our colleagues on Merseyside, the long-deferred crunch has come. It can only be stated categorically: the Arts Council has no spare cash. If the Playhouse is such an artistic and well-loved Elysium, local patronage will have to be seen and counted and surely this is not too much to ask, even in these storm-tossed dog days of the community charge.
>
> (*The Stage* 1988a)

To a degree, the Arts Council's actions had the desired effect. While the Everyman's artistic director, Glen Walford, called the organization's actions 'vandalism of the worst kind', Liverpool City Council greeted the news by publicly proclaiming that the national funding body had 'stabbed [them] in the back' (*Liverpool Echo* 1988). Not only had the city council been willing to increase their funding, they claimed, but they had also been in the middle of negotiations with the Arts Council at the time of the latter's announcement. The chairman of the council's finance committee, Keith Hackett, told the *Liverpool Echo*: 'We offered to put money in and they ignored the offer' (*Liverpool Echo* 1988). According to Hackett, prior to the Arts Council's decision, the city council had already agreed to increase financial support for the theatres despite its own crippling financial problems and had simply postponed the announcement while it tried to find the most effective way to secure the money. Emergency talks held subsequent to the Arts Council's announcement between Arts Council chairman William Rees-Mogg and Keva Coombes, the leader of the city council, resulted in Liverpool agreeing to increase its support for the two theatres by a further £200,000 on the condition that the Arts Council suspended its reduction. The national funding body agreed to do so pending the outcome of a working party report on theatre provision on Merseyside. In the event, Arts Council support to the theatres was only cut by £30,000 in the financial year 1988/9, bringing the national funding body's contribution closer in line with that of the local authorities' after their £200,000 increase. While increasing such contributions from other public funding bodies was the theoretical ideal behind parity funding, the situation nevertheless negatively affected the theatres in other ways.

The year after Wright's departure from Liverpool Playhouse, the Everyman's popular and successful artistic director of five years, Walford, also gave his notice. Despite continued backing from the board of directors, who had supported his decision to ignore the Arts Council cuts and continue operating the theatre's activities at current levels for as long as possible, Walford told the *Liverpool Post* that he had become weary of fruitless negotiations with the respective funding bodies that took up time and energy that should have been devoted to artistic work. When he announced his departure in October 1988, the Everyman was carrying a £90,000 deficit and because of financial restrictions had only been able to announce three shows for the coming season.

In light of the problems the theatre was experiencing, the board's choice of successor was telling. John Doyle was recruited from Cheltenham Everyman, a provincial theatre that had been devolved to its regional arts association prior to *The Glory of the Garden* and which had consequently for some time relied exclusively on local sources for its income. Cheltenham was also a theatre that had made its name as the successful producer of commercial, mainstream work. Such factors had informed Doyle's background and provided a clear contrast to the traditionally experimental outlook of the Merseyside Everyman. Given the circumstances, there was wide speculation in the local press that the board's choice of Doyle as the new artistic director was a direct indication of the theatre's concern with improving support from the local authorities and safeguarding the future of the Everyman by taking it in a more commercial direction. Although he managed to avoid following such a commercial path, when Doyle took up his post at the Everyman, he adopted a policy intended to make the box office more accessible to the local community while keeping costs down. In his first season, Doyle employed a permanent resident company of fourteen actors, something the Everyman had not done for twelve years, and adopted a traditional repertory system whereby plays were presented on a rotating basis. His first season was devoted to updated versions of Greek classics, including

The Trojan Women, Wild Wild Women (an updated version of *Lysistrata*), *The Gods Are Not to Blame*, produced in conjunction with Talawa Theatre Company, and a half-hour Dario Fo version of *Medea*. Commenting on this choice of artistic policy, Doyle said:

> I think this theatre has always been about risks. Cash is an issue which is always hanging around. There are two schools of thought and one is to say we haven't enough money so we'll cut down on production and do longer runs – or you can say we will do a lot of work here and prove we're worth having and make damn sure we become indispensable.
>
> (Doyle 1989)

Despite clearly aligning himself with the second option, Doyle's artistic policy was a very clear gesture of the financial pressures incumbent on theatre. Adopting the repertory system allowed him to effectively stay true to the Everyman's role as a pioneering venue for controversial work, but was a means of only having to support one set of salaries at any given time. The reappearance of familiar faces in numerous productions could be a valuable asset at the box office, a factor Doyle openly acknowledged. Similarly, the decision to rotate the presentation of plays was no longer based exclusively on questions of quality, as it had been in Granville Barker's day, but the idea that 'If people come to see the second Greek play in the season and like it, it's good to give them the opportunity to see the first one which they might have missed' (Doyle 1989).

The success of Doyle's policy temporarily improved the theatre's financial situation, helping to cut costs through savings on actors' salaries and co-productions, as well as increasing the revenue from the box office. Over the course of the next three years, the Everyman managed to reduce its operating deficit of £90,000 by a third, while extensive fund-raising and a £50,000 renovation grant from the Foundation for Sports and the Arts allowed the Merseyside Everyman Theatre Trust to buy its building from Liverpool City Council, thereby also reducing the rental overheads.

Although there was never any question that such events had solved the theatre's financial problems, at the end of the 1980s the Everyman was in a much stronger position than the Playhouse. In 1988, the latter announced that its operating deficit had doubled to over £180,000 as a consequence of fewer performances – which had lost the theatre an estimated £14,000 in 1987/8 alone – the appointment of three different artistic directors in as many years and financial shortages in the contributions of the collective funding bodies.[4] Concerted efforts had been made to improve this situation by increasing revenue from the box office through the introduction of a new season-ticket subscription scheme. This resulted in a 60 per cent increase in attendances by 1989. Similarly, a high pressured drive to increase revenue from business sponsorship was considered very successful. But as with the Everyman, none of these improvements were enough to solve the ongoing problems caused by the lack of support from their funding bodies.

At the beginning of 1989, continued negotiations between the Arts Council and the five successor local authorities resulted in a promise from the local councils that they would bring their combined support for the two theatres up from 20 per cent of public funding to 50 per cent by 1991. The Arts Council agreed to this time frame to allow the cash-strapped councils the breathing space they needed to sort out questions of responsibility and find the extra money. In 1989/90, the Everyman and Playhouse were able to avoid the threatened further cuts to their Arts Council grants and received standstill funding from the national funding body.

Unfortunately for the theatres, this tenuous agreement did not mean an end to their problems. Notwithstanding the fact that in a year of high inflation, standstill funding in 1989/90 meant a collective loss of £60,000 in real terms, the local authorities were not able to come through with the promised levels of funding. In part, the councils' collective social obligations and cash crises meant they were simply not able to find the money, particularly given that primary responsibility was delegated to the rate-capped, politically embattled Liverpool City Council. In 1990, the city's deficit was £6 million, and when the threat of bankruptcy and central government pressure forced the council to make substantial reductions in the city's spending, arts funding was once again designated a secondary consideration.

The low priority afforded the arts by the city was reinforced by the fallout of the council's attempts to reduce spending, which, initially at least, cost Liverpool as much money as it saved. To offer one example, in 1991, Liverpool City Council started to make substantial cutbacks in its 29,000-strong workforce, the size of which had long been seen as out of proportion with the city's declining population. But compulsory redundancies made by the city were greeted with months of trade union action that threatened to once again cripple the council's activities, cause it to default on loans and send it into bankruptcy. In June 1991, the dismissal of 460 garbage men, made redundant when the city's refuse work was privatized and the franchise given to a French company, resulted in the city's binmen going on strike for three months. At its height, the strike saw the city immersed in 12,000 tons of uncollected rubbish and a rather nasty stench. The refuse collectors were supported by other council employees, who also went on strike under the direction of the union, the National and Local Government Officers' Association (NALGO). Amongst others, these included council employees responsible for overseeing collection of the new local tax, the poll tax, the revenue from which combined with central government grants to provide the mainstay of the city's budget. Hostility to the unpopular new tax was most effectively expressed through widespread non-payment, particularly encouraged by the Militant group who were still influential in Liverpool. In parts of the city, non-payment of the poll tax was running at 70 per cent, and the consequent costs of collection outweighed the value of the levy. NALGO strike action exacerbated the situation considerably, and by November 1991 £150 million worth of poll tax had not been collected from the Liverpool area alone. Interest on bridging loans was costing the council a further £16,000 a day. Under such circumstances, the city council was unable to follow through on its promise to the Arts Council and bring its contribution to the Everyman and Playhouse in line with that of the national funding body. Although it managed to provide its share of the extra £200,000 promised between 1988/9 and 1989/90, in the circumstances this did not become a permanent arrangement and subsequently Liverpool was unable to promise an annual base rate for the two theatres exceeding £100,000.

The Arts Council's own actions did little to persuade the city to increase this sum. In 1990/1, the national funding body received a substantial increase of £20 million from the government in its annual grant-aid. But while this translated into a boost of between 7 and 35 per cent in the grants for certain theatre companies, the Liverpool Playhouse and Everyman received cuts of 9 per cent and 7 per cent respectively, reducing Arts Council support to £527,000 and £280,000. The decision to cut their grants was made following an agreement with a regional independent arts funding organization, Merseyside Funders' Forum. The latter agreed to provide the £80,000 cut from the theatres' grants in the belief that the money saved by the Arts Council would be allocated to other arts organizations in the region that had also been severely affected by abolition of the metropolitan council and Merseyside's socio-economic deprivations. Both the Everyman and Playhouse were furious at the cuts; neither theatre was consulted about the deal or given the opportunity to have any part in the decision-making process. They were also worried about Merseyside Funders' Forum's ability to provide replacement funding. This fear proved founded, less because of the organization's inability to pay than because the Arts Council did not specifically allocate the retained £80,000 for Merseyside arts projects. While this failure could arguably be put down to a lack of communication between the two funding bodies, Merseyside Funders' Forum felt understandably cheated by the Arts Council and no longer obligated to the Everyman and Playhouse. Subsequently, only a portion of the promised money was given to the theatres, while the remainder went to support other Merseyside arts projects that the Funders' Forum had intended to benefit from the deal. Even more ominous was the fact that the initial agreement had only been for one year. So even if Merseyside Funders' Forum had come through with the money in 1990/1, it would have had no obligation to repeat the grant the following year. Meanwhile, as the theatres were aware, historically, cuts in Arts Council's support had tended to be permanent. As Doyle commented to the press, 'The amount they are taking away in their terms is very small, but in our eyes it is very big. It is so difficult when you hear them getting £20 million more from the government to see them take it away from an area already suffering great deprivation' (*The Stage* 1990a). Adding insult to injury, this action effectively meant that the Arts Council had reneged on its part in the parity deal it had worked so hard to enforce with the local councils. Thus, good intentions aside, there was now no obligation beyond a sense of civic duty with which to pressure the successor authorities to follow through with the agreed levels of funding for the two theatres.

These events culminated in financial crises for both theatres. In January 1991, Liverpool Playhouse became the first regional theatre in the country to be operating while technically insolvent. It was given two months to trade its way out of insolvency and avoid going into receivership. The theatre's administrator, John Stalker, estimated that when inflationary considerations were added to the cuts made in the collective funding bodies' grants, the value of the Playhouse's grant had dropped by £250,000 a year in real terms since 1988. In 1991, total local authority contributions to the Playhouse amounted to £127,000 less than the theatre had been receiving in 1986. The operating deficit of £500,000 had increased from the previous year, and when the cost of urgent repairs on the 122-year-old building, which hadn't been renovated for over twenty years, were taken into consideration, it was estimated that the Playhouse needed a minimum of £900,000 to continue trading past March.

The war years excluded, the Playhouse faced the threat of going dark for the first time in its 80-year history and the loss of 70 jobs. Manchester High Court appointed an insolvency expert from accountants Ernst and Young as the theatre's official administrator to try to save the theatre. Given full authority over the Playhouse's affairs, Frank Taylor cancelled a projected youth theatre festival and much of the theatre's planned programme, including the premier of Beryl Bainbridge's adaptation of her novel, *An Awfully Big Adventure*, based on her experiences as an assistant stage manager at Liverpool Playhouse in the fifties. While it was considered artistically interesting, Taylor thought this type of programming was too risky for the theatre. He replaced it with more commercial fare, including three toured-in performances of co-productions between the Leatherhead Thorndike Theatre and Bill Kenwright, a new Francis Durbridge murder-mystery thriller called *Small Hours*, starring the well-known actor Patrick Mowber, and two plays by Russell, *Shirley Valentine* and *Our Day Out*, the former being both commercially attractive and cheap because it required one actress and no set. While the new artistic programme proved both popular and cost effective, what actually saved the Playhouse from going dark was a five-year partnership deal with the commercial production company, Bill Kenwright Ltd. In return for absolute autonomy in dealing with the Playhouse's affairs for the next five years, including artistic programming and control of an agreed level of public funding from the local authorities and the Arts Council, the West End impresario Kenwright, a Liverpudlian by birth, agreed to underwrite the Playhouse's debts for the duration of the term.

In many ways, Kenwright's association with Liverpool Playhouse resembled his partnership with the Thorndike Theatre in Leatherhead (see chapter six). Under his leadership, the theatre functioned as a testing ground for planned national tours and a touring date for commercial productions sent out from the Thorndike or the West End. And while there is no question that the Playhouse would have closed at this time had it not been for Kenwright's intervention, the long-term ramifications of his involvement for the theatre are nonetheless ambiguous. When Kenwright ended his five-year partnership with Liverpool Playhouse in 1996, he estimated that his involvement had personally cost him in excess of £2 million. As with Leatherhead, however, such figures were only based on the costs of activities carried out at the Playhouse and did not take into account profits generated by co-productions that went on to successful national tours after they left the theatre. While the proceeds of these tours should have been split equally between BKL and the Playhouse, part of BKL's agreement with the Playhouse included a majority of seats on the board and the appointment of BKL employees to senior administrative positions in the theatre. As such, all accounting was ultimately dealt with by BKL rather than being channelled through the Playhouse. After the partnership came to an end, despite Kenwright's agreement to underwrite all debts incurred during the association, the Playhouse was left with a sizeable deficit of half a million pounds. Moreover, while the Playhouse attempted to revert to its traditional repertory role, five years of commercial vehicles with named casts had raised the audience's expectations beyond the capabilities of a regional producing theatre. Attendances were consequently very disappointing. In October 1997, a year after Kenwright's departure, the Playhouse's debts had increased to £800,000, with £250,000 owed to the Inland Revenue in unpaid taxes. With the Playhouse's total grant from funding bodies amounting to just £650,000 that year, directors of the theatre went to court to win an administration order to prevent creditors calling in the receivers. The autumn season went ahead, but the theatre nevertheless went into receivership at the beginning of 1998 and remained closed for the next three years.

For a time at the beginning of the 1990s, the Everyman fared a little better than the Playhouse. In part, this was simply due to the fact that, as a smaller outfit, its overheads were substantially lower. In a cruel twist of fate, however, the fact that the Playhouse survived its 1991 insolvency crisis precipitated the Everyman's downfall in 1992. Although the disparate artistic programmes of the theatres meant they had rarely considered the other a rival at the box office, the dearth of funds available from the local authorities had increasingly raised questions of the viability of having two producing theatres in Liverpool. This question was brought to a head by the Playhouse's association with Kenwright, where part of BKL's agreement rested on an assurance from the funding bodies of a minimum level of public support being pledged to the Playhouse for the course of the agreed partnership. With the growing socio-economic problems facing Liverpool City Council, by 1991/2, the paucity of the city's funds meant that the share intended for the Everyman had to be reduced to ensure the agreed levels could be provided for the Playhouse.

In July 1992, the Merseyside Everyman called in the consultants Peat Marwick to try to help resolve the theatre's financial problems. Despite the achievements of the theatre in cutting its deficit in previous years, the renovation and purchase of the building, made possible by the grant from the Foundation of Sports and the Arts, and an increase in its Arts Council grant, combined with public funding in 1991/2 was simply not enough to allow the Everyman to sustain its activities. Although Arts Council support for 1992/3 was increased by £35,000, the grant of £315,000 was the same as the theatre had received in 1987 and was worth considerably less when inflation was taken into consideration. The same year, local authorities were only able to promise the Everyman a base grant of £33,000. According to Peat Marwick, the theatre needed at least £100,000 more than this to be able to sustain its activities until the following March. Without any guarantee that such funds would be forthcoming, the Everyman was unable to plan a programme for 1993, while only three productions were scheduled for the second half of 1992. Questions were also raised over the efficacy, in the circumstances, of continuing the Everyman's costly young people's programme, the Hope Street Project. As the administrator Ros Robbins commented, 'The whole organization has been under review. It would be irresponsible to operate at the current level without knowing how much money we've got at our disposal' (*The Stage* 1992).

Despite his insistence that he had not been frightened out of his job by the theatre's cash crisis, when Doyle subsequently announced his resignation in October 1992 his actions were widely seen as a sign that the theatre was on the verge of imminent collapse. Without the finances to plan a programme for the new year, no vacancy was advertised and no artistic director was appointed to succeed him.

At the beginning of 1993, the problems at the Everyman reached crisis point when the issue of parity funding resulted in a further cut in the theatre's public funding. When Liverpool City Council announced that local authority grants to the Everyman were to be slashed by 50 per cent to provide the extra funding for the Playhouse, the blow to the theatre was compounded by the Arts Council's response of cutting their grant by an equal proportion. Thus, at a time when the Everyman was experiencing its most severe financial crisis, total public funding fell from £440,000 to £240,000.

The decision, made by the funding bodies after a series of discussions at the beginning of the year, was deliberate and made with full knowledge of the consequences. Following years of sustained crises, a joint statement released by the collective bodies revealed their new policy:

> It became clear last year that there was no longer any possibility of finding the money to continue both companies with a year-round producing role. The main reason for this was the severe financial limitations affecting local authorities.
> (*The Stage* 1993)

While the Playhouse and Everyman's needs were estimated at £860,000 and £530,000 respectively, the total funding available to the two theatres from both the Arts Council and the local authorities amounted to only £600,000. Rather than continuing to share the misery in a way they believed would ensure both theatres continue to experience sustained crises, and place them both constantly on the brink of closure, the funding bodies opted to devote a more substantial share of the available monies to the Playhouse in the hope that at least one theatre would be able to continue operating securely. While the Playhouse effectively had priority because of the history and size of its operation, it was also seen as having a better chance of success following Kenwright's investment. In turn, the funding bodies recommended that the Everyman scale down its operation to become a mixture of producing and receiving house. Recognizing the severity of the theatre's financial problems, the Arts Council offered a one-off rescue package from its contingency fund to help the theatre remain open, on the condition that it altered its operation in the way the Council outlined.

The funding bodies' actions catapulted the Everyman into turmoil. Following the news of the cutbacks, and Doyle's departure in March 1993, the board announced that the theatre was in imminent danger of closure. Efforts to avoid this fate, however, were thwarted by acrimonious machinations within the board and various departments of the Everyman that prevented the theatre from launching an effective survival strategy.

Following the 1988 Insolvency Act, which placed responsibility for keeping the theatre solvent in the hands of the board, concerns about the future of the Everyman resulted in a bitter split amongst the directors. Initially, the board was divided over the issue of artistic policy. Following the redundancy notices issued to fifteen of the remaining twenty full-time staff in June, the majority of the board accepted the idea that the Everyman's only chance to avoid going dark was to follow the recommendations of its funders and, for the time being at least, become a receiving house. A plan involving 'artistic tendering' to local and national professional and amateur companies had been drawn up by two councillors from Liverpool City Council, Hackett and Nick Stanley, the latter having once worked as an administrator at the theatre. A small caucus of board members, however, under the leadership of board chairman Peter Howell Williams, felt that following such a path undermined the very reason for the theatre's existence. A long-standing board member from the Everyman's heyday as a pioneering venue of experimental theatre, Williams was insistent that the theatre should remain a producing house and fight for subsidy at levels that would offer the Everyman that cherished 'right to fail'. In an ideal situation, he would probably have had unanimous support for this policy. Under the circumstances, the majority of the board were more concerned about finding an immediate practical solution that would allow the theatre to stay open.

The power struggle that arose resulted in three extraordinary general meetings being called during the summer of 1993. In these meetings, the majority of the board voted to set up a three-member caretaker board, on which Williams was not included. The attempts failed, however, after Williams sought legal advice and was able to declare one meeting invalid on the grounds that the votes of five members, including Russell's wife, Annie, were illegal, given that the voters were 'stand-ins' who had not been formally elected. The attrition rate of board members had increased as the stalemate continued over the summer. Following Williams' actions, the residue of those who had supported the rescue package proposed by the Arts Council resigned, partly in protest at the way fellow board members had been treated. While such dissent rendered the board incapable of working on a survival strategy for the theatre, by September so few members were left anyway that the board effectively no longer existed.

This situation was not helped by the rebellion of the Hope Street Project. The youth and community development arm of the Everyman had become disillusioned by what they claimed was the apathy and lack of interest with which the board had recently regarded its work. The Everyman's ongoing financial crisis and predicted closure provided the impetus to formally break away from the theatre, and in June 1993 it proposed operating as an independent company. Earlier the same year, a group of workers from the Project had applied for, and been granted, charitable status for the company and had assembled a separate board to run it. Moreover, their plans had received official approval from the Arts Council and local government. The Everyman board, meanwhile, put a spoke in the works. The Hope Street Project's request that the board agree to the separation and release the £80,000 grants that they claimed had been allocated to the theatre specifically for the project was refused. Regardless of the alleged indifference of the board, the Hope Street Project was still considered a core part of the grass-roots work of the Everyman theatre, particularly with regard to its original objective of development work for young people (*The Stage* 1993). Moreover, the release of £80,000 in grants would have put the main theatre into immediate liquidation.

The board-room machinations, both in terms of internal dissent amongst the directors and their treatment of the Hope Street Project, lost the theatre a great deal of support in the local community. The letters pages of the local newspapers were filled with angry remonstrances from parents outraged at the 'selfish' and 'high-handed' manner with which the Everyman board had jeopardized the Hope Street Project. Following years of predictions of the theatre's imminent closure, the Project was widely seen as the one branch of the Everyman's work that could still be saved. Under such circumstances, the actions of the board of directors were perceived as having wantonly condemned the one vital branch of the theatre to a needless demise.

In turn, such actions further impaired relations between the Everyman and Liverpool City Council, its primary local funding body. The negative feelings stirred up locally aggravated an already tense situation that had escalated following the board's refusal to explore the city's recommendations for 'artistic tendering' and to offer the Hope Street Project autonomy. In September, Liverpool refused to hand over even its reduced share of the agreed local authority grant for the financial year 1993/4. Although an interim 'rescue lifeline package' was arranged from the reserves of the Arts Council and the other local authorities in Wirral, Sefton and Knowsley to cover wages and overheads for a few weeks, with no programme, no artistic director and a substantial operating deficit, the theatre was put into receivership and forced to go dark in October 1993.

At the end of 1993, the Everyman building was put up for sale, and it was widely believed that, after 29 years, the theatre had closed for good. The building was bought, however, by David Scott and Paddy Byrne, the proprietors of the Everyman bistro, the successful restaurant that operated in the basement of the building and that had previously received much of its custom from theatre patrons. The sale was approved by the council on the agreement that a new company be formed, the New Everyman, to whom Scott and Byrne would lease the theatre. Money to buy the lease was provided through funds amounting to more than £250,000 raised by the Everyman Supporters' Group, a high-profile support group for the theatre founded in the wake of its closure that included many celebrated local artists, such as Bleasdale, Russell and Barbara Dickson, all of whom had had early successes at the Everyman. With the funds raised, a new board was set up chaired by one of the theatre's original co-founders, Terry Hands, and a policy of operating the theatre as a touring venue for the rest of the year was adopted, with the aim of extending the policy to offer a mixture of toured-in and in-house productions the following year depending on financial viability. To increase profits and raise the profile of the theatre, it was also decided to use the Everyman as a venue for dance, comedy and certain types of music, jazz in particular, that were seen to be under-represented in the city at the time. The theatre reopened in February 1994 with a production of Kaboodle Theatre Company's *King Lear*.

While there was enormous local community support for the reopening of the Everyman, the situation with regard to available public monies had not changed. Despite the efforts of the new artistic director, Peter Rowe, and administrator, Kevin Fearon, the local authorities refused to acknowledge the Everyman's 40 per cent claim on available drama funds for the region. Although the new regional arts board, North West Arts, to which the theatre was now delegated, attempted to compensate by offering a grant that was £40,000 larger than that of the Arts Council at the time of the theatre's closure in 1993, following its reopening in 1994 the Everyman found its combined funds came to £170,000 less than it had received in 1992. Thus, even though it received a capital award from the lottery of £100,000, and ticket sales saw a rise from 22,000 in 1992/3 to 84,000 in 1993/4, to continue operating the theatre had to substantially scale back its previous operation. This was particularly true in the area of outreach work. It also had to increase its ticket prices and was only able to produce two in-house productions while taking in touring dates the rest of the year. Subsequent years saw the theatre continue to operate as a mixed venue on a shoestring budget, with financial problems continuing even when a portion of the local authority funds that had gone to the Playhouse were allocated to the Everyman when the older theatre closed in 1998.

In 2001, a new solution was offered to relieve the ongoing financial problems of the Everyman and to restore the Playhouse, which by now had been dark for three years. By this time, there was a general recognition that the socio-economic problems of the area meant that Liverpool could not sustain two theatres functioning exclusively as producing houses. Money provided through the European Community contributed to substantial urban regeneration, and extra funding also became available to the Arts Council following the Treasury's response to the findings of the Boyden Report and the Arts Council's *Theatre Review*. Under these circumstances, discussions resumed between the local authorities and North West Arts, whereby it was decided to offer a significantly increased funding package that would allow the Playhouse to reopen, on the condition that the Everyman and Playhouse companies merge and each function as mixed venues. Under the guidance of Josephine Beddoe, the Playhouse's administrator from the early 1980s who was brought back from New York to oversee the project, the Playhouse and Everyman were merged under a single trust, the Liverpool and Merseyside Theatres Trust, in 2001. They were subsequently given a single visual identity in terms of logo, company and policy, but the in-house productions presented at each were decided on the basis of their distinct historical styles, stages and auditoria. The two theatres continue to operate under these auspices, with a mixture of productions ranging from Shakespeare and the classics to new writings and experimental dramas being presented alternately in the venue considered most suitable.

After the theatres' dances with death in the 1990s, their recovery under the trust in the early years of the twenty-first century has been remarkable: an upbeat annual report for 2004/5 showed attendances up 45 per cent; education and community activities up by 55 per cent; earned income by 57 per cent and nineteen full and part-time jobs created. The figures represented a decided thumbs up from the local community for the theatres' new programmes of homegrown 'Made in Liverpool' work, which that year included three premieres. At the same time, plans for a £35 million redevelopment of the theatres were announced, kick-started with the pledge of £8 million from Arts Council England's capital lottery programme and a £2 million fund-raising campaign by the trust.

But there was a stumbling block to carrying out the project: the trust did not own the Everyman – it was still renting the premises from the restaurant proprietors who had bought the site in 1993, when the theatre went into receivership. Into the ring stepped the Northwest Regional Development Agency, and in April 2008 the trust was able to buy back the Everyman with a £1.7 million donation from the agency.

'The Everyman owns its own future again,' commented Deborah Aydon, current executive director of the two theatres. 'It is a milestone in the history of the theatre. The redevelopment of the Everyman and Playhouse is our big legacy project for Liverpool's year as European Capital of Culture' (*The Stage* 2008).

Plans include more facilities at the Everyman, including creating a studio, dressing and rehearsal rooms. Meanwhile, restoration work is planned for the Grade II listed Playhouse. Work is scheduled to begin in 2010. Were it to be completed by 11 November 2011, it would mark the centenary of the founding of Basil Dean's Liverpool Repertory Company.

Notes
1. In 1930, the population of the Merseyside area was 850,000. By 1985, the decline in manufacture and the docks had caused that figure to fall to 460,000.
2. A now defunct political party, the Social Democratic Party (SDP) existed between and 1981 and 1990. It was created as a centrist breakaway group from the Labour Party by Labour MPs who thought the party had moved too far to the left, making it unelectable and leaving the Conservative Party effectively unchallenged. Before the end of 1981, the SDP had allied with the Liberal Party to form the SDP–Liberal alliance.
3. Arts Council of Great Britain, finance correspondence files (m–q): records 1928–97.
4. Jules Wright was replaced by Ian Kellgren in 1987.

10

Harrogate Theatre

When Harrogate Theatre temporarily went dark in 1986, it had been struggling with financial difficulties for almost a decade. One of the oldest repertory theatres in the country, the North Yorkshire theatre was converted from the original Grand Theatre and Opera House, which had first opened on Oxford Street on 13 January 1900. The original title can still be seen on the illumined cupola over the upper corner of the building. At the time of its opening, the Grand Theatre had an auditorium seating 1,300 and was considered one of the top opera houses on the circuit. But the popularity of circuit theatres had dwindled by the 1930s, and the decision was made to convert the building into a repertory theatre. In 1933, the company White Rose Players was founded, with Trevor Howard and Sonia Dresdel among some of the early performers. The theatre continued operating on a repertory basis right through the 1960s when Harrogate Borough Council purchased the building as part of the urban renewal and civic investment sweeping the country. At this time, a trust, the Harrogate (White Rose) Theatre Trust, was set up to run the theatre, and Harrogate became a not-for-profit, subsidized producing house.

For the next couple of decades, Harrogate presented a successful, if traditional, operation, expanding its activities by introducing a TIE programme in the 1970s and, in the same decade, cutting into and remodelling the main auditorium in order to make room for a state-of-the-art lighting room and 50-seat studio theatre on the third floor. Yet, even before the Thatcher administration took office in 1979, the theatre had experienced a series of difficulties that had brought its future into question. Most notably, in 1979, it found itself carrying a sizeable deficit and was only saved from closure following intervention and increased grants from its three main funding bodies: the Arts Council, Harrogate Borough Council and North Yorkshire County Council.

For a number of years, Harrogate had long been one of the five lowest funded regional producing theatres in the country, a situation generally attributed to its small scale; following the remodelling of the theatre to incorporate the studio and lighting room, the auditorium was left with a seating capacity of only 465. While the intimate space translated into lower overheads in the minds of funding bodies, it equally limited Harrogate's own potential for earned income through the box office. In common with the three theatres that constitute The Surrey Cluster, Harrogate also believed it was discriminated against because of the comparative wealth of its catchment area. The 69,000-strong town and surrounding district from which the theatre drew the majority of its audience have traditionally been considered both rural and conservative. More than 33 per cent of the population in this area came from social classes AB, the groups that, as discussed earlier, comprise the highest proportion of theatregoers across Britain. This figure is far higher than the national average, which puts the typical proportion of social groups AB to be found in municipal and regional areas in Britain as, respectively, 23 per cent and 20 per cent. Notwithstanding, in Harrogate's case this did not automatically translate into high attendances at the theatre, a situation the management felt was not taken into consideration by the Arts Council in deciding the level of its grant-in-aid. As early as 1979, Harrogate was complaining that it was being under-funded to the extent of 39 per cent by its collective funding bodies and that this was the absolute minimum increase needed to continue operating at 'present standards' (*The Stage* 1979a).

In 1979, difficulties increased following the arrival of a new artistic director. According to comments featured in the letters pages and articles in the *Harrogate Advertiser* and *Yorkshire Post*, standards in the quality of production dropped significantly with the arrival of Michael Poyner. After an alarming and sudden drop in audiences, by halfway through the season the theatre was projecting that it would be ending the year with an operating deficit of £169,000. Unsurprisingly, the artistic director of only eight months resigned not long after, and Harrogate was forced to become a receiving house for five months to reduce its debts and await a decision on its future. It was widely expected that the theatre would close permanently at this time, but Harrogate was in fact given a reprieve following the collective funding bodies joint decision to increase their grant levels. Even so, these increases fell far below the desired amount. The first year of the Conservative administration saw severe cuts in central government grants to local authorities, which prevented the local funding bodies, Harrogate Borough Council and North Yorkshire County Council, from raising their grants by more than 10 per cent. The Arts Council, meanwhile, did offer a £10,000 increase, bringing their annual grant-in-aid to £78,000, but even so the combined collective subsidy now allocated to the theatre fell far below the 39 per cent increase Harrogate had stated it needed to continue operating even at current levels.

Following the decision to continue operating as a producing house, the theatre was faced with the challenge of not only bringing back the audiences it had lost during the troubled period in 1979, but increasing attendances to make up the continued shortfall in subsidy. The same cuts that prevented the local authorities from offering a more substantial grant equally prevented them from increasing funding levels at a rate ahead of inflation. As such, over the course of the next five years, the theatre saw subsidized support fall from providing 60 per cent of its income to 40 per cent. Rather than creating a climate in which the new artistic director, Mark Piper, could afford to put all his efforts into improving standards, and take risks on new styles and works that might offer a more diverse range, production values had to be severely compromised to make up the increasing financial shortfall.

Since being purchased by the Borough Council in the 1960s and run as a civic theatre, Harrogate's programming had been traditionally conservative. The design of the main house, which was based around a proscenium arch and raked stage with 'Juliet steps' leading to the stalls on either side, lent itself to 'typical box set productions' (*The Stage* 1985). So too did the conservative tastes of the loyal audience. A manual survey taken by the theatre in 1982 put the average age of theatregoers at over 60, and comments made by Piper at the time revealed concern that this audience was dying away (*The Stage* 1979a).

The theatre was fully cognizant of the need to improve audiences in terms of numbers and profile, but nevertheless completely prohibited from doing so by financial strictures. In an attempt to prevent any further decline in attendances, Harrogate retreated yet further into a safe and old-fashioned repertoire, dominated by a proliferation of Christie, Coward and Ayckbourn. These were, as Piper noted, without exception, presented in traditional, realism terms. While this move may have satisfied the loyal audience, who comprised the majority of subscribers to the newly introduced season-ticket scheme, it failed to generate interest amongst other social groups. Simultaneously, financial restrictions ensured that alternative avenues that might be used to foster new interest were also neglected.

The problem of the narrow and diminishing audience was aggravated by reduced activity in the studio theatre during this period. Productions continued to be presented sporadically, but there was an increasing tendency to cut costs by using the studio as a rehearsal room rather than a venue for putting on new or experimental work. The consequences of this policy for the theatre were disastrous. Playing safe artistically may have catered to the tastes of the loyal audience, but it didn't prevent the effects of old age, and box office receipts revealed a steady decline in numbers during the five years Piper was in charge. By 1984, when the Arts Council's 'strategy for a decade' was announced, average attendances at Harrogate were below 45 per cent.

Under the terms of *The Glory of the Garden*, the Arts Council decided to withdraw Harrogate's entire grant of £132,500, beginning in 1985/6. The reasons offered for this decision were grounded in the poor standards of the repertory and the fact that the theatre was not considered to be offering a diverse, innovative or exciting enough programme. The Arts Council also noted that their decision had been influenced by the belief that the theatrical needs of the local community could easily be answered by a number of other producing houses located nearby, most notably Leeds Playhouse, the York Theatre Royal and the Sheffield Crucible. While upset that its funding should be withdrawn for any reason, Harrogate Theatre fundamentally disagreed with this last point, noting that many people from the surrounding environs of Northallerton, Richmond and the Dales were situated too far from any theatre but Harrogate to find performances in any of the other towns easily accessible. They used this argument, along with the outpouring of support that the new threat to the theatre brought with it from the local community, to appeal the Arts Council's decision. A petition, which included 40,000 signatures, and a new business plan for Harrogate's future drawn up by the board of directors were sent to the national funding body. In response to both this appeal and the public outcry that accompanied the 'disastrous' *Glory of the Garden*, four months later the Arts Council agreed to reinstate Harrogate's funding for at least two years. This was less £30,000 that the Arts Council held back, based somewhat unfairly on the grounds that the board of directors' business plan emphasizing expanded outreach activities was considered unfeasible in light of the theatre's lack of funds. The Arts Council's offer was also conditional, based on the proviso that Harrogate adopt a new artistic policy, improve the quality and range of its repertoire and increase houses to an average 60 per cent capacity in the following two years. At this time, responsibility for the theatre was also devolved to Yorkshire Arts Association, who took over responsibility in 1986.

Although the reinstatement of Arts Council funding allowed the theatre to continue operating, a precarious financial situation was made worse by the reduction in size of the reinstated grant. But, as with so many other local authorities, Harrogate Borough Council was in no position to help. In 1984/5, it was forced to further cut public spending to avoid being penalized by the government under the new rate-capping law and was only persuaded to maintain its grant to the theatre, which had also been under threat, by virtue of the need to secure the return of the Arts Council's grant.

The increasingly tight circumstances in which the theatre found itself limited the opportunities of following through on the conditions made by the Arts Council. Despite the appointment of a new, popular artistic director in 1984, Andrew Manley, the opportunities for improving artistic standards were heavily compromised by the need to cuts costs. The theatre's public image suffered heavily in the town when it was forced to make seventeen staff redundant in November 1985, a situation further exacerbated by cuts in other areas.[1]

The closure of the studio theatre, which now became used as a full-time rehearsal space, shut off one possible avenue by which the theatre might have offered a broader spectrum of work and attracted a new audience. The dearth of funds also prevented the theatre from hiring a marketing officer to work on analysing audience trends, make connections with the local community and promote the theatre amongst more diverse sections of the public, despite a specific recommendation by the Arts Council. Most seriously, potential to improve the situation was limited by internal divisions within the theatre, where the conditions imposed on reinstatement of the grant directly conflicted with the conservative ethos of the Harrogate Theatre board of directors.

In 1985, the traditional, long-serving board were largely representative of the old loyal audience, in terms of both artistic tastes and personal profile. More than half the twelve-strong board were over sixty years of age, and a couple of members had served since the theatre was taken over by Harrogate Borough Council, and the White Rose Trust was first formed, two decades earlier. As such, they were heavily resistant to any radical change in the theatre, believing that this would alienate the last remnants of the devoted audience and ultimately sound the final death knell for the theatre.

This situation brought them into direct conflict with the new artistic director. Manley was adamant about the 'need to get away from the tired restrictions of period, box-set productions that had trapped the theatre in a time warp and caused it to lose touch with the local community'.[2] Although he had arrived at Harrogate just prior to The Glory of the Garden, the urgency of bringing in new audiences with a new artistic policy had been heavily emphasized on his appointment. While the need to overcome the Arts Council's withdrawal of funding became the priority in his first year, Manley nevertheless believed that the conditional reinstatement of the grant, with its proviso that artistic policy had to change, would be enough endorsement to quell any doubts the board might have. As he noted, he was wrong in this assumption, and while the board accepted that some changes needed to be made, they were reticent about how radical those could be. Consequently, they asked Manley to make some modifications to the more experimental programme initially proposed for 1985/6 such that it continued to incorporate a large number of familiar and popular names. Moreover, the board was adamant that any change in direction should be phased in gradually and 'almost imperceptibly, so that our loyal audiences are hardly aware it's happening'.[3] Thus, while the theatre was unable to employ a new marketing officer through lack of funds, the decision to avoid a large-scale marketing drive to communicate and promote the new artistic policy was a deliberate decision made at board level and one with which the theatre administration were particularly uncomfortable.

The lack of communication with the public had a devastating effect at the box office. In one arbitrary example, audiences were not warned about the theatre's new policy of colour-blind casting. As a result, 'the letters column of the local weekly became quite apoplectic',[4] following the 1985/6 season's production of Shaw's Pygmalion, which cast a black actress in the role of Eliza Doolittle but white actors in the role of her father and Professor Higgins. Other productions, which introduced nudity, strong language and modern dress for period pieces for the first time in Harrogate, were enough to frighten many long-term audience members away. With the exception of a brief surge in attendances following the publicity gained from The Glory of the Garden threat, by this point the theatre's audiences had been steadily declining for six years. In 1985/6, another substantial drop was recorded, noted most significantly in the lack of subscription renewals in the theatre's season-ticket scheme. The year culminated in a disastrous summer in 1986, when audience figures fell to an average of 25 per cent, with certain shows, such as The Normal Heart, playing to an average 15 per cent capacity.[5]

The difficulties experienced by the theatre were aggravated by the discovery that poor budgetary management had allowed Harrogate to accumulate a substantial deficit far in excess of that projected by the administration at the beginning of the financial year. In the wake of the Arts Council's post-Glory of the Garden grant, and despite substantial cutbacks in numerous areas, the theatre had not pretended it would be able to continue operating without accumulating a debt. The Arts Council had agreed to pay off the £34,000 deficit with which the theatre ended the 1984/5 season over the following two years. However, there was no provision made for any further debts incurred. In November 1985, the theatre projected that it would end the 1985/6 season with a deficit of £9,392. At this point, it turned out that a number of major accounting errors had not yet been discovered owing to an outdated manual system of record keeping. This proved particularly difficult for Amanda Laidler, the new financial administrator, to decipher when she arrived following the death of the incumbent financial administrator at the height of the theatre's 1984 crisis. The following March, revised figures submitted to Harrogate Borough Council revealed the theatre's operational deficit had already reached £69,524. Commenting on the situation to the local paper after the decision was subsequently taken to close the theatre, Harrogate Borough Council's director of financial services said, 'Projected forward for the remainder of the year, it was apparent that the theatre could incur a deficit of over £100,000 if nothing was done to correct the position. This was not a position which could be allowed to materialise' (Woolley 1986).

At the same time, a consultants' report on the theatre noted that the dilapidated state of the building was both uninviting to the public and had deteriorated to the point of being a safety hazard in some backstage areas. The theatre had not had a complete refurbishment since being taken over by Harrogate Borough Council in the 1960s and lacked the 'Good Night Out' ambience the critic Gooch noted as being so important in promoting live theatre. According to comments made in the local paper, it was 'outdated', 'dingy' and 'uninviting'. The consultants' report estimated that the necessary work, which needed to be undertaken immediately for the theatre to be allowed to continue operating safely, would cost £175,000. Costs for a complete refurbishment were placed at £420,000.[6]

Although it was hoped that the theatre would recover some of the financial losses during the summer, the change in artistic policy, lack of marketing and bad publicity generated by the ongoing problems at the theatre contributed instead to the poor houses noted earlier. After a series of emergency meetings with Harrogate's respective funding bodies, it was decided that the theatre would have to close for at least six months from September 1986, entailing the loss of 50 jobs.

From September 1986 to March 1987, when the theatre went dark, the reality of the threat to its future was more forcefully brought home to both the local authorities and the town. While the authorities were unable to increase their levels of funding, a strong feeling of civic pride in Harrogate's history of more than 80 years of theatre meant they had no desire to see the playhouse permanently closed. The local community was realistic about the limited appeal repertory theatre would ever hold in a place like Harrogate – box office income had only exceeded 40 per cent of the theatre's revenue on four occasions since 1970. They were nevertheless encouraged by the show of public support that the closure of theatre generated.[7] The local papers were flooded with letters of protest at the closure decision, and the theatre itself received numerous donations and suggestions for fund-raising. As the administrator at the time of closing, Laidler, noted, 'When the theatre was open, no one wanted to know. You have to actually take it away to get people to care. At that point, they get very irate, and stamp their feet really loudly and shout 'mine', 'mine'!' (*Yorkshire Post* 1986).

Encouraged by this show of support, the collective funding bodies agreed to maintain funding to the theatre. Harrogate Borough Council, as owners of the building, provided the requisite

£175,000 for refurbishments, with an annual promise of a further £25,000 annually for maintenance, and increased their annual subsidy to £72,000. In the interim, a skeleton staff was kept on at the theatre to oversee the day-to-day running, plan a strategy for improving previous operations and spearhead the campaign to save the theatre and pay off its deficit.

Although a radical overhaul of the theatre's administration and policies included a much heavier emphasis on communicating with the local population in order to foster support, Manley emphasized that an almost accidental by-product of going dark was a new audience. Closure raised consciousness amongst the local community, and the 'Long Live Harrogate Theatre' appeal, led by the new chairman of the board, Carolyn Bayliss, actively brought the public into the theatre through a series of benefit activities such as plays, fashion shows, choral recitals, dance school competitions, the Antiques Road Show, gala dances, etc. As such, the town's people were able to support the theatre financially, and many found more incentive and opportunity for personal investment while the theatre was closed than they had when it was open. When it did reopen the following year, through their fund-raising efforts, a new cross-section of the local community now had a vested interest, and, for a short while at least, the problem of the dying audience was solved.

Notwithstanding the accidental discovery of a new audience, the theatre still took note of Yorkshire Arts' recommendation to hire a new marketing officer to increase box office figures. With an increased marketing budget, the new marketing officer was briefed on the need to communicate artistic policy to the local community in a way that was clearly informative and in looks and packaging directly addressed to modern sensibilities. As Manley commented, 'If you do a production called *A Man with Connections* and it's about Perestroika – which it was at the time – it does help if you put a picture of Gorbachev on the cover.'[8] Further incentive schemes were also introduced to encourage people back into the theatre, most notably the introduction of a 'Friends' of' club, the White Rose 500, which offered deals on theatre tickets, access to the venue for special occasions and the chance to help save the theatre for £100. Similarly, the theatre introduced a policy of 'access pricing' at this time, which, even with better attendances, was not considered likely to lose the theatre money given a continued surplus of empty seats. Meanwhile, there was a complete change in the board of directors. Recognition of the ongoing problems of the theatre, and the resistance to change that had prohibited the administration from successfully doing its job, meant that none of the old directors who stood for re-election were successful in their bid. Instead, there was a clear preference for younger, more open-minded individuals who presented a wider cross-section of backgrounds and tastes. As Manley explained, 'The previous members had put in a lot of service, no doubt about that. But the changes brought the average age of the representatives down by 25 years. Now we have a board in its 30s and 40s' (*Harrogate Advertiser* 1988).

With a new board, the artistic director found it considerably easier to change the artistic programming for the theatre. In consultation with the board and community, a new policy was created with the specific intention of at once satisfying Yorkshire Arts Association's criteria for subsidy and making the theatre accessible to the Harrogate community. An increased number of classics and foreign and experimental works took their place alongside the more familiar brand names, but there was a deliberate decision to present these in a more contemporary style and address them to 'the modern needs of a modern audience'.[9] So, for example, after the theatre reopened in April 1987, the first season included a production of *A School for Scandal* set against a backdrop of the contemporary goings-on in and around Whitehall, while a postmodern performance of *Cat on a Hot Tin Roof* was performed against a huge backdrop of Elizabeth Taylor as Maggie. Both board and artistic director acknowledged that such a contemporary style might not be to everyone's taste. But the conscious need to get away from 'safe, boring repertory that offends no-one, but pleases no-one either' (*Yorkshire Post* 1987), meant that the idea of a repertoire that, if not always easy, would at least be involving, engaging, thought provoking and of a high quality, was considered infinitely preferable.

* * *

The theatre spluttered its way through the decade following its temporary closure, maintaining average attendances of between 50 and 60 per cent. The limited income from the box office restricted the theatre's programme, particularly when combined with continued low levels of funding. As such, the length of the theatre's annual season and the size of its production output steadily diminished: initially, when it reopened in April 1987, it was as a repertory theatre with an eight-month season. It was closed during the summer months, except for occasional touring productions that could be taken in and when local amateur groups performed. While Manley acknowledged that using the building in this way reduced the theatre's overheads and was an effective means of keeping the local community in touch and invested in the theatre, he also noted that, from time to time, it had led to confusion over the true nature and quality of the repertory theatre itself. Over the years, continued low levels of subsidy caused the theatre to scale back its operation even further. By the time Manley left Harrogate in 1997, the theatre was only producing four plays a year and the post of artistic director had been reduced to a part-time, rather than a year-round, position.

At the same time, many of the theatre's socially oriented outreach programmes were sporadically reduced or temporarily stopped altogether in years when the box office showed signs of decline or funding was placed on standstill, as it was for three years between 1993 and 1996. In the decade from 1986, the theatre's TIE programme was threatened with closure on three separate occasions before being finally closed down in 1996.

But finally the pendulum began to swing the other way. A substantial increase in funding from Yorkshire and Humberside Arts Board awarded following the Arts Council Theatre Review in 2001, based on the recommendations of the Boyden Report, allowed Harrogate to start expanding its portfolio once again. In 2001, the extra funds restored the job of artistic director to a full-time, permanent position, with the theatre likewise moving to a year-round producing structure by 2004. From this time, the theatre increased its annual output to six repertory performances, taking in touring productions to flesh out the season. In 2001, it also introduced a new outreach and education department, which worked in the Harrogate district to develop new audiences and involve the rural community. It also nurtured a very popular youth theatre.

The year 2007 was especially successful for the Harrogate Theatre. Funding totalled £591,000 in grants from the Arts Council and the two local authorities, Harrogate Borough Council and North Yorkshire County Council; audiences were up, with attendance averaging 72 per cent; and in the first phase of a major refurbishment programme funded entirely by the public and Harrogate Borough Council, the theatre's auditorium and foyer were restored.

So it was with incredulity that the theatre learnt in December 2007, just days before Christmas, that the Arts Council intended to slash its grant to the playhouse from £410,000 in 2007 to £100,000 in 2008. Moreover, the bombshell fell after theatre executives had held what was reportedly an encouraging review session with Arts Council theatre officers in August, when they were told that a positive report would be forwarded to the Council regarding the growing financial strength and proposed artistic direction of the theatre. There was no mention of disinvestment in November, either, when Arts Council Yorkshire met with its funding partners, Harrogate Borough Council and North Yorkshire County Council.

The reason for the cut, according to the Arts Council, was a general decrease in the quality of the work produced at Harrogate. With five other strong producing houses in the area, it decided that Harrogate would operate better as a receiving house, taking in touring productions and not creating its own. In addition, the Council said, there were too many amateur productions and the Christmas pantomime ran for too long. Interestingly, when making this assertion, it did not present comparable statistics on other nearby theatres. At the West Yorkshire Playhouse, one of the 'big ten' regional theatres, the annual Christmas pantomime typically ran for three weeks longer than at Harrogate.

Jim Clark, chairman of the theatre board, was devastated. 'This is a massive setback and we will be appealing,' he said. 'We have achieved the targets set down by the Arts Council over two years ago. This included the magnificent restoration of the auditorium, increased audiences and more than 20,000 young people connecting with a theatre activity' (*Yorkshire Evening Post* 2007).

The appeal was only partially successful. The Arts Council decided to give Harrogate £150,000 rather than £100,000 for 2008/9, in recognition of its outreach work – which translated into a grant cut of 64 per cent rather than 75 per cent. Harrogate Theatre chief executive David Bown did not exactly fall over himself in gratitude. 'Our rural communities work is vital and it is not something that can be done on a budget of £50,000' (*Yorkshire Post* 2008), he commented.

The cuts so incensed local opinion that in a late-night debate in Parliament in March 2008 the Member of Parliament for Harrogate and Knaresborough, Liberal Democrat Phil Willis, urged the minister for culture, Margaret Hodge, to intervene 'to seek a sensible and negotiated outcome'. The Arts Council had presented 'a miscellany of concerns that were an insult to the building and the management of the theatre', he said.[10]

One 2007 production at Harrogate of which the Council had been particularly critical was *Look Back in Anger*, Willis said. The great anomaly was that this had been co-produced in partnership with two other companies; 'To add insult to injury, both Pilot Theatre and the Oldham Coliseum, which collaborated on the production, received funding increases from the Arts Council for their innovative productions.'[11]

Willis did not receive much relief from the minister. She could not challenge the Arts Council's decisions, she said, although she did concede that the Council might want to review the 2007 funding process and see if it could do better next time.

Back in Harrogate, the theatre took the cuts stoically. The 2008/9 programme continued as scheduled, with the second phase of refurbishment, again paid for wholly by Harrogate Borough Council and a supportive public, set to take place in the summer of 2008. But what will happen in 2009/10 and the years beyond is uncertain. 'The theatre will continue to explore ways to offer a vibrant artistic programme of drama, dance, music and comedy' (whatsonstage 2008), said Clark. But theatre executives have admitted that unless alternative sources of funding can be found, it is likely that both in-house productions and the theatre's outreach programme will be jeopardized.

Notes

1. Redundancies included five full-time staff, two part-time and all ten ushers.
2. Andrew Manley, artistic director, Harrogate Theatre, 1984–97, interview with the author, December 1995.
3. Manley, interview with the author, December 1995.
4. Manley interview, 1995.
5. Statistical information supplied by Harrogate Theatre.
6. Statistical information supplied by Harrogate Theatre.
7. A report made to Harrogate Borough Council's leisure services committee at this time estimated that the theatre's poor attendances meant that it was being subsidized at a rate of £3 per seat every night.
8. Manley, interview, 1995
9. Manley, interview, 1995.
10. Phil Willis, Member of Parliament for Knaresborough and Harrogate, House of Commons debates, 10 March 2008.
11. Willis, House of Commons debates, 10 March 2008.

PART FOUR: THE LEGACY

11

TONY'S COUNCIL: ARTFUL OR ARMLESS?

The heart of all our work is one central theme: national renewal. Britain rebuilt as one nation in which each citizen is valued and has a stake; in which no-one is excluded from opportunity and the chance to develop their potential; in which we make it, once more, our national purpose to tackle social division and inequality.[1]

In April 1997, a landslide election victory for New Labour under the leadership of Tony Blair ended eighteen years of Conservative rule, and promises of a new cultural policy brought hope for change amongst the country's regional theatres. The abrasive approach and individualistic ideologies that had characterized the enterprise culture of the previous government, and had such a devastating effect on the nation's playhouses, had also left a widespread feeling of demoralization across the country and a sense that Britain was now a fragmented society. In his work, *The Unprincipled Society*, the Labour MP and critic David Marquand had commented on this legacy of Thatcherism and asked, 'How can a fragmented society make itself whole? How can a culture permeated by possessive individualism restore the bonds of community?' (Marquand 1988: 11). These were the questions that Blair faced when he first arrived at 10 Downing Street. In setting out to find an answer, the new government designated culture as playing a key role.

New Labour had officially added the prefix 'new' to the party's title in the early 1990s. The intention was to distance the party from negative associations attached to its previous affiliation with socialism. That term conjured up images of high taxation, high inflation, a 'bust' rather than 'boom' economy and, not least, a dependency culture in which, in the popular mind, too many people lived on public handouts. New Labour in fact accepted many of the Thatcherite policies, particularly the emphasis on the market, privatization, low taxation and trade union reform. At the same time, they also retained a strong enough belief in ethical socialism for the party to wish to help directly the disenfranchised and protect the fundamental cornerstones of the welfare state. Under Blair, social democracy was recast to accommodate the changes brought about by Thatcherism, which meant that, in New Labour's terms, economic efficiency and social justice were combined as central goals. These ideals were constructed into a new ideology, 'the third way', at the heart of which was the concern to rebuild a new, economically competitive nation with a much more compassionate ethos:

> Our task today is not to fight old battles but to show that there is a third way, a way of marrying together an open, competitive and successful economy with a just, decent and humane society.[2]

The key to building this new society was, in what became a well-known mantra during Blair's first few years in government, 'education, education, education'.

Culture was at the heart of the party's mission to re-educate the nation. New Labour's notorious adoption of traditional media techniques, and employment of powerful 'spin doctors' to control and promote the government's image, testified to their appreciation of the influence culture could wield if used in an effective way. Under Blair, the arts were identified as a powerful tool for realizing the government's objectives of an enterprise culture and social inclusion, offering a possible route to forge community identity, draw people together and overcome isolation and rejection. As such, they were afforded a far more prominent position on New Labour's political agenda than they had achieved under the Conservatives. During the leadership of Labour's first culture secretary, Chris Smith, the Department of Heritage was allocated wider responsibilities and powers and, in line with New Labour's concern for national renewal, a new name: the Department for Culture, Media and Sport (DCMS).

Accompanying the new position afforded the arts, DCMS outlined a set of fresh objectives that focused on wider access, excellence and innovation, educational opportunities and the fostering of creative industries. In response to the years of ambiguity, financial hardships and obstructive bureaucracy, Smith also promised a lateral restructuring of public bodies that would present a more united, coordinated and efficient system of funding. He described this in his book *Creative Britain* as having 'joined-up government in cultural areas' (Smith 1998: 43). Most importantly, appropriate to the elevated position of culture, New Labour promised increased financial support for the arts. These changes appeared to indicate a major sea change in cultural policy and with it the possibility of some relief from the pressures contributing to the crisis regional theatres had been experiencing. Despite such changes, early government legislation not only undermined such optimism, but pointed to a continuation of the problems that had dogged the arts community for decades.

Initially, the higher profile being attached to the arts did not automatically translate into increased government subvention. New Labour's commitment to reduce public expenditure and maintain low levels of income tax meant a commitment to construct their 1997/8 budget within the spending limits set by the previous Conservative government. Consequently, the first year of the new administration saw a reduction in annual grant-aid, only the fourth actual cut in government support to the arts in the history of public subsidy. 1998 subsequently saw the temporary closures of Liverpool Playhouse, the Theatre Royal, Stratford East, the Old Vic and Greenwich Theatre, while Ipswich's Wolsey Theatre closed temporarily in 1999. Although New Labour's arts subvention in 1998/9 offered a substantial increase on the previous budget, the promised rise of £125 million over the course of three years would still leave state support for the arts below 1990 levels. And increased funding came with strings attached. The government emphasized that cultural policy should be used to develop their key political objectives and made it clear that they viewed their contribution to the cultural economy as an investment on which they expected to see a return. Under these circumstances, the Arts Council was expected to demonstrate how arts organizations were contributing to the government's political, social and economic objectives, and DCMS emphasized that it would be developing a much clearer and more exacting funding agreement with the national funding body. Such actions not only undermined early promises of a decreased administrative burden, but also indicated that the invidious question of a politicized culture was no nearer to being solved. They also prompted a new surge of questions from politicians, the arts community and the press about the arm's length principle and the role and purpose of the Arts Council.

If New Labour's actions in the early years of their administration did not inspire confidence within the arts community, new legislation reducing the revenue generated for the arts by the National Lottery made the situation increasingly complicated. For years before the Lottery Act was passed by Parliament in 1994, the introduction of a national lottery had been fiercely resisted by the arts community out of concern that the government might try to shift responsibility for funding away from the Treasury. Following years of below-inflation rises in annual support for the arts, such fears were most dramatically realized in the related resignation of Gowrie as chairman of the Arts Council following New Labour's first budget in 1998. The potential ramifications of this threat were compounded when a second National Lottery Act in 1998 allowed the government to divert lottery funds previously designated for the arts into a newly created 'sixth good cause'. Shortly after Blair's 1997 statement, 'We don't believe it would be right to use lottery money to pay for things which are the government's responsibilities', Smith publicly spoke of the government's desire that Exchequer and lottery grants should 'sit side by side and complement each other'. With the introduction of the 'New Opportunities Fund', the principle of additionality, whereby lottery resources were not supposed to be used by ministers to replace government spending, was, to all intents and purposes, dead.

Despite previous reassurances from all political parties that the National Lottery would not become a 'stealth tax' and be used to support core government spending programmes, the controversial creation of the New Opportunities Fund allowed lottery money to fund innovative projects in line with the government priorities of education, health and the environment. This fund was initially allocated 13 per cent of all money generated by the lottery for the 'good causes', but that figure increased to 60 per cent by the millennium. Meanwhile, the proportion of money going to the original 'five good causes', the arts among them, fell from 16 to 5 per cent. This reduction was particularly keenly felt by the arts community, as a significant decline in lottery receipts at the end of the millennium indicated that the era of huge grants was over.

At the same time, the consequences of limiting revenue from lottery grants to capital projects, was becoming more and more apparent.

Across the country, the benefits of lottery funding for theatre buildings were increasingly visible, but this visibility equally served to underline the disparity between beneficiaries and theatres that had not received assistance from capital grants. Those theatres in receipt of capital grants, meanwhile, rarely saw any change to their revenue funding, and few anticipated the increased running costs such modern or enlarged buildings would require. This situation ensured that views such as those expressed by Peter Longman, the chairman of the Theatres Trust, became commonplace. He blamed the lottery for the creation of a series of 'white elephants that should never have been started, vastly over-elaborate refurbishments, schemes that cannot be completed unless more money is produced, and buildings that cost more to run than anticipated'.[3] Recognition of the validity of his argument, that 'rarely, if ever, in the arts has so much money and effort been wasted' as in the case of the National Lottery, led to the introduction of a new Arts for Everyone scheme in 1997.[4] The policy allowed arts organizations, professional and amateur, to apply for lottery funds of up to £500,000 on a 'new projects' basis. Proceeds could thus be used for revenue funding. However, the haste with which the new policy was enacted ensured that the scheme was widely considered to be a disaster, costing far more to administer than it generated.

One of the major grievances aired by struggling theatres under the Conservatives had been the constant waste of precious resources diverted to cover the increasing administrative burden required by the pressures of attracting sponsorship and functioning in the marketplace. While the changes in lottery funding under Labour offered potential new avenues of revenue, they only served to aggravate this problem. Specifically, the application process was administratively substantial, but offered no guidelines. Many theatres found themselves devoting considerable amounts of time and energy they felt should have been spent marketing the theatres themselves in tendering bids to the National Lottery. As theatre director Dominic Dromgoole said:

> The lottery created an enormous development industry. Whenever you made a lottery pitch or got a lottery grant, you had to create an enormous development department within your organisation to find matching funding, and they became as significant and powerful as any other player within the arts organisation. They haven't gone away. They are still there looking for money and parties and sponsorship from Vanity Fair, and looking to create excitement around buildings which has got nothing to do with what is put on there. The art tends to get less and less priority as these administrators and bureaucrats mushroom.
>
> (Moss 2004)

Many practitioners were equally vocal about the large sums of Arts Council money, often running into tens of thousands, used to prepare feasibility studies for lottery bids they felt would have been better spent on supporting the theatres. Successful applicants were in the minority, and those regional theatres that did succeed often found that the size of the grant was substantially smaller than the amount spent on the application.

Such events inevitably meant that there was scant relief from the crisis afflicting regional theatres before the end of the millennium. As Longman said, '[it is] ironic that, nearly three years into a life of a new government, and in spite of the lottery, the theatre faces a greater crisis of confidence than at any time since the War' (Moss 2004). In 1999, the accumulated deficit of England's regional producing theatres alone was estimated at £4.4 million, with forecasts indicating a substantial increase in the years ahead. And as the Arts Council emphasized, this figure would have been substantially higher except for the fact that a significant 'one-off' windfall of National Insurance rebates had coincided with new legislation concerning the lottery that allowed one-off 'stabilization grants' to be used to help theatres such as Birmingham Repertory Theatre wipe out its debts. With surveys by the Target Group Index conducted the same year indicating that national attendance at plays was at the lowest levels ever recorded, at the end of the century there appeared little on the horizon to relieve the gloom for the country's regional theatres.

Despite its concern over the continuing burden of administration, by this time the situation had become so serious that Arts Council England felt impelled to hire independent consultants Peter Boyden Associates to examine the situation. Following a series of assessments of 45 theatres, a report on *The Roles and Functions of the English Regional Producing Theatres* was published in May 2000 confirming the ongoing crisis in regional theatres and emphasizing that they had been inadequately funded since the early 1980s. The report confirmed that 30 of the total producing companies interviewed were operating with a deficit. According to Boyden, in actuality the situation was even worse than this: when lottery money was taken out of the equation, many more were technically insolvent, based on the fact that their net liabilities exceeded their net assets. The report emphasized that without outside help, most had no realistic hope of clearing these debts.

Citing the consequences for regional theatres – becoming inward looking, territorial, producing poor work and unattractive working conditions, and creating a consequent drain away from theatre on talent and audiences – the report emphasized the importance of the provincial producing houses as one of the country's most vital art forms, and as theatres that should be celebrated by all for their regional distinctiveness and international excellence. The Boyden Report estimated that an extra £25 million, accompanied by a complete overhaul in both the operations and funding mechanisms that characterized regional theatre, would have to be forthcoming were the producing houses to have a future.

The Boyden Report heralded what was perhaps the first genuine ray of hope for the collective body of England's regional playhouses in twenty years. Building on the positive turn marked by the government's pledge in the 2000 Comprehensive Spending Review to increase Arts Council funding from £252 million to £337 million over the subsequent three years, it was published alongside Arts Council England's own theatre review, *The Next Stage*, which considered the future of the English theatre sector as a whole. The findings of the report were the basis on which an extra £25 million was promised by the government in 2001. Together, *The Next Stage* and the Boyden Report were also the motivation for the Arts Council's creation, in 2001, of a National Policy for Theatre in England, the first time a national policy for drama had been drawn up. After years of financial struggles and ambiguity, such events generated genuine optimism, in England at least, that regional theatres' debts could be wiped out and that playhouses would subsequently be funded in three-year cycles at levels that would allow them to carry out effectively the activities prescribed in the now defined requirements for subsidy.

Inevitably, the situation was not as simple as that. While many English regional theatres received a substantial raise in their annual grant, others found themselves excluded from the list of recipients, with the Arts Council once again offering no explanation for its decisions. Certain of these theatres, such as the Swan Theatre in Worcester and Westcliff Palace Theatre in Essex, subsequently closed. The remainder of the country's theatres, while buoyed by the raise, were equally galled by the fact that one-third of funding specifically awarded by the government to save the provincial producing houses was allocated to other theatre sectors. Nor were there any benefits for producing houses in Scotland or Wales. Following the division of the Arts Council of Great Britain in 1994, responsibility for these had been completely delegated to the Scottish Arts Council and the Arts Council of Wales. They ran their own affairs in relation to arts funding and received money through, respectively, the Scottish Executive and, from 1999, the Welsh Assembly. Given that there was no equivalent review conducted in either country at this time, the theatres continued to struggle in the face of the ongoing problems of the previous decades. In addition, they were now subject to the priorities of their specific funding bodies, which brought further concerns into the equation.

Despite initial excitement at the opportunities that might be afforded by devolution, the bonus to the English regional theatres brought the ongoing problems in Scotland into sharp relief. Following devolution, there was increasing disenchantment across the sector at the Scottish Executive's failure to invest in its theatres, despite their considerable record of artistic success. This feeling was particularly acute with regard to the large sums earmarked for a Scottish National Theatre, the realization of which was repeatedly stalled. Resentment equally stemmed from the constant flow of money seemingly needed to shore up the Scottish Opera and Scottish Ballet, which, in a situation reminiscent of the Arts Council of Great Britain's historical dealings with Covent Garden and the Royal Opera House, appeared to claim a disproportionate and ever-increasing share of available funds. In 2001, the situation had degenerated to such a level that the Federation of Scottish Theatres made a plea for an additional £3 million to support existing theatres at current levels. It received £1.1 million. There was no improvement on the position in 2002, when the Scottish Arts Council was told to expect standstill funding the following year, with only minor increases in the years following that.

Noting what was happening south of the border, Heather Baird, director of the Federation of Scottish Theatres, felt compelled to comment:

> If we were still part of the system which receives money from Westminster we would be in a better position because we would be funded on the same basis as provincial theatres in England. Now we're being hit by the same increases in costs, but we haven't had the investment.
>
> (*Scotsman* 2002)

As theatres in Scotland continued lurching from one crisis to another, by 2003 even the bullish chairman of the Scottish Arts Council, James Boyle, admitted that theatres were only producing half the work they had done in 1990. Under such circumstances, an inevitable by-product of the extra support for the English theatres was an increasing drain on talented Scottish practitioners who left to take up more lucrative positions in the neighbouring country. On resigning from Dundee Rep to take over the post of artistic director at Coventry's Belgrade Theatre in 2003, Hamish Glen noted that the different circumstances made it an easy choice: 'At Dundee, despite great council support, we had only £600,000 to play with. At the Belgrade I have £2m a year and another £5m to create a new studio space. Since devolution it has been like getting blood out of a stone' (Gibbons 2003).

Ultimately, the Scottish National Theatre was finally launched in 2006, and while Scottish regional theatres continued to struggle financially, the National Theatre in many ways breathed a renewed sense of vitality and cohesiveness into the national scene. With the increased recognition it brought to the importance of cultural life in the country and, with it, a boost in funding, an important part of its success came from the fact that it functioned not as a company or a building, but rather a commissioning body that worked through Scotland's existing network of major companies to commission work and showcase the best of Scottish-made theatre to the nation and the world.

Theatres in Wales experienced worse hardships, with English-language companies particularly hard hit. Perhaps because, as the Scottish theatre critic Joyce Macmillan suggested, 'we are probably dealing in both countries with a culture to which theatre has traditionally been marginal, perhaps seen as an art-form in which England excels' (Macmillan 2004), in Wales, theatre was not given the same weight as what were regarded as traditionally national forms of culture such as storytelling, poetry, music or song. If true, this might explain why, in the years following devolution, the Arts Council of Wales provided additional funds to establish a Welsh-language national theatre company and put young people's theatre on a firm footing, while making very little provision for the English-language form. By 2003, with only a handful of producing theatres left, all of which were struggling to survive, the situation had deteriorated to such a degree that Peter Boyden was called in to assess the situation. His findings were gloomy at best, noting that an inevitable side effect of the alarming drop in range and volume of production was a substantial drain of practitioners who couldn't find work in the field, lost opportunities to develop creative talent and dwindling audiences. And the three producing theatres that continued operating in Wales – Clwyd Theatr Cymru in Mold, the Sherman Theatre in Cardiff and Torch Theatre at Milford Haven – were stifled by a lack of resources to the extent that they couldn't cope with demand for a product now in short supply or even make the most of existing operations.

Back in England, meanwhile, new levels of funding and a new national policy inevitably brought with them added demands. In particular, the national policy clearly reflected New Labour's own ideas about the function of art, identifying eight priorities for the theatres. These included offering a better range of high-quality work, the need to attract more people from a wider sector of society, diversity and inclusion within the workforce as well as audience, developing new ways of working, establishing an international reputation, ensuring an emphasis on education and, last but not least, maintaining their regional distinctiveness.

Despite Blair's early claim that 'the arts should be supported by government for their intrinsic merit', New Labour quickly became more and more blatant about its perception of the arts as tools for the implementation of social policy and creative enterprise. Shortly after arriving in Downing Street, Blair commented:

> For too long, arts and culture have stood outside the mainstream, their potential unrecognised in government. That has to change, and under Labour it will...in the 21st century, we are going to see the world increasingly influenced by innovation and creative minds. Our future depends on our creativity.
>
> (Mitchell 2001)

Art, he continued, had the task of recreating a sense of community, identity and civic pride.

Labour saw the arts as vital instruments in the transformation of Britain into a multicultural utopian enterprise culture. The creativity to which Blair referred in his speech was something that could be presented to businesses and managers as the way to foster necessary skills in entrepreneurial innovation. For the big corporations, the arts were emphasized as core to productivity in a post-industrial Britain that operated less as a manufacturing economy than an 'economy of the imagination'. In the meantime, major new cultural buildings such as the Lowry Centre in Salford, or the BALTIC Centre for Contemporary Art in Gateshead, could be highlighted to town planners and local authorities as key to regenerating former industrial towns. And in the areas of health care, education and the judicial system, creativity through the arts could be used to combat issues of social exclusion and valued in terms of the possibilities they offered for boosting people's self-esteem, raising morale and empowering individuals. In other words, the role of artists was to help the government deliver ministers' policies. At a seminar entitled 'Can Policy Be Artist-Led?' in 2007, government adviser John Holden noted, 'the world has changed...governments have difficulty trying to engage with the public. They're very good at engaging with business, with big organizations, but they're very bad at engaging with individuals.'[5] For Labour, the arts provided the vehicle to address this problem. As such, those working in the state-funded arts sector were expected to fit their work around the government's agenda.

Following Blair's famous hobnobbing with celebrities from the world of entertainment at Number 10, Britpop sensations Oasis and Blur among them, the first clear move in New Labour's plans to make the arts a creature of government came in 1998 when Smith appointed Gerry Robinson to succeed Gowrie as chair of the Arts Council. A public supporter of Blair, the Granada chairman had previously ignored broadcasting directives on political impartiality to participate in a Labour Party Election broadcast, and many saw the prestigious role of Arts Council chair as his reward. Robinson was a shrewd businessman under whose leadership Granada had become the most commercially successful broadcasting organization in the country, and his appointment served as a good illustration of New Labour's identification of the arts with the creative industries. Based on his dealings at Granada, Robinson was also someone who could be trusted to carry out government policies at the Arts Council. Not long after he arrived in Great Peter Street, the new Arts Council headquarters, Robinson duly launched what he called a 'national debate on the arts', putting all grant recipients on financial notice and warning that they would be closely watched in the coming years. Any 'tired practices' would be rooted out and bad management would not be tolerated. By way of providing a lesson to any would-be dissidents, Robinson ensured there would be little argument from his own staff by starting his tenure as Arts Council chair with the appointment of three new managers to look after the newly defined areas of policy and arts, finance and operations, and public affairs. He also sacked most of the 23-strong council, whom one new appointee referred to as 'old men in suits', and reduced the newly created team to a more manageable, financially stringent and streamlined ten. His own appointment prompted scathing attacks by the press. Citing Robinson's ruthless dealings at Granada, *Times* columnist Richard Morrison commented, 'True, many people feel that the Arts Council needs a good shake-up. Whether it needs to be purged, downsized, gutted, rationalised and hung out to dry is another matter' (Morrison 1998).

Robinson's appointment was followed in quick succession by the introduction of a series of measures that would facilitate and reflect the Arts Council's change in direction in line with the government emphasis on advocacy. Guidelines for worthy projects emphasized a clear social function: giving children the opportunity to interface with professional actors; making the arts an integral part of health care; putting the arts at the centre of urban renewal; showing greater commitment to cultural diversity. At the same time, the Arts Council launched a series of initiatives to encourage such practices. In 2001 for instance, it was responsible for organizing the Eclipse conference to discuss ways the theatre industry might develop strategies to combat racism in theatre. In addition to increased pressure on all client theatres to re-examine the diversity of their staffing and adopt policies such as colour-blind casting, the conference resulted in an added incentive to follow Arts Council policy: the Eclipse Award has since become a regular fixture at the annual Theatre Management Association awards ceremony. It is given out alongside awards for best director and best new play to the theatre recognized as having made the most outstanding contribution to cultural diversity that year.

For regional theatres, the effects of this shift in emphasis were manifold. The need to address the areas of access, education and diversity while following the National Policy directives on excellence and innovation meant a return to many of the contradictions of programming experienced under Harold Wilson. Once again, subsidized theatres found themselves pressured to reassess their artistic policies and present high quality programmes that would have mass appeal and bring in new audiences while still retaining the old. It also required they re-examine the diversity of their staffing and ensure that their buildings were accessible to all, something that could entail expensive modifications to often dilapidated buildings. Given that the increase in financial support following the Boyden Report only brought government spending on the arts back to 1993 levels, companies were not necessarily in a position to address such a vast array of requirements, and it by no means meant an end to the theatres' financial difficulties.

The problems experienced by Leicester Haymarket are a case in point. In 2000, the theatre introduced the 'New Audiences Development' scheme to meet the needs of the Asian community in Leicester, as identified by the ' NATAK' Asian Theatre initiative. In addition to bringing in Kully Tiaira as co-artistic director alongside Paul Kerryson, the first Asian to fill this role in a British regional theatre, the programme included a new transport subsidy scheme, targeted to reach a broader range of new audiences, and an integrated audience development programme based around a diverse season of programming at the Haymarket. Ticket subsidies were offered for target audiences. Additional outreach projects and community networking around individual productions such as *Bali – the Sacrifice* also specifically focused on the Asian community. While substantial strides were made in attracting audiences from this group, other sectors of the community felt alienated. Angry letters to the local paper variously complained of 'the ludicrously PC Asian theme that alienates everybody not from Bangladesh. And the namby-pamby programming policy that serves less to satisfy a local audience than to promote a particular sexual orientation' (Smith 2003). And while such comments might fairly be said to be representative of the feelings of the Haymarket's older, loyal audience, the specific targeting of one particular minority group was recognized as perpetuating a sense of marginalization both within that community and in others. As box office figures fell, consultants brought in to assess the situation in 2003 noted:

> While it is important to be proactive in targeting communities that do not usually engage with the theatre, a reductive approach that targets Asian communities exclusively with Asian work is limiting at best, damaging at worst. The work is distinct and so are the audiences, distinguishing 'Asian' audiences from the other diverse communities of Leicester, perpetuating a sense of marginalisation and otherness, failing to encourage cross over and dialogue between the diverse communities.
> (J. Wilson Associates 2002)

By 2003, the Haymarket was riddled with debts totalling £450,000, a sum one official from the Broadcast Entertainment, Cinematograph and Theatre Union (BECTU) cannily pointed out as being almost identical to the theatre's overestimate of budgeted box office income for the previous financial year. On top of claims that the Haymarket had never had sufficient resources to mount such initiatives in the first place, the theatre's problems were exacerbated by a strike amongst theatre workers, the majority of whom BECTU claimed were paid less than levels acknowledged by the Low Pay Unit and the Council of Europe as poverty pay. Adding insult to injury, that same year, Leicester County Council withdrew its entire grant of £100,000 on the grounds that the theatre was the exclusive responsibility of the City Council. In July 2003, the Haymarket was forced to temporarily close its doors and 60 staff were made redundant.

Despite attempts to increase efficiency and reduce bureaucracy, a widespread managerial obsession with social inclusion, and an equally onerous government obsession with what became known as 'targetology', meant the excessive administrative machine that theatres had been forced to adopt under the Tories was now replaced by the equally onerous burden of collecting data and constantly proving how far artistic programmes were driven by advocacy. Over the course of New Labour's first two terms, there was a noticeable rise of corporate jargon in the government's spin on arts funding; the intrinsic value of the arts was increasingly sidelined as the government demanded 'value for money' that could be measured in terms of 'tangible benefits to stakeholders'. In response to Labour's call for such evidence-based policy, the Arts Council increasingly demanded that all projects be evaluated in terms of 'measurable success factors' to determine the accomplishments of organizations in which they had made an investment. While taking up vital funds many felt could better have been spent elsewhere, the resulting tick-box culture inevitably also had a profound effect on programming.

A question that increasingly dogged arts funding over the course of New Labour's incumbency concerned the effects of the government's politically correct attitude towards the arts, bringing the perennial debate between high art and social art once again into the foreground. For the first ten years under New Labour, the official line from the Arts Council was that there was no conflict between these two agendas. As Christopher Frayling, Robinson's successor as Arts Council chair, noted in 2004, 'I can't bear the thought that the artistic experience is somehow diminished if everyone can have access to it. Maybe it's because of my provenance, coming through art schools – I was once called professor of the sort of art you lean against. Some people see me as the enemy: I like opening doors, I like building bridges between high art and people's everyday experience' (Moss 2004). Many disagreed, and the concern that democratization was leading to a culture of mediocrity became increasingly widespread.

In his book *Where Have All the Intellectuals Gone?*, sociologist Frank Furedi wrote, 'We want democratic participation in the arts, but that should be a reaction to the art, not a premise for it. The arts have become an appendage to the political agenda and we need to create more distance between the Arts Council and the people who produce the arts; otherwise we will get dull art' (Moss 2004). The Millennium Dome has often been held up as the most extreme manifestation of New Labour's cultural vision and as evidence of such problems. At a cost of almost £1 billion, the government's cultural showpiece was so mired in New Labour rhetoric, and so lacking in artistic vision, that it only attracted half the forecast number of visitors. The same flaws also afflicted regional theatres. Under pressure to make advocacy central to their artistic programmes, many discovered that diversity and education did not always go hand-in-hand with high quality or appealing work.

Even with increased subvention, many theatres were unable to reconcile the often conflicting requirements they continued to face. And the creation of a national policy did not necessarily clarify what was expected. Terms such as 'high quality', for example, remained undefined. In practice, the Arts Council emphasis on new work, access and diversity meant a move away from the text-based classics to more trendy recent works that specifically addressed current issues, or extended beyond the traditional parameters of the text and proscenium. Alliances with street performance, circus arts, multi-media productions and site-specific ventures ticked many of the desired boxes. But for the same reasons, particularly when the educational imperative was added into the mix, the new emphasis was also widely seen in terms of the dumbing down of interpretation and over-intrusive, simplistic and preachy labelling. Under these conditions, retaining the old audience while appealing to the new, advocating creativity while ensuring social inclusion, and juggling the multiple and various demands of the partner funding bodies proved too much for some theatres. And rather than encouraging good management practices, such demands often created an intolerable strain for staff. The case of Basingstoke Haymarket provides a good example.

Responding to the Arts Council's directives to introduce a more innovative programme that would reach wider audiences, in 2003 Haymarket theatre director Alasdair Ramsay presented an ambitious series of international drama seasons with French, Russian and Irish themes. The programme saw a 10 per cent rise in new audience members at Basingstoke, but the long-term loyalty of this new group was questionable and by no means offset the loss in regular subscribers, who dropped by 15 per cent that same season. Within just six months, the Haymarket was boasting a deficit of £143,000, and, on the advice of consultants, the board of directors instigated a major reorganization of senior management to address the financial crisis. Although Ramsay was subsequently offered the role of artistic director within the reshuffle, he refused the position. In particular, he was unhappy with the fact that the role would be secondary to that of the chief executive, a position the board was concerned should sit at the apex of the hierarchy to ensure the theatre would prioritize administration and finances. The reorganization went entirely contrary to Ramsay's own feelings, and he expressed resentment at what he referred to as 'inhumane' treatment by the trustees. Despite the subsequent resignation of board chairman David Smith, the tensions between board and management escalated to such a degree that Ramsay subsequently took the Haymarket Theatre Trust to an employment tribunal on the grounds of unfair dismissal. Crediting the theatre's problems to 'the seemingly irreconcilable tension between the funders, board, staff, volunteers and audiences as to what the Haymarket should be', he explained his own programming ideas by asking, 'Should it be an exciting, challenging, risk-taking and live-producing theatre, or a purveyor of easy-listening "entertainment" which we are told the people of Basingstoke supposedly want and which appears to offer more financial security?' Ramsay went on to say, 'My dismissal, I believe, was purely a means of certain members of the board wanting to abandon the three-year programme of international plays they had collectively signed up for only six months before. In order to do this, they had to get rid of me' (*Hampshire Gazette* 2005).

Evidence of just how far relations between senior management and the board of directors had deteriorated became apparent with the disclosure of various e-mails concerning Ramsay. One, from the then chair of the board, Catherine Hopkins, openly criticized Ramsay, saying, 'Secretly, I'm hoping he takes all this rope and hangs himself.' Although Ramsay was unsuccessful in his case, the continuing tensions and consequent bad press, which saw the board try to self-impose a gagging order to prevent internal divisions from being leaked, ensured the theatre's problems could only get worse. In particular, they attracted increased attention from Arts Council England South East (ACESE). If concerned by the in-fighting their own policies had precipitated, ACESE were equally disturbed by the Haymarket's return to a programme of safe, more traditional repertory, which in 2005 included productions of *Emma*, *The Wind in the Willows*, *Shirley Valentine* and *Hamlet*.

The board of directors were possibly correct in their assumption that this was what local audiences wanted. The 2004/5 season set new box office records, with audiences increasing by 15 per cent and performances up 10 per cent, allowing the theatre to halve the inherited debt by turning its annual trading deficit of £75,000 around to produce a net profit of £55,000. Notwithstanding, in January 2006, ACESE announced the withdrawal of their entire £250,000 grant to Basingstoke. In their report, they said, '[the Haymarket is] old fashioned, unexciting and provincial [and] trying to recreate a golden age of regional repertory theatre but is in danger of ending up with a parochial repertory' (ACESE 2006). With Basingstoke and Deane Borough Council unable to make up the shortfall, the theatre was forced to cease trading as a producing theatre in 2006.

One of the eight criteria informing the National Policy was an emphasis on retaining individual theatres' regional distinctiveness. In other words, theatres should not only express their own character, but speak to their specific community. But, despite the fact that there was no official hierarchy in the National Policy's criteria, this concern was constantly relegated in the interests of diversity and access. On occasion, the funding body's quest for democratization even extended to a rejection of the very word 'arts'. As Peter Hewitt, Arts Council chief executive 1998–2007, said, 'It is associated with a narrow definition of the arts. Too many people still think of the arts either as the visual arts or as certain kinds of arts that take place in posh places' (Moss 2004). So pervasive had these emphases become that in 2008, responding to the withdrawal of Arts Council funding from a small theatre in a predominantly white middle-class area, the *Sunday Times* columnist Jeremy Clarkson felt compelled to write an article entitled, 'It seems it ain't art if it ain't ethnic'. As he saw it, the problem in Chipping Norton was that

> plans for 2008 include a play about space travel, devised by Niki McCretton, who I'm afraid is white. Then there's a tribute to Abba, who were a very popular Swedish pop group featuring no disabled Bangladeshis, and a talk by Arabella Weir, who is the daughter of a notable diplomat. You can see immediately why none of this fits in with the Arts Council's "agenda". And I'm afraid the concert planned for next Saturday doesn't work either. Yes, the pianist, Hélène Tysman, is foreign, which is good, but I'm afraid she's only French. And that's hopeless because they had an empire too, the bastards. What the management should be doing to maintain its grip on the Arts Council's funding is hosting a celebration of haiku poetry, in silence, by the Al Gore polar-bear workers' collective. Of course nobody would come, but hey – serving the needs of the area? Since when did that ever matter?
>
> (Clarkson 2008)

In practice, Arts Council policy left little room for regional theatres to present programmes that reflected their communities if those communities did not fit the Arts Council's own definition of a diverse, multicultural nation. Similar to their dealings with Basingstoke, the funding body's decision in 2007 to respectively withdraw and reduce funding to the Yvonne Arnaud and Harrogate theatres was heavily influenced by the concern that the theatres were presenting old-fashioned, safe, elitist repertory. But in each case, as the theatres themselves argued, such programming reflected the predominant tastes of their community, and a significant change risked seriously alienating the loyal audience without necessarily presenting an alternative one to target. In the case of Harrogate, which had attempted to develop its programming in line with the changing emphasis from Great Peter Street, the Arts Council's decision appeared to hinge on just one production – a period proscenium performance of *Look Back in Anger*. Interestingly, this was a co-production with Oldham Coliseum and touring company Pilot Theatre. At the time Harrogate saw the majority of funding removed, both of these companies were simultaneously given boosts to their grants based on their innovative work.

It is also worth noting here that as the Arts Council developed a track record of withdrawing funding from theatres with old-fashioned or safe programmes, even when they were successfully filling auditoriums, equally it became something of a pattern to bail out theatres that were clearly following its directives but steadily losing money. In 2004, after being dark for a year, Leicester Haymarket, one of the Arts Council's flagship theatres, was rescued from its sizeable debts by a package to the tune of £1.3 million. After reopening, the theatre's artistic policy was altered somewhat to address the issues made by the consultants. The new programme, however, focused mainly on community and outreach work, and translated less into improving the number of bums on seats, particularly in the main auditorium. When one critic put it to chief executive Mandy Stewart that this should be an important consideration in ensuring the theatre's success, Stewart responded,

> What needs to be successful is the array of theatre. It's really important as we move our journey towards our brand new theatre in Leicester that we're able to go to all sorts of places to meet all sorts of people to perform theatre...it's really important in that context that occasionally the Haymarket Theatre stage and the Haymarket Studio stage can be open to the public. But if theatre is only up those steps or through that car park into the old Haymarket theatre, it's not going to connect enough with the people of Leicester and Leicestershire. So the journey is about broadening out the way in which theatre is produced and presented across our area.
> (British Theatre Guide 2004)

Since then, despite continuing problems with the Haymarket's box office, which saw the theatre back in debt and its doors temporarily closed once again in January 2007, the Arts Council has contributed £12 million to the theatre's new home, a state-of-the-art Performing Arts Centre on Rutland Street in the city's new cultural quarter.

The year 2007, in fact, proved a watershed for many theatres. The Chester Gateway went dark the same month as Leicester Haymarket. And in July, the board of Bristol Old Vic, the country's oldest continuously running theatre, announced that the venue would close, ostensibly for 'refurbishment'. The abruptness of the announcement indicated there was probably more to it than that. The announcement came on the back of a year marked by artistic and financial problems, followed years of difficulties with the theatre's various funding partners and was made after an autumn season of high-profile performances, including a production of *Ivanov* directed by Kenneth Branagh and a visit by Kneehigh theatre company, had been scheduled. The resignation of artistic director Simon Reade, whose position was subsequently left unfilled, fuelled concerns that the future looked bleak for the Old Vic. Meanwhile, in December, staff at Derby Playhouse were shocked to discover that Derby City Council had refused to advance a funding grant due in January. In consequence, the theatre was forced into liquidation just one day after the opening night of *Treasure Island*, its Christmas show. Almost simultaneously, the Northcott Theatre in Exeter, which had been closed for refurbishment for much of the year following a long period of falling attendances, reopened in December only to discover that the Arts Council proposed cutting its entire budget from the beginning of the following financial year.

Although the creation of a national policy, and increased funding in 2001, had indicated a more positive turn in the regional theatres' history, they also led to further complications in the perennially uneasy relationship between the funding bodies. The creation of the DCMS raised the profile of the arts and afforded it a clearer role in the re-building of a new Britain, but the extensive control exercised by central government caused accusations of impotence to be increasingly levelled at the Arts Council. The national funding body inevitably therefore looked for a new way to reassert its position. In the same month that increased financial support for regional theatres was announced following the Boyden Report, the Arts Council initiated yet another restructuring of the funding system. Only seven years after the costly policy of devolution to the regional arts boards had been completed in 1994, reducing the powers and responsibilities of the Arts Council, the new buzzwords of 'streamlining' and 'integration' translated into further reorganization. In March 2001, the Arts Council published *The Prospectus for Change*, outlining plans to merge the country's ten regional arts boards to create a single funding body. It proposed changing the regional arts boards from independent bodies that reported to the national funding organization to regional arms of the Arts Council that were effectively nothing more than subsidiary branches. In other words, it was a reversion to the days of the regional offices dissolved by Williams in the 1950s.

Following the government's mantra of cost-cutting and efficiency, the Arts Council presented restructuring as a means of reducing bureaucracy and of introducing a coordinated national policy. Robinson also put forward the argument that a single organization was better placed to make a case for funding to central government. Even so, the restructure was costly to implement and took the main funds, and powers of decision making, back to the centre, in line with the Arts Council's perceived metropolitan bias. Proud of having built up distinctive and accountable regionalism, the regional arts boards were outraged by this 'unilateral attempt to remove local responsibility from the arts funding system'.[6] Not least, they were particularly wounded by the high-handed manner in which it was conducted. In the spirit of tradition, the decision to reorganize was exclusively the Arts Council's, taken without consultation and conducted as a 'sort of dawn raid more familiar to the City':

> It was a surprise when, in mid-March, the Arts Council announced its plan to abolish all 10 regional arts boards by the end of April. The plans were sprung on the world and politicians without prior consultation. Whatever the chairman, Gerry Robinson, and his chief executive, Peter Hewitt, had in mind, they have disastrously mishandled their plan.[7]

Designated 'Gerry's smash and grab' by journalists, the reorganization was greeted largely in terms of a 'hostile takeover' and heavily resisted. After the initial unveiling of the plans, the regional arts boards were given just six weeks to hand over all their staff contracts and assets to the Arts Council. By the end of that period, not a single one had conceded any contracts, London Arts' chief executive had resigned in protest and eight boards had publicly rebelled. South West Arts' comment, 'It would be wrong to under-estimate the offence this has caused and the extent to which it has undermined trust and confidence in ACE',[8] could be fairly said to have echoed their collective sentiment. A debate in the House of Commons equally condemned the plans, and while the decision publicly had the government's support, even Chris Smith managed to make his nervousness clear in a conveniently leaked letter.

Celebrations over the financial bonus awarded following the Boyden Report were also short-lived after several new and unforeseen threats to the theatres' financial security entered the arena. Despite Labour's public affirmation of its continued commitment to the arts, the 2004 spending review saw the government announce that its Arts Council grant would be frozen for the subsequent three-year period, entailing a loss of £34 million in real terms. The government tried to ease any potential damage by allowing the funding body to divert funds previously earmarked for the 'Creative Partnerships' scheme to make up the shortfall in revenue funding. But this did little to reassure an increasingly anxious theatre community, particularly at a time that saw increasing threats to their income from other sources.

While direct government funding for the arts doubled during New Labour's first ten years in government, there was increasing strain on money from other funding bodies, particularly the local authorities, who fared less well under Blair. In 2005, 85 per cent of local authorities received standstill funding. Combined with a cap on council taxes, and central government's insistence on improved statutory services for education and transport in the face of heavy inflationary rises, there was increased concern that non-statutory obligations such as arts funding would suffer. Echoes of the problems under Thatcher began to surface when, as in the case of Wandsworth and Battersea Arts Centre, headlines were made by stories of local councils withholding arts funding on the basis that a theatre's national prominence, or, conversely, specific geographical location, made it someone else's responsibility. The Arts Council had quietly dropped parity funding as a major condition of theatre support following the receipt of extra government money in the wake of the Boyden Report. Nevertheless, local authorities were still expected to contribute their share, and a loss of support from one funding body continued to pose a threat to funding from others. Nor at any time were theatres in such a strong financial position that they could afford to lose any amount of their grants from even one source.

The now-closed Derby Playhouse was ultimately a victim of such problems. The theatre suffered prolonged difficulties at the box office in 2006 when ten of its shows were disrupted by the city council-sponsored development of the surrounding Westfield shopping centre. The construction work compromised access to the theatre and unleashed a plague of further problems for the Playhouse that included rat infestation and faulty sewerage. Despite good sales for the two shows that followed completion of the building work, with the Christmas production of *Treasure Island* taking an estimated £200,000 in advanced sales, a financial crisis at the beginning of December saw the board make the decision to put the company into liquidation. Notwithstanding prolonged difficulties between the trustees and management, the crisis could have been averted had Derby City Council agreed to give the theatre a £40,000 cash advance on money due to be released to the theatre in the new year. Its refusal to do so was made in spite of the knowledge that the Arts Council had promised an advance of £70,000 and was prepared to offer a further loan if Derby would be forthcoming with its advance. And the city council's silence on its reasoning inevitably gave rise to rumours that the local authority had ulterior motives. As the local paper noted, Derby City Council had expressed an interest in buying back the freehold for the theatre, which it had sold in 1999. Located in a prime position for the new shopping centre, the theatre's site had obvious potential for retail development. The Playhouse's lease was protected so long as it continued to operate. However, a business cannot carry on trading when insolvent. Publicly, the city council claimed it was committed to theatre in Derby, but as a number of critics pointed out at the time, the council's wording was interesting because it did not specifically mention a commitment to Derby Playhouse. Despite subsequently allowing the theatre to go into administration rather than liquidation to allow a completion of the Christmas show's run, it is perhaps not surprising that the Arts Council withdrew its funding to the Playhouse not long after.

While John Lewis may have been putting itself forward as a contender for Derby Playhouse's site, a significantly more powerful rival to the nation's theatres had also entered the ring. Britain's bid to host the 2012 Olympic Games, originally formulated in 2002, was successfully realized in 2005 when the International Olympic Committee awarded the tender to London. At the time of the original bid, the total cost of hosting the games was placed at approximately £2.4 billion: £1.5 billion of this, about two-thirds of the costs, were earmarked to come from the lottery, with £410 million to be taken from the existing 'good causes', of which the arts was one. Although the lottery had by this point generated almost £2 billion for arts and heritage, estimates claimed that a further £1.5 billion had been lost to government spending. The news that further funds considered by many to be the rightful property of the arts were to be diverted to finance the Olympics infuriated the arts community, who argued that this was little more than an outright raid by the government. Making matters worse, by November 2006, the secretary of state admitted that costs had already risen by a further £900 million. Despite fears voiced by the Select Committee on Culture, Media and Sport, and by many arts and heritage organizations, about the likely impact on lottery 'good causes', the government announced a further diversion of £675 million from this source. At the same time, party officials told the Arts Council to consider the effects of significant cuts for the arts in the next spending round. In February 2007, Arts Council chief executive Peter Hewitt revealed that the funding body had been asked to look at the implications of either a 5 per cent cut every year until 2011, standstill funding or, at best, an annual increase in line with inflation.

In the event, months of intense lobbying that emphasized the dangers of undoing the goodwill built up with the arts community over the previous decade, and the potential fallout of a return to stop–start funding, persuaded the government to have a change of heart. In October 2007, rather than the expected loss of £112.5 million, it was announced that the Arts Council could expect an increase of £50 million over the next three years, with central funding rising to £467 million by 2010/11. The victory, however, was hard won: government pressure ensured that as with all cash bonuses, increased subvention wouldn't be given without strings. In this case, the strings came in the form of one of the most radical revisions of funding policy in the Arts Council's history.

In 2007, something of a sea change was signalled when the new culture secretary, James Purnell, announced that the pursuit of targets would henceforth be superseded by a new emphasis on excellence. Numerous motives were inevitably put forward to account for such a change in government attitude. These included the growing anger of the arts community at being treated as creatures of government, preparations for significant cuts in arts funding and a recognition by New Labour of its wholesale failure to meet its own targets. Whatever the reason, within days of taking over, Purnell had commissioned Sir Brian McMaster, the former director of the Edinburgh Festival, to undertake a comprehensive review of the funding and management of the arts and assess how best to encourage excellence.

Published in January 2008, the findings of the report noted that the inevitable effect of directing funding at social objectives was that excellence and innovation suffered. McMaster argued that the obstructive target-driven approach should be replaced with more judgement, self-assessment and input from artists. And his report provided the guidelines by which the Arts Council rationalized its own funding rethink. True to the spirit of tradition, however, in doing so, the central funding body failed to consult the organizations involved or make public the thinking behind its decisions. At a time when the Arts Council could have justifiably been flaunting its triumph in staving off the Olympic threat, and presenting itself as the saviour of the arts, it instead found itself at one of its lowest ebbs in the minds of its own clients.

As noted previously, threats to Arts Council pre-eminence or autonomy have historically seen the central funding body respond with major revisions to either its organizational structure or funding policies. Ten years into the New Labour regime, and proportionate to the number of state-funded arts organizations and size of the funds it was handling, Arts Council England found itself, in many ways, as diminished as it had been at any time in its history. The extent of government interference was publicly and embarrassingly demonstrated for all to see in 2005 when, via the Freedom of Information Act, *The Stage* obtained and printed a vital letter from the culture secretary, Tessa Jowell, explicitly instructing the Arts Council to concentrate grants on schemes in line with key New Labour policies.[9] By this point, Christopher Frayling, Arts Council chair since 2004, had become so concerned at the extent of government interference that he complained that the arm's length principle had been reduced to 'Venus de Milo length', with the government considering the Arts Council as nothing more than an extension of the DCMS. And if the funding body felt increasingly impotent in this capacity, its reduced role as a result of Robinson's 2001 restructuring ensured the wound was far more deeply felt. While many considered devolution mainly superficial and a nod to New Labour policy, the reduced Arts Council in Great Peter Street nevertheless announced a further extension of this principle in 2006, whereby it would restrict itself to determining funds and taking direct responsibility for just fifteen national organizations, each of which had a grant of £5 million or above. Responsibility for all other funds would be devolved to the regional branches. Frayling denied this was in response to a critical speech by Culture Minister David Lammy that called on the Arts Council to 'slim down' its operation. He equally rejected the idea that there were any fears about an associated government agenda when Lammy's attack coincided with proposals for the abolition of the Scottish Arts Council and in seeing their Welsh counterpart substantially reduced and more directly subject to the dictates of the Welsh Assembly.[10] Equally, Frayling refuted the suggestion that the subsequent haemorrhaging of senior executives from the Arts Council was in any way related to feelings of frustration or impotence. Nevertheless, few were under the illusion that the organization was happy with its role at this point in time. In periods of trouble, the Arts Council has traditionally been seen to flex its muscles, and, in 2007, that is exactly what it did.

Just before Christmas 2007, the Arts Council announced that 194 of its 990 regularly funded organizations and individuals would have their grants substantially cut or completely withdrawn. While the majority of the remaining clients received substantial increases in their regular funding, and numerous new companies were added to the Arts Council's portfolio, any good news inevitably got buried amid outrage at what was called the funding body's bloodiest cull since its inception in 1946. Theatre companies were amongst those most severely affected, and four regional producing theatres – Derby Playhouse, Exeter Northcott, the Yvonne Arnaud, Guildford, and the Bristol Old Vic – were included on the list of clients who would see their entire funding withdrawn from the end of the financial year.

It had long been widely agreed across the arts sector that the Arts Council needed to conduct a comprehensive review of its revenue funding. Nonetheless, this news was greeted with widespread fury. In part, the outrage was provoked by the manner in which the decisions had been made and delivered. In a move almost identical to the unpopular Christmas Cuts of 1980, without warning or consultation, the Arts Council announced the shake-up on 12 December and gave affected organizations just five weeks to appeal the decision. With the approaching holiday period, this amounted to a mere eighteen working days between receiving the bad news and the deadline for objections, and many organizations' staff had to give up their yuletide celebrations in a frantic rush to assemble responses. Others were incensed by the perception that the Arts Council had once again effectively passed the buck, requiring the regional offices to convey the bad news and conduct the appeal reviews. As Richard Pulford, former deputy secretary general of the Arts Council, and now chief executive of the Society of London Theatre and the Theatrical Management Association, commented:

> It seems extraordinary to me there could have been nearly 200 organisations that were worth funding this year, that aren't next year. It looks like cutting for the sake of cutting. I don't understand the rationale for it. We are very concerned that many organisations were given little or no forewarning and some have been cut by regional offices when they aren't regional organisations. There seems to be no central policy
> (*The Observer* 2008)

Despite the implication that decisions were taken in line with McMaster's recommendations, feelings ran high over the apparent lack of any clear rationale or consistency governing decisions. As Pulford went on to say,

> Some organisations have been told they're cut because they're not adventurous; others because they have a risky artistic agenda...there's no coherence. It's astounding.
> (*The Observer* 2008)

Exeter's Northcott Theatre received the news that it was to lose its entire grant of £547,000 the day before it was due to reopen following a substantial refurbishment, funded in part by the Arts Council. One of the reasons for its original closure had been to allow for a major rethink of its artistic policy, and the theatre had made concerted efforts to address Arts Council concerns and expand its portfolio. Plans unveiled prior to the reopening included ventures that incorporated new media work for and by young people evolving from MySpace and YouTube projects, alongside collaborations with street-theatre practitioners and school and community groups. Despite the fact that the previously safe programme had been agreed with the Arts Council prior to the refurbishment as a way of stabilizing the Northcott amidst falling audiences, the central funding body argued that while the theatre had made progress, it was not substantial enough to answer the new priorities. Responding to the news, Northcott Theatre's acting chief executive, Claire Middleton, said, 'If you look at our aspirations over the next five years, we hit every button in Arts Council priorities: new work, diversification, innovation – it's all there in embryo but they've pushed the abort button...It's like planting a bulb but as soon as a shoot appears, you cut it off' (*The Observer* 2008). Theatre staff and audiences were not the only ones outraged by the Arts Council's decision. Its funding partners, in this case Exeter City Council, Exeter University and Devon County Council, were understandably put out by a decision of which they were given no warning and for which they were given no clear reason. This was particularly galling considering that they had just contributed £1.5 million to the Northcott's refurbishment based on assurances from the Arts Council that it was 'committed' to the theatre's future.

London's Bush Theatre, meanwhile, was told that it would receive a 40 per cent drop in its annual funding. As artistic director Josie Rourke pointed out, with the Bush Theatre being the capital's powerhouse of new writing, this clearly went against the Arts Council's new emphasis on excellence and innovation. Using freedom of information laws to scrutinize the proposals underlining the decision, Rourke discovered that the central funding body had under-recorded the theatre's audiences by two-thirds and thus arguably based their decision on faulty data. With the lack of clear information outlining the reasons for the cuts, accusations of bullyboy tactics and outright madness were aggravated by speculation about the Arts Council's motives. These ranged from its being an incompetent organization acting in haste as a result of the late date of the government settlement, to a central funding body that still retained its London bias. Certainly, none of the capital's leading organizations found that their grants were detrimentally affected. None of these arguments did anything to repair the beleaguered Council's reputation.

On 10 January 2008, the day before McMaster's report was published, and a day when the Arts Council should have been riding high in the popularity stakes after its victory in securing government support against the odds, the actors' union Equity invited outgoing chief executive Peter Hewitt to address an emergency meeting at London's Young Vic Theatre. Facing a packed house of angry theatre practitioners, Hewitt had little chance to have his voice against the onslaught of accusations of high-handed behaviour, incompetence and secrecy in the Arts Council. The actor Malcolm Sinclair spoke for many in the auditorium when he said he had 'no confidence in the people who are making the choices' (*The Guardian* 2008). Patrick Malahide was similarly applauded when he accused the funding body of acting as an overbearing agent of social change and attempting to manipulate theatre's output. And his outcry that 'the theatre is about people and over the last month the Arts Council has treated these people with contempt', was widely echoed throughout the hall, not least by one outraged artist who exclaimed, 'If this had been the behaviour of a private individual, they would have been sectioned by now' (*The Guardian* 2008). Miriam Karlin, famous for her role as a sullen shop steward in the 1970s sitcom *The Rag Trade*, wound up the meeting by calling for a vote of no confidence. She didn't exactly say 'everybody out'. Nonetheless, everybody quickly left after the vote was swiftly and unanimously passed.

With echoes of the fallout from the Christmas Cuts and *The Glory of the Garden* in the 1980s, in the face of such vocal criticism from stars and ministers alike, the Arts Council was inevitably forced once again into a partial climbdown. Attempting to justify its actions, and repair some of the damage done to its image, the Council denied that the cuts were ever a fait accompli. Nor was there any acknowledgement that the beleaguered funding body was giving in to such strident criticism. Talking to *The Sunday Times*, Frayling emphasized, 'It is not the decibel count which has influenced us, but reasoned argument' (*The Sunday Times* 2008). He was equally critical of the aggressive nature of the protests. As he said of National Theatre director Nick Hytner's comments, 'I don't think calling us "bollocks" is what would pass as a critical judgment' (*The Sunday Times* 2008). Notwithstanding, some 25 of the 194 organizations originally earmarked to lose their funding were successful in their appeals. Amongst them were Exeter's Northcott Theatre, Bristol Old Vic, the Bush Theatre and the National Student Drama Festival. But while these organizations were given a reprieve, the actions of the Arts Council indicate that the problems regional theatres thought had been laid to rest long ago may very well continue to haunt them for some time yet.

Frayling recently argued that we are currently living in a golden age of the arts in this country. And there is no question that the last decade under New Labour has indeed provided some desperately needed financial relief, in England at least, to the problems that propelled regional theatres into a perpetual state of crisis under the Tories. Yet, when examined in terms of the pattern of events that conspired to make subsidy both a blessing and a curse in the history of regional theatres, it seems that many issues remain unsolved. The scales continue to fluctuate precariously in the ongoing battle between metropolitan and regional concerns, high art and populist entertainment, and in the arguments over government interference and independent cultural policy. With the threat of recession, and Equity issuing a statement following the release of the McMaster's Report commenting that the Arts Council is not 'as it currently operates...fit to judge what is excellent in theatre', it would be safe to say that the problems for the country's regional theatres are far from over.

Notes

1. Blair, speaking at the Labour party annual conference following his election to the leadership in 1994.
2. Blair, from an address made at a meeting of the European Socialists' Congress in Malmo, Sweden, quoted in Driver and Martell 1988: 7.
3. Peter Longman, *Theatres Trust Annual Report, 1997/8*, 9 December 1998.
4. Longman, *Theatres Trust Annual Report, 1997/8*, 9 December 1998
5. John Holden, from lecture *Know Your Place*, Birmingham, 8 March 2007.
6. Robert Maclennan, culture spokesman for the Liberal Democrats, speaking at the Westminster Hall debates, 2 May 2001.
7. Maclennan, speaking at the Westminster Hall debates, 2 May 2001.
8. Robert Maclennan (MP for Caithness, Sutherland & Easter Ross, Liberal Democrat), quoted an official statement from South West Arts, in the Westminster Hall Debates on Regional Arts Boards, Wednesday, 2 May 2001
9. Tessa Jowell replaced Smith as culture secretary in 2001.
10. In 2004, funding control of the Arts Council of Wales was transferred to the Welsh Assembly. Six national companies, including Clwyd Theatr Cymru and Theatr Genedlaethol, came under their direct control, and all strategic planning and policy functions, including research and evaluation, were relocated to the Assembly Government. In Spring 2008, the Scottish Executive announced plans to establish a new cultural development body, merging the Scottish Arts Council with Scottish Screen to create a new funding body, Creative Scotland.

REFERENCES

Addison, Paul (1994), *The Road to 1945: British Politics and the Second World War*, London: Pimlico.
Anderson, Bette (1994), *Salisbury Journal*, 22 November.
Arnold, Matthew (1879), 'The French play in London', *The Nineteenth Century*, London: August.
Arts Council England (ACE) (2001), *A National Policy for Theatre in England*, London: Arts Council England.
Arts Council England (2001), *A Prospectus for Change*, London: Arts Council England.
Arts Council England (1995), *Drama in England*, London: Arts Council England.
Arts Council England (1994/5–2002/3), *Annual Reports*, London: Arts Council England.
Arts Council of Great Britain (ACGB) (1988), *Better Business for the Arts* (pamphlet), London: Arts Council of Great Britain.
Arts Council of Great Britain (1985a), *A Great British Success Story*, London: Arts Council of Great Britain.
Arts Council of Great Britain (1985b), *Theatre Investment Fund*, London: Arts Council of Great Britain.
Arts Council of Great Britain (1984), *The Glory of the Garden*, London: Arts Council of Great Britain.
Arts Council of Great Britain (1980), *The Arts Council of Great Britain and the Regional Arts Associations: Towards a New Relationship*, report on an informal AGCB/RAA working group, London: Arts Council of Great Britain.
Arts Council of Great Britain (1970), *The Theatre Today in England and Wales*, London: Arts Council of Great Britain.
Arts Council of Great Britain (1967), 'A chairman's note', *A New Charter: Twenty-second Annual Report, 1966/7*, London: Arts Council of Great Britain.
Arts Council of Great Britain (1961), *The Needs of the English Provinces*, London: Arts Council of Great Britain.
Arts Council of Great Britain (1945/6–1993/4), *Annual Reports*, London: Arts Council of Great Britain.
Arts Council of Great Britain National Arts and Media Strategy Unit (1991), *Drama Discussion Document*, London: Arts Council of Great Britain.

Arts Council South East England (ACESE) (2006), *Haymarket Theatre Review 2006*, ACESE.

Baumol, H. and W. J. Baumol (1994), *Inflation and the Performing Arts*, New York: New York University Press.

Blacklock, Peter (1994), *Salisbury Journal*, 10 November.

Blackstock, Anthony (1997), *The Thorndike Theatre (Leatherhead)*, consultants' report commissioned by South East Arts Board.

Bonnar-Keenlyside (1994), *Salisbury Playhouse Business Plan*, consultants' report, Salisbury: Bonnar-Keenlyside Consultants.

Bonnar-Keenlyside (1993), *South East Arts Board Producing Theatres Review*, consultants' report, Salisbury: Bonnar-Keenlyside Consultants.

Peter Boyden Associates (2000), *Roles and Functions of the English Regional Producing Theatres: Final Report to the Arts Council England, May 2000*, Bristol: Peter Boyden Associates.

Brannen, Rob and Ian Brown (1996), 'When theatre was for all: The Cork Report after ten years', *New Theatre Quarterly* 12, no. 48 (November 1996): 367–83.

— (1986), *The Cork Report: Theatre IS for All*, London: Arts Council of Great Britain.

Brind, D. G. W. (1994), *Salisbury Journal*, 24 November.

British Theatre Guide (2004), 'Taking the Haymarket to new heights', http://www.britishtheatreguide.info/otherresources/interviews/MandyStewart.htm. Accessed 14 May 2008.

Chisholm, Cecil (1934), *Repertory: An Outline of the Modern Theatre Movement*, London: Peter Davies Ltd.

Church, Jonathan (1995), 'Playhouse gifts to welcome new duo', *Salisbury Journal*, 1 June.

Clarkson, Jeremy (2008), 'It seems it ain't art if it ain't ethnic', *The Sunday Times*, 20 January.

Colston, Elizabeth (1994), *Salisbury Journal*, 1 November.

Council for Encouragement of Music and the Arts (CEMA) (1943), *The Arts in Wartime: A Report on the Work of CEMA, 1942 and 1943*, London: CEMA.

Cultural Trends (1994–2008), quarterly periodicals, London: Policy Studies Institute.

Devlin, Graham and Sue Hoyle (2000), *Committing to Culture*, London: Franco-British Council.

Docherty, Peter W. (1991), *Salisbury Journal*, 1 August.

Doyle, John (1989), 'Tampering with ingredients', *The Stage*, 2 November.

Driver, Stephen and Luke Martell (1998), *New Labour: Politics after Thatcherism*, Cambridge: Polity Press.

Elsom, John (1971), *Theatre outside London*, London: Macmillan.

Farnham Herald (1995a), 'Job axe falls on artistic director', 11 August.

Farnham Herald (1995b), 'Redgrave must be a producing theatre', 18 August.

Farnham Herald (1994a), 'Theatre funding row takes centre stage', 1 April.

Farnham Herald (1994b), 'Redgrave will remain a Surrey theatre for a Surrey audience', 25 November.

Farnham Herald (1994c), 'Board hits back', 2 December.

Farnham Herald (1991), 'Show stoppers', 22 February.

Feversham, Lord (1974), 'The role of regional arts associations', paper presented at the Standing Conference of Regional Arts Associations (CoRAA) *The Arts and the Regions*, University of Sussex, Great Britain, June.

Forgacs, David (1988), *An Antonio Gramsci Reader: Selected Writings 1916–1935*, New York: Schocken Books.

Gahan, Paul (1991), *Salisbury Journal*, 25 July.
Gibbons, Fiachra (2003), 'Scottish arts community stares into the abyss', *The Guardian*, 26 August.
Gooch, Steve (1984), *All Together Now*, London: Methuen.
Gowrie, Lord (1994), 'Never enough cash for casualties', *The Stage*, 27 October.
The Guardian (2008), 'Actors boo Arts Council over swinging cuts', 10 January.
Guildford Herald (1994), 'Higher funding needed to save Arnaud Theatre', 2 December.
Gurney, David (1997), 'Final curtain call at the Thorndike', *Surrey Advertiser*, 10 March.
Hall, Peter (1985), 'J'Accuse...', *Plays and Players*, 379, April, pp. 6–7.
Hamilton, Roger (1994), *Salisbury Journal*, 24 November.
Hampshire Gazette (2005), 'Former director claims he was forced to leave', 16 February.
Harrogate Advertiser (1988), 'Theatre-lovers star in a revival', 24 June.
Hawkins, Robert (1993), *Salisbury Journal*, 22 February.
Hewison, Robert (1995), *Culture and Consensus: England, Art and Politics since 1940*, London: Methuen.
Hoggart, Richard (1992), *An Imagined Life: Life and Times 1959–91*, London: Chatto and Windus.
Hutchison, Robert (1982), *The Politics of the Arts Council*, London: Sinclair-Browne, 1982.
The Independent (1995), 'Making a drama out of a crisis', 23 February.
J. Wilson Associates (2002), *Audiences for the Leicester Haymarket Theatre: A Future-scoping Report*, J. Wilson Associates.
Jackson, Anthony and George Rowell (1984), *The Repertory Movement*, Cambridge: Cambridge University Press.
Jenkins, Hugh (1979), *The Culture Gap*, London: Marion Boyars.
Johnstone, Karen (1994), *Salisbury Journal*, 4 August.
Jones, Derek (1992), *Salisbury Journal*, 21 May.
Kavanagh, Dennis (1987), *Thatcherism and British Politics: The End of Consensus?*, London: Oxford University Press.
Keynes, J. M. (1945), 'The Arts Council: its policy and hopes', *The Listener*, 34:861, 12 July.
Landstone, Charles (1953), *Offstage*, London and New York: Elek.
Leversuch, Christine (1991), *Salisbury Journal*, 11 July.
Liverpool Echo (1988), 'Everyman fury at Arts Council "stab in back"', 10 March.
Macmillan, Joyce (2004), 'Creating a scene', *Western Mail*, 14 May.
Marquand, David (1988), *The Unprincipled Society: New Demands and Old Politics*, London: Jonathan Cape.
McClean, Margaret (1994), *Salisbury Journal*, 1 December.
Meweezen, Judy (1990), 'Clearing the stage for the money men', *The Sunday Times*, 29 April.
Mitchell, Paul (2001) 'Britain: Labour government outlines the next stage in its assault on the arts', World Socialist Website, http://www.wsws.org/articles/2001/apr2001/arts-a10.shtml. Accessed 15 May 2008.
Morrison, Richard (1998), 'Dawn raid on the Arts Council', *The Times*, 1 November.
Moss, Stephen (2004), 'Luck and brass', *The Guardian*, 4 November.
The Observer (2008), 'Is this the best way to run the arts?', 13 January.
Peacock, D. Keith (1999), *Thatcher's Theatre: British Theatre and Drama in the Eighties*, Westport, Ct: Greenwood Press.

Penycate, Jack (1985), Yvonne Arnaud Theatre press release, 7 January.
Peter, John (1995), 'Facing the final curtain', *The Sunday Times*, 15 January.
Pick, John (1986), *Managing the Arts? The British Experience*, London: Rhinegold Publishing Ltd.
Pinder, John and Mary Pinder (1994), *Salisbury Journal*, 24 November.
Rayner, Lord (1995), *The Rayner Report*, London: National Theatre.
Rees-Mogg, William (1985), *The Political Economy of Art*, London: Arts Council of Great Britain.
—— (1983), 'Arts Council looks to "Big Four" companies in its own defence', *The Stage*, 6 October.
Rix, Sir Brian (1991), 'A scheme to avoid disaster', *The Times*, 17 January.
St. John Stevas, N. (1979), 'The Tories and the arts', *The Observer*, 14 October.
Sayer, Philip (1991), letters page, *Salisbury Journal*, 8 July.
Scotsman (2002), 'Art experts doubt theatre plan', 29 November.
Sinclair, Andrew (1995), *Arts and Culture: The History of the 50 Years of the Arts Council of Great Britain*, London: Sinclair-Stevenson.
Smith, Daniel (2003), 'No love for Leicester', *Leicester Mercury*, 21 August.
Smith, Chris (1998), *Creative Britain*, London: Faber and Faber.
Soutar, Jim (1994), *Salisbury Playhouse*, 10 August.
South West Arts (1980), *Annual Report and Accounts, 1979–80*.
The Stage (2008), 'Liverpool's Everyman "owns its own future"', 15 April.
The Stage (1993), 'Doom looms for the Liverpool Everyman', 14 October.
The Stage (1992), 'Everyman calls in business consultants', 20 July.
The Stage (1990a), 'Liverpool theatres angry over grant cut', 4 January.
The Stage (1990b), 'Boss slams theatre policy as "elitist"', 12 July.
The Stage (1988a), 'Equal means misery for more', 12 March.
The Stage (1988b), 'Business sponsors get only a bit-part claims NCA survey', 21 April.
The Stage (1986a), 'Theatre director quits in despair', 27 February.
The Stage (1986b), 9 October.
The Stage (1985), 'Harrogate in cash drama', 3 November.
The Stage (1984a), 'Cold winds that will follow White Paper', 5 January.
The Stage (1984b), 31 January.
The Stage (1984c), 'Theatre bosses quite age of the strain', 7 July.
The Stage (1983), 'Report will put arts minister on the spot', 1 September.
The Stage (1982), 'More power planned for regions', 6 May.
The Stage (1979a), 'Reprieve for Harrogate', 22 March.
The Stage (1979b), 12 July.
The Stage (1979c), 2 August.
The Stage (1979d), 27 September.
Stewart, Hugo (1991), *Salisbury Journal*, 22 February.
Strand, Timothy (1994), *Salisbury Journal*, 24 November.
Stride, Marie (1994), *Salisbury Journal*, 10 August.
The Sunday Times (2008), 'Stars force Arts Council to drop cut', 27 January.
Surrey Advertiser (2007), 'Theatre in jeopardy after main grant is axed', 21 December.
Surrey Advertiser (1997a), 'Lack of cash is cause', 3 March.
Surrey Advertiser (1997b), 'Closure of Thorndike is "a disgrace"', 13 March.

Surrey Advertiser (1996), 'Lifting the curtain on a theatre's "mixed blessing"', 16 May.
Surrey Advertiser (1994a), 'Attack on funding as town theatre fights for its life', 18 February.
Surrey Advertiser (1994b), 'MP seeks fair deal for Arnaud', 21 October.
Surrey Advertiser (1992a), 'Cash crisis hits Arnaud Theatre', 27 November.
Surrey Advertiser (1992b), 'Civic Hall can't show the way to viability', 4 December.
Surrey Advertiser (1992c), 'Funding bodies must increase their subsidy', 4 December.
Surrey Advertiser (1985), 'Blaze destroyed theatre but fired drive for Arnaud', 2 June.
Surrey Advertiser (1980), 'Theatre's future is on knife edge', 1 February.
Tanner, Doreen (1974), *Everyman: The First Ten Years*, Liverpool: Merseyside Everyman Theatre Trust.
Taylor, P. (1995), 'Making a drama out of a crisis', *The Independent*, 23 January.
Thatcher, Margaret (1993), *The Downing Street Years*, London: HarperCollins.
The Times (1993), 15 July.
The Times (1986), 'Councils blamed for danger to arts', 28 February.
Vines, Sidney (1994), *Salisbury Journal*, 13 August.
Watkins, Graham (1984), 'Art grows where seed is sown', *The Stage*, 17 May.
whatsonstage (2008), 'Harrogate Theatre faces Arts Council cuts', http://www.whatsonstage.com/blogs/yorkshire/2008/02/01/harrogate-theatre-faces-arts-council-cuts/. Accessed 26 May 2008.
White, Eric Walter (1975), *The Arts Council of Great Britain*, London: Davis-Poynter.
Williams, Raymond (1989), *Resources of Hope: Culture, Democracy, Socialism*, London and New York: Verso.
Woolley, Ronald (1986), 'Theatre faced £100,000 loss', *Harrogate Advertiser*, 4 September.
Wootton, Ena (1994), *Salisbury Journal*, 28 July.
Wright, Michael (1994), 'Theatre goes bust', *The Daily Telegraph*, 24 December.
Yorkshire Evening Post (2007), 'Devastating blow as theatre faces £300,000 arts funding cut', 24 December.
Yorkshire Post (2008), 'Funding cuts to theatres cause regional anger', 8 February.
Yorkshire Post (1987), 'Ideal start to the season', 15 April.
Yorkshire Post (1986), 'Financial crisis closes theatre', 24 July.

Further Reading
Agnew, J.-C. (1986), *World Apart: The Market and the Theatre in Anglo-American Thought*, Cambridge: Cambridge University Press.
Amis, Kingsley (1979), *An Arts Policy?*, London: Centre for Policy Studies.
Aragay, Mireia, Hildegard Klein, Enric Monforte and Pilar Zozaya (eds) (2007), *British Theatre of the 1990s: Interviews with Directors, Playwrights, Critics and Academics*, Basingstoke: Palgrave Macmillan.
Archer, William (1889), 'A plea for an endowed theatre', *The Fortnightly Review*, May.
Arts Council England (2000), *The Next Stage: Towards a National Policy for Theatre in England*, London: Arts Council England.
Arts Council England (1996), *Policy for Drama of the English Arts Funding System*, London: Arts Council England.
Arts Council of Great Britain (ACGB) (1989), *An Urban Renaissance: Sixteen Case Studies Showing the Role of the Arts in Urban Regeneration*, London: Arts Council of Great Britain.

Arts Council of Great Britain (1989), *Glory Reflected: A Progress Report on 'The Glory of the Garden'*, London: Arts Council of Great Britain.

Baldry, Harold (1981), *The Case for the Arts*, London: Secker and Warburg.

Barker, Kathleen (1974), *The Theatre Royal, Bristol, 1766–1966, Two Centuries of Stage History*, London: The Society for Theatre Research.

—— (1973), *Entertainment in the Nineties*, Bristol: Bristol Branch of the Historical Association.

Bavin, J. (1976), *Heart of the City: The Story of the Salisbury Playhouse*, Salisbury: Salisbury Playhouse.

Beeche, Matt and Simon Lee (2008), *Ten Years of New Labour*, Basingstoke: Palgrave Macmillan.

Billington, Michael (2007), *State Of The Nation: British Theatre Since 1945*, London: Faber & Faber.

Brown, Ian, Robert Brannen and Douglas Brown (2000), 'The Arts Council touring franchise and English political theatre after 1986', *New Theatre Quarterly*, 16:64, pp. 379–87.

Bull, John (1994), *Stage Right*, London: Macmillan.

Clark, Kenneth (1977), *The Other Half: A Self-Portrait*, London: John Murray.

Conservative Party, (1982), *Private and Public Funding of the Arts*, vol. 1, London: HMSO, 18 October.

Davis, Tracy (2000), *The Economics of the British Stage, 1800–1914*, Cambridge: Cambridge University Press.

Department of Culture, Music and Sport (DCMS) (1998), *Culture and Creativity: The Next Ten Years*, London: Department of Culture, Music and Sport.

D'Monté, Rebecca and Graham Saunders (2007), *Cool Britannia? British Political Drama in the 1990s*, Basingstoke: Palgrave Macmillan.

Drummond, John (1999), *Tainted by Experience*, London: Faber and Faber.

Dunn, Kate (1998), *Exit through the Fireplace: The Great Days of Rep*, London: John Murray.

Ellis, Adrian (2002), *Valuing Culture*, Demos.

Elsom, J. and N. Tomalin (1978), *The History of the National Theatre*, London: Cape.

English Tourist Board Socio-Economic Research Unit (1982), *The Provincial Theatre and Tourism in England: An Analysis of Trends between 1975 and 1981/2*, London: English Tourist Board.

Fielding, Steven, Peter Thompson and Nick Tiratsoo (1995), *'England Arise!': The Labour Party and Popular Politics in 1940s Britain*, Manchester and New York: Manchester University Press.

Goldie, Grace Wyndham (1935), *The Liverpool Repertory Theatre, 1911–1934*, Liverpool: Liverpool University Press.

Goodman, Arnold (1993), *Tell Them I'm on My Way*, London: Chapmans.

Gottlieb, Vera and Colin Chambers (1999), *Theatre in a Cool Climate*, London: Amber Lane Press.

Granville Barker, H. (1910), 'The theatre: the next phase', *Forum*, 44, August, pp. 159–70.

Hall, Peter (1983), *Peter Hall's Diaries: The Story of a Dramatic Battle*, London: Hamish Hamilton.

Harris, John S. (1970), *Government Patronage of the Arts in Great Britain*, Chicago: University of Chicago Press.

Harvie, Jen (2005), *Staging the UK*, Manchester: Manchester University Press.

Hewison, Robert (1987), *Too Much: Art and Society in the Sixties*, New York: Oxford University Press.

Hibbard, G. R. (1968), *The Neville Affair: The Facts by G. R. Hibbard with the Assistance of R. G. Bateman, H. B. Mattingly, and Allan Rodway*, Nottingham: Nottingham Playhouse.

Holden, John and Robert Hewison (2004), *The Right to Make Art. Making Aspirations Reality*, Demos.

Holland, Philip (1981), *The Governance of Quangos*, London: Adam Smith Institute.
Hollis, Patricia (1997), *Jennie Lee: A Life*, Oxford: Oxford University Press.
Howe, P. P. (1910), *The Repertory Theatre*, London: M. Secker.
Hutchison, Robert (1982), *A Hard Fact to Swallow: The Division of Arts Council Expenditure between London and the English Regions*, London: Policy Studies Institute.
Itzin, Catherine (1980), *Stages in the Revolution: Political Theatre in Britain since 1968*, London: Methuen.
Jackson, Tony (ed.) (1980), *Learning Through Theatre: Essays and Casebooks on Theatre in Education*, Manchester: Manchester University Press.
Kershaw, Baz (2004), *The Cambridge History of British Theatre, vol. 3.*, Cambridge University Press.
—— (1992), *The Politics of Performance*, London: Routledge.
Keynes, W. M. (1975), *Essays on John Maynard Keynes*, Cambridge: Cambridge University Press.
Labour Party (1997), *Our Creative Future: A Strategy for Cultural Policy, Arts, and the Creative Economy*, London: Labour Party.
—— (1977), *The Arts and the People: Labour's Policy towards the Arts*, London: Labour Party.
Lavender, Andy (1989), 'Theatre in Thatcher's Britain: organizing the opposition', *New Theatre Quarterly*, 5:19, pp. 113–23.
Lee, Jennie (1965), *A Policy for the Arts: The First Steps*, London: HMSO.
Leggett, Phyllis (1972), 'The repertory movement in Great Britain', *Who's Who in the Theatre*, 15, London.
Leventhal, F. M. (1990), 'The best for the most: CEMA and state sponsorship of the arts in wartime, 1939–1945', *Twentieth Century British History*, 1:3.
Ludlam, Steve and Martin J. Smith (2001), *New Labour in Government*, Basingstoke and London: Macmillan.
McGrath, John (1981), *A Good Night Out: Popular Theatre: Audience, Class, and Form*, London: Nick Hern Books.
McGuigan, Jim (1996), *Culture and the Public Sphere*, London and New York: Routledge.
Marwick, Arthur (2000), *A History of the Modern British Isles, 1914–1999*, Oxford: Blackwell Publishers.
Matthews, W. Bache (1924), *A History of the Birmingham Repertory Theatre*, London: Chatto and Windus.
Minihan, Janet (1977), *The Nationalisation of Culture*, London: Hamish Hamilton.
Mirza, Munira (2007), *Culture Vultures: Is UK Arts Policy Damaging the Arts?*, London: Policy Exchange.
Mulgan, Geoff, and Ken Worpole (1986), *Saturday Night or Sunday Morning? From Arts to Industry – New Forms of Cultural Policy*, London: Comedia.
Myerscough, John (1988), *The Economic Importance of the Arts*, London: Policy Studies Institute.
National Campaign for the Arts (1993), *Facts about the Arts*, London: National Campaign for the Arts.
Pelham, David (1986), *Aspects of Funding Regional Theatres Subsidized by the ACGB*, London: University of Westminster.
Pick, John (1988), *The Arts in a State: A Study of Government Arts Policies from Ancient Greece to the Present*, Exeter: Bristol Classical Press.
—— (1985), *The Theatre Industry*, London: Comedia.

—— (1980), *The State of the Arts*, Eastbourne: John Offord.

Ray, Larry and Andrew Sayer (1999), *Culture and Economy after the Cultural Turn*, London: Sage Publications.

Redcliffe-Maud, Lord (1976), *Support for the Arts in England and Wales*, London: Calouste Gulbenkian Foundation.

Selwood, Sara (ed.) (2000), *The Cultural Sector*, London: PSI.

Shank, Theodore (1994), *Contemporary British Theatre*, London: St Martin's Press.

Strong, Judith (1999), *Encore: Strategies for Theatre Renewal*, London: The Theatres Trust.

Toynbee, Polly and David Walker (2001), *Did Things Get Better? An Audit of Labour's Successes and Failures*, London: Penguin.

Trewin, J. C. (1963), *The Birmingham Repertory Theatre, 1913–63*, London: Barrie and Rockliff.

Wallinger, Mark (2000), *Art for All?*, London: The Peer Trust.

Wareing, Alfred (1928), 'The Little Theatre movement', *The Stage Year Book: 1928*, London: HMSO.

Wilding, Richard (1989), *Supporting the Arts: A Review of the Arts Funding Structure*, London.

Williams, Raymond (1979), 'The Arts Council', *Political Quarterly*, Spring.

INDEX

Theatres and other arts venues are listed under the town in which they are located (London excepted)

Abercrombie, Nigel, 61, 62–3, 64
ABSA (Association for Business Sponsorship of the Arts), 78, 81, 82, 91
ACESE (Arts Council England South East), 211
Acts of Parliament: 1916 Finance Act, 26; 1925 Public Health Act, 29, 47; 1944 Education Act, 57; 1948 Local Government Act, 47–8; 1972 Local Government Act, 52; 1988 Education Reform Act, 92, 116; 1988 Insolvency Act, 97, 182; 1994 National Lottery Act, 201; 1998 National Lottery Act, 201
Addison, Paul, 35, 221
Albery, Sir Bronson, 32, 33–4
animateurs, 22, 28
Apollo Leisure Group, 151
Archer, William, 10, 17, 18
Arnold, Matthew, 10, 17
Arts Council (of Great Britain; post 1994, England), 9, 11, 12, 13, 19, 21, 24, 25, 26, 27, 291; annual reports, 31–2, 39, 41, 43, 48, 49, 73; arm's length status, 12, 21, 56, 78, 80, 201, 217; becomes responsibility of Treasury, 38; chairmen, see individual names; Christmas Cuts of 1980, 77–8, 92, 100, 170; closes its regional offices, 34, 43, 48, 55, 56; delegates regional responsibility to arts boards,102–5; directly manages regional theatres, 28–9, 31–2, 33–4, 37, 113; drama panel of, 27, 32, 54; embraces enterprise culture, 88–9; emphasizes standards, 31, 36–7, 43, 51, 103; executive committee (council) of, 27, 32, 33, 35, 36; funding of regional theatres, 12, 39, 41, 51–2, 75–99; grows out of CEMA, 21, 24; Housing the Arts, 1965 scheme, 29, 49, 60, 63, 64,106, 130, 149, 157; Keynes and, 11, 27; National Policy for Theatre in England, 2001, 204, 206, 207, 209, 211, 213; origins and establishment, 10, 11, 12, 19, 30–1; prioritizes London artistically, 32, 34, 42, 83, 103; quango, 72; relationship with local authorities, 48, 50, 51–3, 92; relationship with regional arts associations, 55–6, 83–5; reverts to Department of Education and Science, 58; split into three, 103; under Conservatives (1979–97), 72–80, 82–6, 87–96, 99, 101–7; under Labour (post-war, 1960s and 70s), 36, 37, 38–9, 58–65; under New Labour, 201, 202–4, 207, 209–20; young people's theatre and, 84–5, 92–3; *see also* Arts Council of Wales, Scottish Arts Council
Arts Council of Wales, 103, 204, 220
Arts Council publications: *Better Business for the Arts*, 1988 pamphlet, 91; *Drama in England*,

1995 consultative paper, 74; *The First Ten Years*, 1995/6 review, 39; *A Great British Success Story*, 1985 document, 88, 93, 95; *The Needs of the English Provinces*, 1961 report, 49; *The Next Stage*, 2001 Theatre Review, 185, 194, 203-4; *A Prospectus for Change*, 2001, 213; *The Theatre Today*, 1970 enquiry, 39, 40; *Towards a New Relationship*, 1982 study, 83; *An Urban Renaissance*, 1988 document, 89; see also Glory of the Garden
Aydon, Deborah, 186

Baird, Heather, 204
Baldry, Harold, 73
Barber, James, 163, 164, 165
Barclays bank, 108
Barrington, Ross, 129
Basingstoke, Haymarket Theatre, 146, 154, 210-11
BBC (British Broadcasting Corporation), 26, 28, 72, 80, 81, 124
Beardon, Sue, 87
Beaumont, Hugh ("Binkie"), 25-6
BECTU (Broadcast Entertainment, Cinematograph and Theatre Union), 208
Beddoe, Josephine, 173, 185
Birmingham Repertory Theatre, 18-20, 50, 91, 103-4, 203
BKL (Bill Kenwright Ltd), 96, 137-44, 180-1; see also Kenwright, Bill
Blackstock, Anthony, 88, 90, 134, 135, 137, 140, 141, 142
Blair, Tony, 9, 108, 199-201, 206-7, 214
Bleasdale, Alan, 172, 184
Bond, Chris, 172, 173
Bonnar-Keenlyside, consultants, 113, 120, 122, 124, 127, 142, 154
Bourne, Nick, 118, 127
Bown, David, 195
Boyden Report, 13, 164, 185, 194, 203-4, 208, 213, 214; see also Peter Boyden Associates
Boyle, James, 205
Brenton, Howard, 89

Bristol Old Vic, see Bristol Theatre Royal
Bristol Theatre Royal (after 1946, Bristol Old Vic), 28-9, 31, 52, 63, 66, 101, 212, 217, 219
British Drama League, 29
Brown, Ian, and Rob Brannen, 101, 170
Browne, Martin, 22
Burnley, Victoria Theatre, 23-4
Bush Theatre, 218, 219
Business Sponsorship Incentive scheme, 81
Butler, R. A., 24

Cambridge Arts Theatre, 25, 26
Canterbury, Marlowe Theatre, 52, 77, 106, 130
Casson, Lewis, 23
Celestina, 117, 119, 122
CEMA (Council for the Encouragement of Music and the Arts), 21-30, 31, 35, 42; attitude to London-based companies, 24; Keynes becomes chairman of, 24; liaises with Tennents, 25-7; precursor of Arts Council, 21; principles, 21-2; shifts emphasis, 25; sponsors Old Vic, 22-3; supports Bristol Theatre Royal, 28-9
Channon, Paul, 80
Cheeseman, Peter, 40
Cheltenham Everyman Theatre, 77, 106, 176
Chester Gateway Theatre, 49, 86, 212
Chichester Festival Theatre, 50, 164
Chipping Norton Theatre, 211
Christmas Cuts, see Arts Council
Church, Jonathan, 127
Clark, Jim, 195, 196
Clark, Sir Kenneth, 38, 58
Clarkson, Jeremy, 211
Clissold, Roger, 117, 121, 135, 136-8
colour-blind casting, 191, 207
community arts, 51, 59, 63, 64, 149
Conservative (Tory) governments: 1945, 35; 1950s, 35, 37, 57; 1979-1997, 9, 10, 11, 12-13, 20, 52, 53, 56, 64, 65, 69-108, 112, 143, 154, 157, 171, 173, 187, 188, 199, 200, 202; see also Thatcher, Margaret
Conservative Party, 12, 69, 81; election victories, 12, 61, 81, 89

Considien, John, 104
Coombes, Keva, 176
Cooper, Chris, 138, 153, 155
CoRAA (Conference of Regional Arts Associations), 56, 105
Cork Report, 1986, 84, 92, 94, 95, 96, 99, 101, 102, 127, 170
Cottesloe, Lord, 62
Coventry, Belgrade Theatre, 49, 50, 59, 65, 96, 205
Crewe, Lyceum Theatre, 52, 77
Cultural Trends, 100

DCMS (Department for Culture, Media and Sport), 200, 201, 213, 217
Dean, Basil, 19, 167, 186
Derby City Council, 213, 215
Derby Playhouse, 97, 213, 215, 217
Devlin, Graham, 105
Digby-Day, Richard, 90
Dossor, Alan, 169
Downing Street Years, The, 73, 74
Doyle, John, 176-7, 179, 181, 182
D'Oyly Carte Opera Company, 42
Dromgoole, Dominic, 202

East Midlands Arts Association, 104
Enhancement Funding scheme, 76, 86
Entertainment Tax, 36
Epsom Playhouse 133, 143
Equity, 219, 220
European Community, 103, 106, 185
Europeans, The, 117, 122
Everyman Theatre, see Merseyside Everyman Theatre
Exeter, Northcott Theatre, 49, 213, 217, 218, 219

Fanshawe, Antony, 105, 115, 125
Farnham, Castle Theatre, 149
Farnham, Redgrave Theatre, 13, 49, 93, 99, 112, 127, 131, 136, 145-56, 162, 163; and young people, 148-9; audiences, 147-8; Board of Directors, 153-4; building and location, 148, 149, 154; funding problems, 146-8, 154-6; goes dark, 145-6, 155; programme, 147, 150-3; relations with local authorities, 149, 153-6; see also Farnham, Castle Theatre
Farnham Herald, 150, 153, 155
Farnham Theatre Productions, 156
Fearon, Kevin, 184
Feversham, Lord, 56
Field, Anthony, 62, 64
First World War, 18
Frayling, Christopher, 209, 217, 219, 220
Friedman, Milton, 71
Furedi, Frank, 209

Garrick, David, 28
Gateshead, BALTIC Centre for Contemporary Art, 206
Gibson, Lord, 62
GLC (Greater London Council), 79-80, 99, 171
Glen, Hamish, 205
Glory of the Garden, The, 1984 Arts Council strategy paper, 33, 37, 82, 90, 92, 104, 133; and devolution, 57, 83-6, 103; and efficiency, 85, 87-8; Harrogate Theatre and, 189-90, 191; origins and contents, 82-3; Surrey Cluster and, 132, 134, 164; theatres lose funding under, 50, 84, 85, 96, 100; Yvonne Arnaud Theatre and, 96, 112, 158-9, 161-2
Gooch, Steve, 95, 96, 147, 192
Goodman, Lord, 53, 56, 58-9, 62
Goodrham, Peter, 146, 148
Gowrie, Lord, 70, 81, 90, 107, 201, 207
Gramsci, Antonio, 34-5
Granville Barker, Harley, 17, 177
great and the good, the, 32, 35, 36, 72
Greenwich Theatre, 49, 59, 201
Grein, J. T., 17
Guildford, Yvonne Arnaud Theatre, 49, 85, 112, 131, 142, 143, 147, 157-65; and Arts Council, 112, 158-9, 161, 164-5, 211, 217; and South East Arts, 112, 158, 159, 160, 161-4; audience, 136, 161; collaborates with West End

producers, 159; financial problems, 158–60, 161–5; history, 157; location, 160; repertoire seen as overly commercial, 85, 96, 112, 158–9
Guildford Borough Council, 157, 158
Guthrie, Tyrone, 23

Hackett, Keith, 176, 183
Hall, Peter, 78, 81, 93, 96, 138, 141; see also Peter Hall Company
Hall, Stuart, 71
Ham, Roderick, 130, 135
Hands, Terry, 168, 184
Harris, John, 35
Harrogate Advertiser, 188
Harrogate Borough Council, 187–8, 190,192, 195, 196
Harrogate Theatre, 13, 85, 112, 187–96, 212; and Arts Council, 37, 187–91, 195–6, 211; and local authorities, 187–8, 189, 190, 192–3; Board of Directors, 190, 193; cuts costs, 190; early history, 187; goes dark, 192; outreach programmes, 187, 194–6; repertoire, 189, 191, 193–4
Hatton, Derek, 173
Hawser/ Findlater Report, 1979, 96
Hayek, Friedman August von, 71, 72
Haynes, Jim, 60
Hedley, Philip, 14, 98, 105
Hewison, Robert, 22
Hewitt, Peter, 211, 214, 216, 219
Hibberd, Judith, 139, 142
Hodge, Margaret, 195
Hoggart, Richard, 36, 72
Holden, John, 206
Hopkins, Catherine, 210
Horlock, David, 114, 116, 117, 118, 121, 127
Hornchurch, Queen's Theatre, 85, 86
Horniman, Miss A. E. F., 18–19
Hutchison, Robert, 57
Hytner, Nick, 219

Ilkley Letter, 82
Ipswich, Wolsey Theatre, 31, 201

Jackson, Barry, 18–19
Jaquarello, Roland, 145, 147, 152–3, 156
James, Peter, 168
Jenkins, Hugh, 21
Jones, Dr Thomas, 21–2, 24–5, 28
Joseph, Sir Keith, 71
Jowell, Tessa, 217, 220

Karlin, Miriam, 219
Keith, Penelope, 163
Kenwright, A. T., 140
Kenwright, Bill, 137–44, 160, 163, 180–2; see also BKL
Kerryson, Paul, 107, 208
Keynes, John Maynard, 11, 24–31, 32, 36, 37, 38, 47, 58, 69; advocates plural funding of arts, 29; and Arts Council, 11, 27, 31, 32; and development of provincial theatres, 28–9; and Trickle down theory, 69; becomes chairman of CEMA, 24; character and interests, 24–5; his policy of excellence, 25, 28, 29; relationship with Tennents, 25–7
Keynesian economics, 71, 172
Kinsella, Denys, 155
Kipling, Rudyard, 82, 83

Labour government: post-war, 30, 34, 35, 36–7, 38; 1960s/70s, 57–61; see also New Labour
Labour Party, 58, 61, 74, 108; see also New Labour
Laidler, Amanda, 192
Lammy, David, 217
Lamont, Norman, 71
Lancaster Repertory Theatre, 59, 97
Landstone, Charles, 24, 32, 33
Leatherhead, Thorndike Theatre, 13, 49, 50, 94, 96, 112, 129–43, 151, 157, 158, 160, 162, 163, 180; and Bill Kenwright, 137–43; and Hazel Vincent Wallace, 129–30, 135, 136, 138, 140–1; and Arts Council, 130, 132; audience statistics, 136–7; design and purpose, 130–1, 140; funding 130, 131–5; history, 129–30; Green Room Club, 131, 135,

140; Leatherhead Theatre Club, 135, 136; location, 133; programme, 136; Roger Clissold artistic director of, 135–7; Theatre Exchange (TIE), 131, 132, 140; Young Stagers, 131, 132, 135; see also Leatherhead Theatre
Leatherhead Theatre, 49, 130
Leatherhead Urban District Council, 130
Lee, Jennie, 11, 37, 58, 61, 62
Leeds Playhouse, 59, 189
Leeds, West Yorkshire Playhouse, 106, 195
Leicester, Haymarket Theatre, 84, 97, 107, 208, 212
Leicester, Phoenix Theatre, 50, 84, 104
Liverpool (Merseyside), 167, 172, 178; local authorities, 171–2, 174, 178, 185
Liverpool and Merseyside Theatres Trust, 185
Liverpool City Corporation, 168
Liverpool City Council, 101, 109, 171, 173, 175, 177–8, 181–4
Liverpool Echo, 176
Liverpool Playhouse, 23, 53, 90, 101, 106, 112, 167–86, 201; and Arts Council, 168, 173, 174–6, 179, 182; and Bill Kenwright, 180–1; and local authorities, 171–6, 182; closes, 181; effects of Liverpool's decline upon, 171; history, 167; insolvency, 179, 181; merges companies with Merseyside Everyman, 185–6; Theatre Upstairs, 168, 175
Liverpool Post, 176
Liverpool Repertory Theatre, 19, 20, 167; see also Liverpool Playhouse
local authorities, 12, 29, 38, 47–8, 61, 75, 76, 92–3, 170, 174–6, 178; and social role of art, 51, 64, 13; arts funding under New Labour, 214; Bristol Old Vic and, 52; erratic support for arts, 47–8; Liverpool theatres and, 174–9; membership of regional arts associations/boards, 104; membership of regional theatres' boards, 54; Nottingham Playhouse and, 50; outdo Arts Council arts spending, 75; promote civic notion of theatre, 29; Redgrave Theatre and, 153–5; relationship with Arts Council, 48, 50, 51–3;

relationship with regional arts associations, 56–7, 170; revenue reduced, 100; support for arts increases in 1980s, 100, 101; support subject to politics, 52
Longman, Peter, 202, 203
Look Back in Anger, 196, 212
Lopokova, Lydia, 25
lottery, see National Lottery
Lucas, Allanah, 117, 119–20
Luce, Richard, 75–6, 102, 104

Macmillan, Joyce, 205
Major, John, 13, 20, 71, 105, 107, 143
Malahide, Patrick, 219
Manchester, Gaiety Theatre, 14, 18, 19
Manchester Royal Exchange Theatre, 50, 91, 103, 171
Manley, Andrew, 190–1, 193, 194
Marquand, David, 199
Marriott, Michael, 129, 130
Matcham, Frank, 49
May, Douglas, 160
May, Val, 159
McMaster, Brian, 216, 218, 219, 220
Mellor, David, 76, 103, 104, 105, 109
Merseyside County (Metropolitan) Council, 101, 172, 173, 175
Merseyside Everyman Theatre, 13, 50, 53, 77, 101, 112, 168–86; and Arts Council, 170, 174–6, 179, 181–2, 184; and local authorities, 171–6, 182, 184; board differences, 183–4; buys its building, 177; closes and reopens, 184–6; history, 168–9; merges companies with Liverpool Playhouse, 185–6; outreach work (Hope Street Project), 169, 181, 183–4; programming, 168–9, 176–7
Merseyside Funders' Forum, 179
metropolitan councils, 13, 74, 79, 80, 99, 100, 101, 171
Middleton, Claire, 218
Militant, 173, 175, 178
Millennium Dome, 209
Moar, Danny, 121

Mole Valley District Council, 133, 143, 158
monetarism, 71–2, 154, 157
Morgan, Perry, 55
Morrison, Bill, 90, 172, 173, 175
Morrison, Richard, 207
Mullins, Ian, 145, 149, 151
Murray, Braham, 103

National Campaign for the Arts, 91, 99
National Health Service (NHS), 72, 82
National Lottery, 74, 106–7, 201–2
National Theatre, 78, 83, 84, 96, 171, 205, 219
National Youth Theatre, 59, 66, 77, 92
New Labour, 12, 13, 108, 199, 214; arts funding, 200–3; cultural vision, 200–1, 206–7, 209; goals, 199–200; origins, 199–200; targetology, 209
Neville Affair, 27, 53–4
Neville, John, 53–4, 125
New Farnham Repertory Theatre, 145, 151
New Opportunities Fund, 201
New Right, 12, 71–2, 73, 80, 81, 82, 85, 88
Newcastle, New Victoria Theatre, 101
North West Arts Board, 185
North Yorkshire County Council, 187, 188, 195
Norwich Playhouse, 107–8
Nottingham Playhouse, 27, 49–50, 53–4, 59, 89, 92, 97–8, 125

Office Party, The, 117, 119–20
Old Vic, 9, 22–4, 25, 26, 32, 37, 38, 201
Olympic Games, 215

Paige, Deborah, 97, 113–14, 116, 117–26, 153
parity (matching) funding, 29, 51, 52, 56–7, 64, 100, 101, 104, 112, 115, 133, 154, 162, 170–1, 174, 176, 182, 214
Peacock, D. Keith, 75, 90, 95
Peat, Henry, 21
Penycate, Jack, 158
Peter Boyden Associates, 13, 36, 203, 205; see also Boyden Report

Peter Hall Company, 138, 140, 144; see also Hall, Peter
Pick, John, 27, 59
Pilgrim Players, 18, 22
Pilgrim Trust, 21, 22, 24
Piper, Mark, 188–9
plural funding, 12–13, 29, 47–52, 56–7, 63–4, 70, 100, 112, 153, 154
Plymouth, Theatre Royal, 106
Policy for the Arts, 1965 White Paper, 11, 58, 60, 61
poll tax, 75, 100, 106, 154, 178
Pooley, Sir Ernest, 33, 38
Poyner, Michael, 188
Priestley, Clive, 78, 80
Priestley Report, 79–80
Pulford, Richard, 218
Purnell, James, 216
Pygmalion, 301

Quality of Living, The, Labour Party document, 61
quangos, 72–3, 175

Ramsay, Alasdair, 210
Reade, Simon, 213
Redgrave Theatre, see Farnham, Redgrave Theatre
Rees-Mogg, William, 79, 80, 81–5, 88, 89, 176
Redfern, Richard, 141
regional arts associations, 12, 26–7, 36, 61, 62–3, 75, 96, 112, 132, 159; affected by *The Glory of the Garden*, 83–5; creation of, 54–5; funding of, 56–7; grow under Labour, 61; reduced and transformed into regional arts boards, 102–4; relationship with Arts Council, 22, 55–6; successors to animateurs, 22; see also entries for individual associations
regional arts boards, 102–5, 115, 213–14
regional theatres, 10, 13, 14, 20, 29, 30; affected by Arts Council 2007 funding decisions, 37–8, 217–18; affected by television, 39–40; Arts Council imposes its own standards on, 36, 63, 207–8; and deficit

budgeting, 26-7; as try-out and training sites, 95, 141, 150-1, 155, 160; audience statistics, 94; audiences diminish, 39-41, 106; board problems, 53-4, 97-8; boom in 1960s, 49-50, 59-61; community arts programmes in, 51, 60, 64, 207-10; constraints on artistic directors in, 96-9; cut costs, reduce activities and repertoire, 92-4; decline under Conservatives, 9-10, 70, 76-8; devolved to regional arts associations/boards, 103-5; directly managed by CEMA/Arts Council, 28-9, 31-2, 33-4, 37, 113; experimental work in, 60; in Scotland, 205; in Wales, 205; increasingly rely on subsidy, 41; maintenance and operating costs of, 50, 63; non-profit-distributing status, 41, 42, 51; permanent ensemble companies in, 40; play-by-play casting in, 40; poor pay in, 98-9; relationship with local authorities, 50; relationship with regional arts associations, 57, 84-5; repertoire statistics, 95, 160; rise in private-public partnerships, 95; state of buildings, 106-7; suffer from *Glory of the Garden*, 83-6; try to adapt to enterprise culture, 89-96; under New Labour, 13, 208-20; young people's educational programmes in, 59, 63, 64, 92-3; *see also* entries for individual theatres, Boyden Report
repertory system, 18, 19, 20, 93, 151, 176, 177
repertory theatres, 10, 18-20, 27, 31, 39, 41, 42, 59, 70, 129-30, 145, 149, 151, 155, 167, 187, 192, 194, 211
Rennie, Michael, 156
Rittner, Luke, 82, 174
Robbins, Ros, 181
Robinson, Gerry, 206-7, 209, 213-14, 217
Robinson, Sir Kenneth, 73, 81
Rourke, Josie, 218-19
Rowe, Peter, 184
Rowell, George, and Anthony Jackson, 54, 168
Royal Court Theatre, 60, 95, 97
Royal Opera House, Covent Garden, 25, 32, 43, 55, 78, 79, 204

Royal Shakespeare Company, 60, 78, 79, 83, 84, 91
Russell, Willy, 169, 172, 180, 184; wife, Annie, 287

Sadler's Wells, 23, 25, 32, 38, 43, 55, 78
St. John Stevas, Norman, 73, 74, 80
Salberg, Reggie, 117, 121, 124-5
Salford, Lowry Centre, 206
Salisbury, 27, 31, 33, 34
Salisbury Arts Theatre, 27, 33-4, 37, 113; *see also* Salisbury Playhouse
Salisbury District Council, 115, 126-7
Salisbury Journal, 117, 119, 120, 123, 127
Salisbury Playhouse, 13, 49, 54, 64, 93, 94, 96, 101, 105, 107, 112, 113-27, 135, 145, 146, 147, 149, 153, 154; and Arts Council, 113-14, 115, 118; artistic directors, 114, 116, 117, 120, 121, 124; audiences, 118-20, 122; Board of Directors, 105, 115, 117, 120, 123, 124-6; comments in local press, 116, 117, 119, 121-3, 125; finances, 113-16, 123; funding bodies, 112, 115, 126; management, 119, 120; programming, 117-18, 119,122; Salberg (studio) Theatre, 116; Stage '65, 116, 120, 122-3, 124; Theatrescope (TIE), 113, 116, 120, 122-3, 124
Scotland, 204; Arts Council, see Scottish Arts Council; Dundee Repertory Theatre, 205; Edinburgh Traverse Theatre, 60; Federation of Scottish Theatres, 204; Glasgow, 32, 53, 59; Pitlochry Festival Theatre, 69; Scottish Executive, 204; Scottish National Theatre, 204-5
Scott, David, and Paddy Byrne, 184
Scottish Arts Council, 44, 103, 109, 204, 205, 217, 220
Second World War, 10, 13, 14, 17, 20, 21, 30, 32, 113, 129, 167
Select Committees: on Education, Science and the Arts, 1982, 77-8, 80; on Estimates, 1949, 34, 38; on Culture, Media and Sport, 215
Shaw, George Bernard, 17, 19, 37, 191

Shaw, Roy, 82
Sheffield Crucible Theatre, 49, 50, 84, 97–8, 101, 174, 189
Sheffield Repertory Theatre, 20
Shirley Valentine, 41, 180
Sinclair, Andrew, 24, 28, 87
Sinclair, Malcolm, 219
Smith, Chris, 200, 201, 206, 214, 220
Smith, David, 210
South East Arts Association (later Board), 55, 112; and Redgrave Theatre, 145, 146, 153, 154–6; and Surrey Cluster, 105, 132; and Thorndike Theatre, 133–4, 136, 137, 138–40, 142–3; and Yvonne Arnaud Theatre, 96, 112, 158, 159–64; Arts Council grants to, 132
South West Arts Association, 55, 57
Southampton, Nuffield Theatre, 101, 146
Southern Arts Board, 105, 113, 115, 118, 126, 127
Standard Drama Agreement, 25, 36
Stafford-Clark, Max, 97
Stage, The, 76–7, 102, 173, 175, 217
Stalker, John, 179
Stanley, Nick, 183
Step in Time, A, 151
Stewart, Mandy, 212
Stevens, Briar, 147–8, 150, 151, 154
Stoke-on-Trent, Victoria Theatre, 40, 50, 53
Stratford East, Theatre Royal, 91, 93, 98, 106, 201
Streamlining the Cities, 1983 White Paper, 80, 85, 171
Sunday Times, The, 71, 211, 219
Surrey Advertiser, 141, 142
Surrey Cluster, 105, 112, 131, 132, 134, 154, 157, 158, 160, 163, 164, 188
Surrey County Council, 154; and Redgrave Theatre, 145, 153–6; and Thorndike Theatre, 134, 137, 140, 142, 144; and Yvonne Arnaud Theatre, 158

Tanner, Doreen, 168
Taylor, Kenneth Alan, 98
television, its effect on theatre, 39–40

Tennent Plays Ltd., 26
Tennent Productions Ltd., 25–6, 27, 42
Thatcher, Margaret, 10, 12, 13, 20, 51, 65, 78, 102, 105, 118, 172, 173, 187; abolishes metropolitan county councils, 171; and dissenters, 72, 80; and Priestley Report, 78; approves arts role in regenerating urban areas, 89; attitude to post-war consensus, 70, 72; conviction politician, 70; economic philosophy, 71–2; election victories, 69, 89; extends Thatcherism to embrace arts, 73–4; leaves office, 105; rejects lottery, 107
Thatcherism, 70–2, 108, 199, 200
Theatres Trust, 202
Theatrical Management Association, 76, 106, 109, 207, 218
Thorndike Theatre, see Leatherhead, Thorndike Theatre
Tiaira, Kully, 208
TIE (Theatre in Education), 59, 92, 113, 116, 123, 131, 132, 140, 169, 187, 194
Times, The, 28, 81, 82, 103, 148, 207
Tories, see Conservative governments
touring theatre companies, 24, 33, 42, 75, 102, 138, 156, 194, 195, 212
Trickle down theory, 69
Triumph Apollo, 159

Under Thirty Theatre Group, 129, 131

VAT (Value Added Tax), 76–7, 88, 99
Venables, Claire, 98, 174

Wales, 103, 204, 205; Cardiff, Sherman Theatre, 205; Milford Haven, Torch Theatre, 205; Mold, Clwyd Theatre Cymru, 50, 205; Swansea Theatre, 31, 32, 37, 38, 48; see also Arts Council of Wales
Walford, Glen, 175–6
Wallace, Hazel Vincent, 129–30, 135–6, 138, 140–2
Watkins, Graham, 99, 104, 147–56
Waverley Borough Council, 149, 151, 153–6
West, Timothy, 94, 161

Westcliff Palace Theatre, 321
West End, 17, 19, 25, 26, 32, 33, 34, 50, 132, 133, 137, 141, 143, 160; productions,154, 180; producers/impresarios, 129, 134, 137, 142, 151, 157, 159, 160; transfers, 93, 95, 137, 138, 139, 140, 159; try-outs, 33, 151, 155
West Midland Arts Association, 103
West Riding Theatre, 31, 32, 37
West Yorkshire County Council, 174
Wilding Report, 102
Williams, Peter Howell, 183
Williams, Raymond, 35
Williams, William Emrys, 42, 43, 55, 56, 61, 64, 112, 213
Willis, Phil, 195, 196

Wilson, Harold, 57, 58, 59, 207
Wiltshire County Council, 115, 126
Woking, New Victoria Theatre, 133, 143, 160
Wolfit, Donald, 26
Worcester, Swan Theatre, 49, 204
Wright, Jules, 175, 176
Wyndhams Theatres Ltd, 32

York, Theatre Royal, 106, 189
Yorkshire and Humberside Arts Board, 194
Yorkshire Arts Association, 190, 193
Yorkshire Post, 188
YPT (Young People's Theatre), 59, 92, 116, 169
Yvonne Arnaud Theatre, see Guildford, Yvonne Arnaud Theatre